MARY CASSATT

Prints and Drawings from the Artist's Studio

MARY
Prints and Drawings

CASSATT

from the Artist's Studio

CATALOGUE BY

Marc Rosen and Susan Pinsky

ESSAYS BY

Warren Adelson
Jay E. Cantor
Marc Rosen and Susan Pinsky
Barbara Stern Shapiro

PRINCETON UNIVERSITY PRESS

This volume is dedicated to Adelyn Dohme Breeskin (1896–1986), whose pioneering scholarship on Mary Cassatt set the stage for all subsequent research.

Presented by

Marc Rosen Fine Art, Ltd.

220 EAST 73RD STREET
NEW YORK, NY 10023-4319
WWW.MARCROSENFINEART.COM

This book was published on the occasion of the exhibition

From the Artist's Studio:
Unknown Prints and Drawings
by Mary Cassatt

November 10 to December 29, 2000

Adelson Galleries, Inc.

THE MARK HOTEL
25 EAST 77TH STREET
NEW YORK, NY 10021
WWW.ADELSONGALLERIES.COM

Meredith Long & Company

2323 SAN FELIPE
HOUSTON, TX 77019
WWW.MEREDITHLONGGALLERY.COM

ISBN 0-691-08887-X

Library of Congress Card Number: 00-109349

Printed in the United Sates of America
10 9 8 7 6 5 4 3 2 1

Published by Princeton University Press, 41 William Street, Princeton, NJ 08540

Front cover: *The Fitting* [detail] (Breeskin 147), proof of seventh state (see pages 87 and 89)
Back cover: *Mother Marie Dressing Her Baby after Its Bath* (Breeskin 142), (see page 74)

CONTENTS

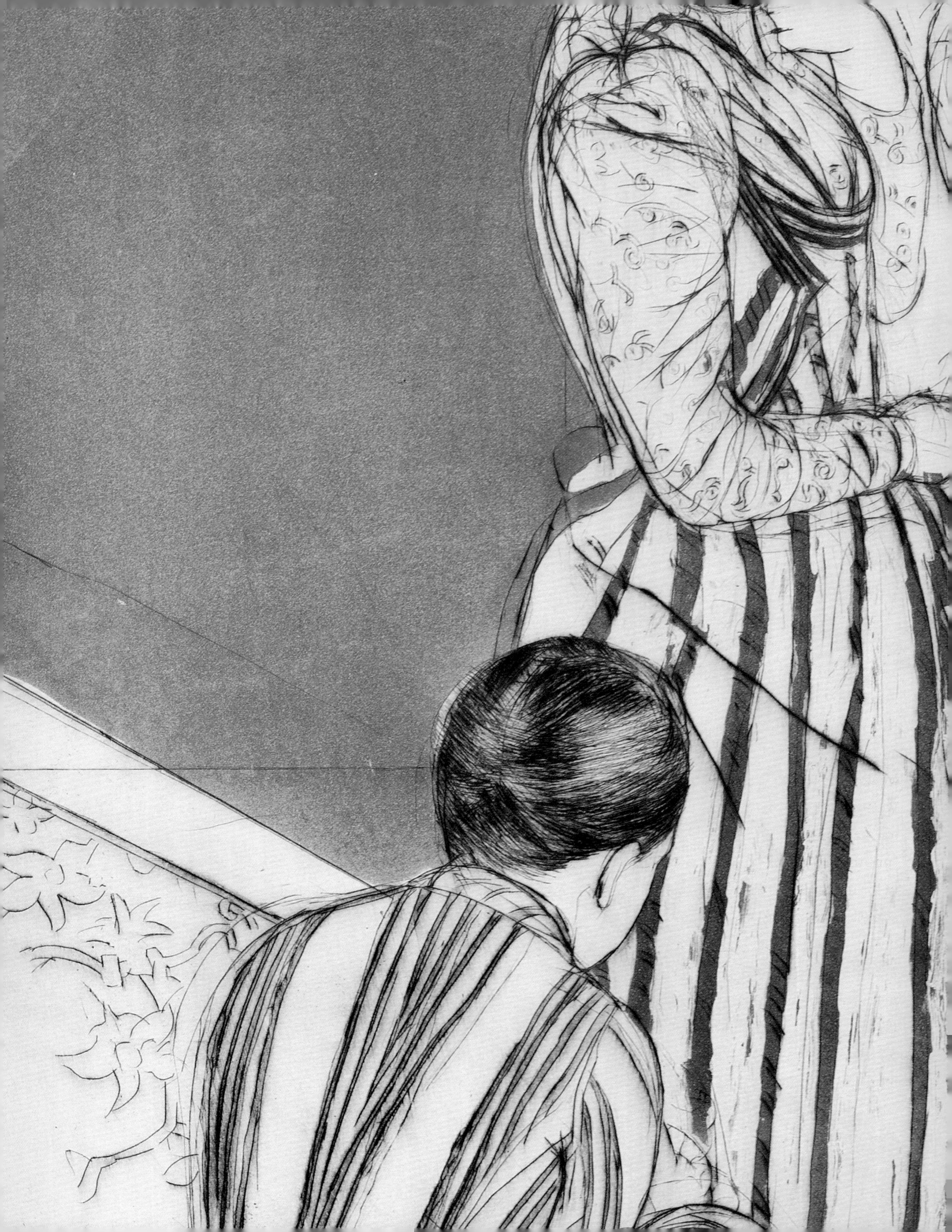

FOREWORD

Ambroise Vollard and the "Studio Collection"

Monographic exhibitions of artists are inevitably flawed. Art critics, collectors, scholars, dealers, and gallery visitors often question the inclusion of this, regret the deletion of that. Where is the Chicago picture? Why was that collector's piece included and not the other's? We at Adelson Galleries have witnessed this during the three decades we have produced one-man shows of turn-of-the-century American art. Some criticisms have been justified; others are more arguable. That said, our current exhibition differs from past productions. *From the Artist's Studio: Unknown Prints and Drawings by Mary Cassatt* presents a comprehensive review of the artist's graphic work. What makes this show unique in our experience is that we have not selected it. Cassatt's dealer, Ambroise Vollard, did that—almost one hundred years ago.

Ambroise Vollard took Paris by storm in the last decade of the nineteenth century. He opened a small gallery in the heart of the art world, Montmartre, and 6, rue Laffitte became the epicenter of modernism. At the suggestion of Renoir and Pissarro, Vollard held the first solo exhibition of the paintings of Paul Cézanne in 1895. Though critically scorned, the show launched both artist and dealer. In the following year he published his first print by Pierre Bonnard, a color lithograph used as a poster for the exhibition *Les Peintres-Graveurs*. Vollard had made his first foray in print publishing in 1893 and it was his idea to convince painters to make prints, expanding the genre beyond traditional "printmakers." This brilliant concept opened a new world of art production. In his remarkable career Vollard published vast numbers of prints by painters as well as books exquisitely illustrated by the leading artists of the time. As a dealer, he sold works by the Impressionists, who were by then well established in the marketplace, and he was in the vanguard in his promotion of the modernists: Bonnard, Cézanne, Chagall, Denis, Gauguin, Maillol, Picasso, Pissarro, Redon, Rouault, and Vuillard. He gave Pablo Picasso and Henri Matisse their first solo exhibitions in 1901 and 1904 respectively. Ambroise Vollard was inquisitive and daring, and he was not afraid to compete with the older firms, especially the formidable Durand-Ruel Gallery. Their exhibitions in Paris and New York helped to establish Impressionist painting as the most desirable art to collect in the 1880s and 1890s. In the process, they helped make Impressionist artists such as Claude Monet world-renowned. Among the new painters in Durand-Ruel's stable, the only American was Mary Cassatt (1844–1926).

Frustrated in her artistic ambitions, Cassatt had left her native Pennsylvania and traveled to Europe in 1866. She was twenty-two years old and determined to be a professional artist. *The Mandolin Player* (private collection), a portrait of a soulful peasant girl, was accepted at the Salon of 1868, but within time Cassatt's independent nature and keen intelligence led her to reject her academic training and to pursue modern painting. Despite her sex and nationality, she exhibited her work along with Edgar Degas, her friend and mentor, and the other new painters. "Degas made me promise never to submit anything to the Salon again, and to exhibit with his friends in the group of the Impressionists," she told her biographer Achille Segard, "I agreed gladly . . . I hated conventional art. I was beginning to live."[1] Like Degas, she considered herself an "Independent," and exhibited twelve works in the Fourth Impressionist Exhibition in 1879; she continued to exhibit with them in 1880, 1881, and 1886. Her work was well received by the critics and the public began to take notice. Her alliance with the dealer Paul Durand-Ruel began in this decade and continued, albeit fitfully, throughout her career.

Cassatt had experimented with etching and drypoint, pulling black-and-white prints on her own press, and gaining hands-on experience with the medium. These prints were shown with those by her friends, including Degas, Pissarro, Rodin, Tissot, and Redon, at the annual print exhibitions of the Society of Painter-Printmakers, held at Durand-Ruel. In 1890 Cassatt, along with Morisot, Pissarro, and Tissot, became interested in adding color to the images, inspired by the woodblocks in the spectacular exhibition of Japanese art at the École des Beaux-Arts, which had set Paris aflame that spring. Her resultant set of ten color prints was the highlight of her first one-person show at Durand-Ruel in 1891 and received positive acclaim, both critical and commercial. Upon seeing the prints, Camille Pissarro wrote to his son Lucien, "subtle, delicate, without stains on seams: adorable blues, fresh rose . . . the result is admirable, as beautiful as Japanese work, and it's done with printer's ink!"[2] The set of ten established Cassatt's fame as a printmaker, especially in France, where the reception for these elegant works was more enthusiastic than in America. Her second solo show, held at Durand-Ruel, Paris, in 1893, featured a retrospective selection of oil paintings, pastels, and prints. Two years later, in 1895, Durand-Ruel organized her first major exhibition in the United States at their Fifth Avenue galleries. Cassatt had agreed to an exclusive contract with Durand-Ruel in 1890, and the gallery's frequent exhibitions of her work sold well and provided the artist with her first sense of financial security.

Cassatt's career expanded in the 1890s, but her relationship with Durand-Ruel faltered from time to time. As early as 1891, Pissarro wrote to his son, "she [Cassatt] is incensed at Durand on her own account and asked me if I would go along with her if she left Durand. She will use all the influence she has to push our paintings and engravings in New York, she is very desirous of upsetting Durand. She has a lot of influence and Durand, who suspects that she is irritated with him, is trying to calm her down with promises and offers which he does not make good."[3] In addition to conflicts over money, Durand-Ruel's marketing of Cassatt's work was not always to her liking. The French dealer sometimes included her in exhibitions she did not approve (such as those showing pictures by women artists only) or entered her meagerly in others; the firm actively promoted some works, but passed over other material she felt should be shown. Notably, Durand-Ruel "discouraged her printmaking efforts, sensing that other works, particularly pastels, were in greater demand."[4] Vollard provided a needed alternative. Unlike the older dealer, he was willing to take whatever he could get from her, and his aggressive approach gained her approval. Cassatt wrote to her friend Louisine Havemeyer that Joseph Durand-Ruel "would not buy the things from Degas that Vollard gladly took and sold again at large profits. Vollard is a genius in his line he seems to be able to sell *anything*."[5] In 1905 she broke her long-standing contract with Durand-Ruel, infuriated that she was not included in an Impressionist exhibition in London, and she turned increasingly to Vollard in response. (Eventually Cassatt and Durand-Ruel did reconcile.)

After the turn of the century, Mary Cassatt was recognized as a great artist by her own countrymen. She proceeded to win awards and prizes: the Lippincott Prize of the Pennsylvania Academy of the Fine Arts, the Norman Wait Harris Prize of the Art Institute of Chicago, and others. She was gratified to receive the attention, but stood by her principles and would not accept the medals or the prize money. She had long ago rejected the Salon system, and still called herself an "Independent," i.e. no juries, no prizes. In 1904 she was named a Chevalier of the French Legion of Honor, an exceptional award for an American woman. Demand for her work was at a high point, and she began to produce and distribute more material than ever before. Vollard boldly purchased many dozens of pastels and oils from her, often unfinished works that in the past would not have left her studio. It was at this time, between 1904–1906, that she evidently decided to sell her collection of prints to Vollard.[6]

His appetite for graphic art was voracious, as attested by his voluminous publication and sales of prints by his expanding stable of artists. Cassatt had been making prints since 1879 and by the first decade of the twentieth century had amassed hundreds of works in her "studio collection." Included were a fascinating range of print states (experimental versions) and final proofs, early images of family members, as well as unique and hitherto unpublished examples. Printmaking had been the medium for which she had received great accolades as an artist; it had placed her in the vanguard. Clearly the collection in her studio had significant meaning to her, and Vollard's overt predilection for graphic arts as a publisher and dealer was unique in the art world. He was the obvious person for her to consult. He bought a large group of material, which included dozens of color prints, scores of black-and-white etchings and drawings, and several series of small drawings. He left behind about one hundred drypoints and pastel sketches, which Cassatt sold to Durand-Ruel in 1920, near the end of her life.[7]

Acquisitive by nature, Vollard supplemented the collection with purchases from other key contemporary collectors, adding Cassatt prints originally owned by figures such as the critics Roger Marx and André Mellerio and the collectors Alexis Rouart and Pierre Demany to the already large inventory. His method as a dealer was to hold works for long periods of time. He thought nothing of keeping unpublished plates of an artist for fifteen or twenty years before producing them. He held Cassatt's works together as a collection, storing them throughout World War I and the ensuing years. Following his untimely death in an automobile accident in 1939, the collection was sold by his heirs to a distinguished print dealer and collector in Paris, who reserved them for his personal collection. They remained sequestered for decades, kept safely in portfolios, and rarely handled. Upon the owner's death in 1980, this prized collection descended to his family, which has now decided to reveal the collection's existence to the public. These marvelous prints can be seen today, as fresh and subtle as when they were initially pulled from the printing plates.

This publication serves a dual purpose. It accompanies the exhibition *From the Artist's Studio: Unknown Prints and Drawings by Mary Cassatt*, held simultaneously at Adelson Galleries in New York and Meredith Long & Company in Houston. Of greater importance to those interested in Mary Cassatt, this volume serves as a record of an extraordinary collection of graphic art, acquired in the artist's lifetime by the one person who was most aware of the nuances of her technique and uniquely suited to appreciate her printed work. These two hundred works on paper have been preserved untouched for nearly a century, creating a time capsule of her art to be seen by us now in its entirety.

We are grateful to Marc Rosen Fine Art, Ltd.; Marc Rosen and Susan Pinsky steadfastly pursued this collection to bring it to the public. Marc had befriended the Parisian owner and then his family for over three decades, resulting in their confidence to release their remarkable holdings to him. We are especially grateful to Marc and Susan for letting us produce this show and for their contribution of the catalogue entries herein. Thanks to Barbara Shapiro, Curator for Special Projects at the Museum of Fine Arts, Boston, for her essay, which links this material with her extensive work on Cassatt's graphic art. Jay Cantor, Director of the Mary Cassatt Catalogue Raisonné Committee, has added to our understanding of Cassatt's working process with his contribution. Dr. William H. Gerdts as a Committee member has lent his expertise. Pamela A. Ivinski, Senior Research Associate, has added immeasurably to the quality and accuracy of this volume. Andrea Maltese has aided in the production of this catalogue, and Caroline Owens has helped coordinate our efforts in this entire project. Again it has been a pleasure to exhibit this collection jointly with our friend and colleague Meredith Long in Houston. On a personal note, I wanted to mention my particular interest in working on this project. Since the Mary Cassatt Catalogue Raisonné came to Adelson Galleries three years ago, this has been our first opportunity to engage the services and expertise of our many friends in the field, some mentioned above, and others, including Nancy Mowll Mathews, who have worked extensively on the artist. Although graphic arts are not the domain of our catalogue raisonné project, the work on the "studio collection" has been invaluable to our understanding of Mary Cassatt.

Warren Adelson
Adelson Galleries, Inc.

NOTES

1. Quoted in Nancy Mowll Mathews, ed., *Mary Cassatt: A Retrospective*, p. 100.
2. Letter of April 3, 1891, in Nancy Mowll Mathews, ed., *Cassatt and Her Circle: Selected Letters*, p. 219.
3. Letter of April 25, 1891, in Mathews, ed., *Cassatt and Her Circle: Selected Letters*, p. 220.
4. Nancy Mowll Mathews, *Mary Cassatt*, p. 91.
5. Letter of December 3, 1913, in Mathews, ed., *Cassatt and Her Circle: Selected Letters*, p. 313.
6. Our research for the catalogue raisonné suggests that Cassatt sold very infrequently, if at all, to Durand-Ruel during this period, while at the same time Vollard may also have been buying from the artist many of the pastels of girls with dogs dated ca. 1901–1904 which he handled.
7. Cassatt letter to Louisine Havemeyer, March 22, 1920, in Mathews, ed., *Cassatt and Her Circle: Selected Letters*, p. 332.

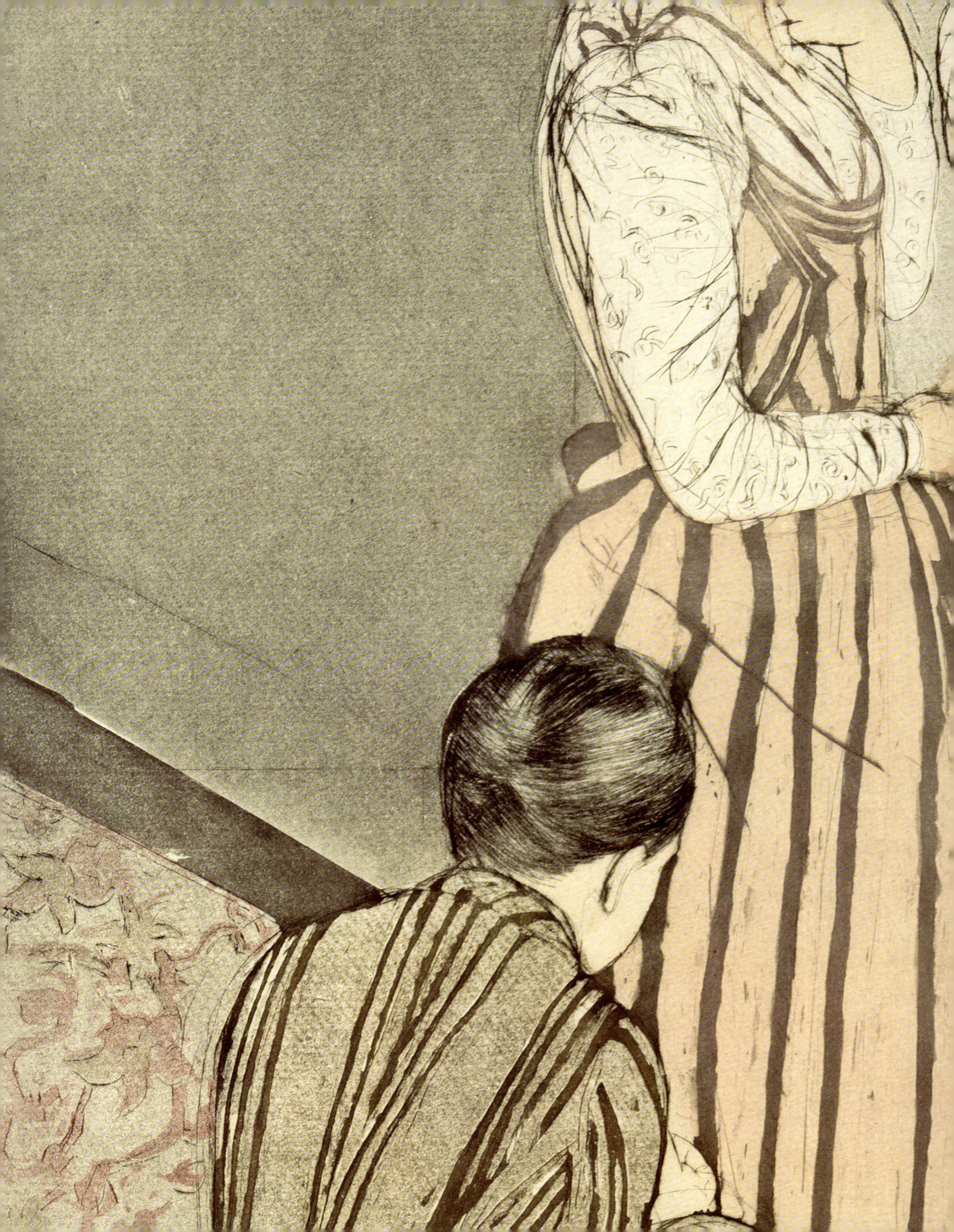

Mary Cassatt Prints – An Appreciation

Mary Cassatt's prints are widely known and hold great appeal. Thus, the appearance of this large cache of her printed work is an event to be applauded. It is also an opportunity to reexamine her important contribution to the graphic arts.[1] The collection presented here comprises more than 170 prints and some thirty-one drawings. By 1903, Cassatt's disenchantment with her longtime dealer Paul Durand-Ruel (1831–1922) deepened and she began to work with Ambroise Vollard (1866–1939), a lively French colonial who had come to Paris determined to succeed in the art trade. Vollard undertook to publish original prints and books, and to make a successful enterprise for himself and to promote his stable of artists. It has been said that great painters make great prints, a concept endorsed by Vollard, whose original idea was to commission prints from artists who were not printmakers by profession.

Vollard admired Cassatt as a painter, so it is not surprising that over a period of time, he brought together this remarkable archive of her works on paper. By 1906 she had invited Vollard to her country home, Beaufresne, at Mesnil-Théribus to select and purchase items from her studio. He had already acquired work from her as early as 1904 and continued to do so sporadically, leading up to what may have been a series of major purchases in 1914. By that time, Cassatt was reviewing the body of works still in her possession for distribution to her family or to put into the market. Those offered for sale usually went to either Vollard or Durand-Ruel.

Vollard's own collection also included significant examples that were acquired later from other collections, including prints previously owned by Edgar Degas (sold at the Atelier or studio sales in 1918, a year after the artist's death), Roger Marx (art critic, Minister at Large in the Ministry of Public Instruction and Beaux-Arts, and editor of art journals, who supported innovative printmakers and owned some 130 of Cassatt's prints), Marcel Mirault (who assembled fine impressions of major nineteenth-century prints), Alexis Rouart (a Parisian industrialist who acquired prints by Degas and Cassatt), and André Mellerio (art critic, author of books on art, and an astute collector), among others. It is worth noting that Vollard acquired and retained so much of her graphic art considering that he never actually published a print by Cassatt.

Mary Cassatt's first serious efforts as a printmaker occurred in the company of Degas, who created a studio environment in which Cassatt and several of her colleagues flourished. There she became proficient in the use of unconventional ways of creating tonal images, and some of her most inventive prints evolved from this "cuisine" or "cookery" approach. The current collection includes at least a dozen images derived from this richly productive encounter. Degas had conceived of a journal of original prints and the distinctive image that Cassatt prepared as her contribution for the never-realized publication was entitled *In the Opera Box (No. 3)* [*Woman at the Theater*] (pp. 28–29: Breeskin 22), an unusual mélange of soft-ground etching and aquatint.[2] This print was executed in 1879–1880 and was printed in an edition of fifty.

A fine example of Cassatt's rich tonal technique can be seen in the study of *Mlle Luguet Seated on a Couch* (p. 35: Breeskin 49) from ca. 1883, also created during this period of great technical exploration associated with Degas's "cuisine" environment. This impression is of the first state before the detail on the flowered couch and without the darkening of the dress. The sheet is boldly initialed in pencil with the frequently used *M. C.* It is interesting to note that Vollard questioned this practice, when he wrote to the artist in 1914 stating that some of the prints and drawings were initialed when "habitually you sign Mary Cassatt."[3] This document disproves the oft-stated assumption that these works may have been signed posthumously.

In the late 1880s, Cassatt turned to working with drypoint, an exacting medium that she employed throughout her printmaking career. Durand-Ruel gave the artist an opportunity to exhibit in a group show, *Exposition des Peintres-Graveurs*, held at the gallery in March 1890. In a series of twelve drypoints which she produced for the show [among them *The Map* (p. 53: Breeskin 127) and *Reflection* (pp. 60–61: Breeskin 131)], the refined images foreshadowed the expertise that Cassatt would develop with the technique when she embarked upon her major color prints in late 1890. There are twenty-eight different impressions of these twelve drypoints in this collection. Originally, Durand-Ruel promoted them as a set of twelve and took credit for the concept of selling Cassatt's prints in a series.[4] These depictions of women and children established a range of subject matter that would engage Cassatt throughout her career.

A massive exhibition of Japanese art that took place soon after the close of the *Peintres-Graveurs* show at Durand-Ruel's proved to be the most important influence on Cassatt's career. From this great visual experience, the artist was inspired to produce a magnificent group of ten drypoint and aquatint color prints that are renowned among Western works on paper. A major effort in

1989 to document the various states of Cassatt's color prints and to explicate her working methods resulted in an exhibition and catalogue.[5] However, significant impressions in the Vollard holdings, shown here, dramatically alter the sequence in the color applications. Our conception of the order and distribution of the drypoint and aquatint work on the multiple plates remains unchanged. It is always noteworthy when new examples expand the efforts of print cataloguers and enhance our knowledge of an artist's work. *The Bath* [*The Child's Bath*] (pp. 76–79: Breeskin 143), which is the first in the sequence of Cassatt's color prints, went through seventeen identifiable states or stages in development while Cassatt explored her direction, techniques, and color harmonies. Mathews and Shapiro knew of forty-three impressions of this print and now eight more sheets can be added to the group, documenting a remarkable journey as the artist laboriously probed her way in color toward a unique unfolding of daily scenes of women performing domestic tasks and activities.[6]

Several other color impressions reveal a different approach to the application of the colored inks on the plate. In a brilliant trial proof of the sixth state of *The Fitting* [*Young Woman Trying on a Dress*] (p. 88: Breeskin 147), the coloration is unlike any of the known impressions; here, the patterned wall and baseboard were printed in a vivid russet brown. In another trial proof of the same image in the seventh and final state, the patterned back wall was printed in a dramatic blue balanced against other subdued tints (p. 89). Is it possible that the work on the sleeve reflected in the mirror that changes from aquatint to scratch drypoint lines is a new development in the sequence of states?

The Bath [*The Child's Bath*] (pp. 76–79: Breeskin 143) and *Mother's Kiss* [*The Kiss*] (pp. 92–93: Breeskin 149) from the Vollard collection reveal additional experimentation with the various effects that the artist wished to convey; here, the use of different colors on three plates produced atmospheric changes. With the exception of *The Fitting* [*Young Woman Trying on a Dress*] (pp. 86–89: Breeskin 147) and *The Lamp* (pp. 80–81: Breeskin 144), there may not be any new development of states in the other eight prints, but the dramatic colorations of several images add to our profound appreciation of Cassatt's experimental working methods. Although she executed the set of ten with an expert printer, M. Leroy, it was her individual decisions that effected this major contribution to printmaking. A print in the collection of Eric Carlson by Paul Renouard, dedicated, *à Monsieur Modeste Leroy/souvenir d'un atelier de la rue de l'arbre – sec 46, tout au fond et tout en haut de tout cour/ P Renouard 1913*, provides us with the previously unknown first name of this talented printer.[7] Mary Cassatt's signature and her dedication to M. Leroy are often found on the sets of ten and on those impressions destined for sale by the artist or Durand-Ruel, who marketed them in Paris and New York. Many examples such as these in the Vollard collection may have been put aside for future commerce.

Cassatt's last color prints are noticeably different from the "ten" and were executed as the result of various circumstances. *Gathering Fruit* [*The Kitchen Garden*] (pp. 100–101: Breeskin 157) was the printed adaptation of a large mural called *Modern Woman* that Cassatt produced for the World's Columbian Exposition held in Chicago in 1893. The color print, based on the central panel of the mural, went through eleven states and was prepared on three plates. Given that there is no inscription to M. Leroy, one can assume that another skillful printer worked with the artist. *The Banjo Lesson* (p. 99: Breeskin 156), simpler in design and execution, utilized two plates with the introduction of sensitive monotype inking and the manipulation of aquatint grain. Both of these prints were shown in the first large retrospective exhibition of Cassatt's paintings, pastels, and prints held in Paris at the Galerie Durand-Ruel in the late fall of 1893. In the Vollard collection, exhibited here, there are seven additional impressions of the two prints that were previously unknown, including some outstanding examples of state and inking changes. Mathews and Shapiro knew of seventeen impressions of *The Kitchen Garden* that are now joined by four more impressions. For *The Banjo Lesson,* there is included a previously unknown state between the first and second states of this charming print.

In April 1895 Cassatt was offered another major exhibition by Durand-Ruel, this time in New York City, and a new color print, unrelated to the earlier set of ten, was unveiled. *Peasant Mother and Child* (pp 104–105: Breeskin 159) derives from a group of pastels. It was influenced by the techniques used in *The Banjo Lesson,* with the delicate aquatint tones and the same monotype inking. One impression of the eighth state, previously unknown, is seen here with an experimental color combination.

Cassatt's last color prints—*Feeding the Ducks, The Barefooted Child, Under the Horse-Chestnut Tree, By the Pond,* and the unfinished *Picking Daisies in a Field* (Breeskin 156+, not in this collection)—were probably designed and printed at the country home that Cassatt had acquired in 1894; even though she maintained her long-owned Paris apartment, she was most content at Beaufresne and produced some color prints and many drypoints in this country locale. *Under the Horse-Chestnut Tree* (pp. 110–111: Breeskin 162), 1896–1897, published by *L'Estampe nouvelle,* was the only print executed for a commercial publication and not controlled by Durand-Ruel. Four impressions from the Vollard collection include two from the published edition and two impressions with distinctive coloring. These last examples bring to a close Cassatt's experiments and great accomplishments in color printmaking. Indeed, her passionate interest in color printing seems to have abruptly ended in 1898, when she decided to undertake a long-postponed journey to America—her first trip abroad since settling in France in 1875.

When Cassatt returned after a year of visiting family and friends and working on important commissions, she altered her concentration in the graphic field. She no longer attempted making prints in color and worked exclusively in the drypoint medium, sketching her country neighbors—children (mostly older models), attentive mothers, and nursemaids. Some of these later prints exhibit the rich drypoint burr that Cassatt successfully achieved on her copperplates. Many of these were acquired by Roger Marx (and then Vollard) who preferred bold drypoint impressions with warm plate tone; see, for example, *Reine and Margot Seated on a Sofa (No. 2)* and *The Crocheting Lesson* (pp. 115–117: Breeskin 177 and 178). Marx also sought the intermediate "black" working proofs of Cassatt's color prints.

By 1910 Cassatt suffered from failing eyesight, and her prints became a method for recording "pictures" of her neighbors. The Vollard collection offers a significant archive of printmaking for an artist who was forced prematurely to abandon her innovative endeavors in the medium. This exhibition is a tribute to Cassatt's skills as well as to Ambroise Vollard, who recognized her abilities and who made a profound commitment to an artist he admired and whose work he greatly respected.

Barbara Stern Shapiro
Curator for Special Projects, Museum of Fine Arts, Boston

NOTES

1. On behalf of the Museum of Fine Arts, Boston, I appreciate that Marc Rosen, Susan Pinsky, and Warren Adelson have invited me to make some comments about this collection of Mary Cassatt prints.
2. Based on a study of early documents and exhibition brochures, many titles of Cassatt's works have been changed to reflect these original listings. Those changes are identified here by including the original title in brackets following the title published by Breeskin. See *Mary Cassatt: Modern Woman*, p. 319, cat. no. 23, for this print.
3. See Shapiro essay in *The Private Collection of Edgar Degas*, p. 245.
4. A set of the drypoints was given to the National Academy of Design, New York, in 1903 by the well-known watercolorist Samuel Colman, who was a friend of Cassatt's patrons, Henry and Louisine Havemeyer.
5. See Mathews and Shapiro, *Mary Cassatt: The Color Prints*, 1989.
6. Many impressions of *The Bath* in the National Gallery of Art, Washington, DC, were originally owned by Vollard. These prints along with hundreds of sheets by other major printmakers were given to the Gallery by Lessing J. Rosenwald. They were acquired from Jean Goriany who was associated with Henri M. Petiet, both of whom were important dealers to Mr. Rosenwald in the 1940s and 1950s.
7. I would like to thank Eric Carlson for bringing this to my attention.

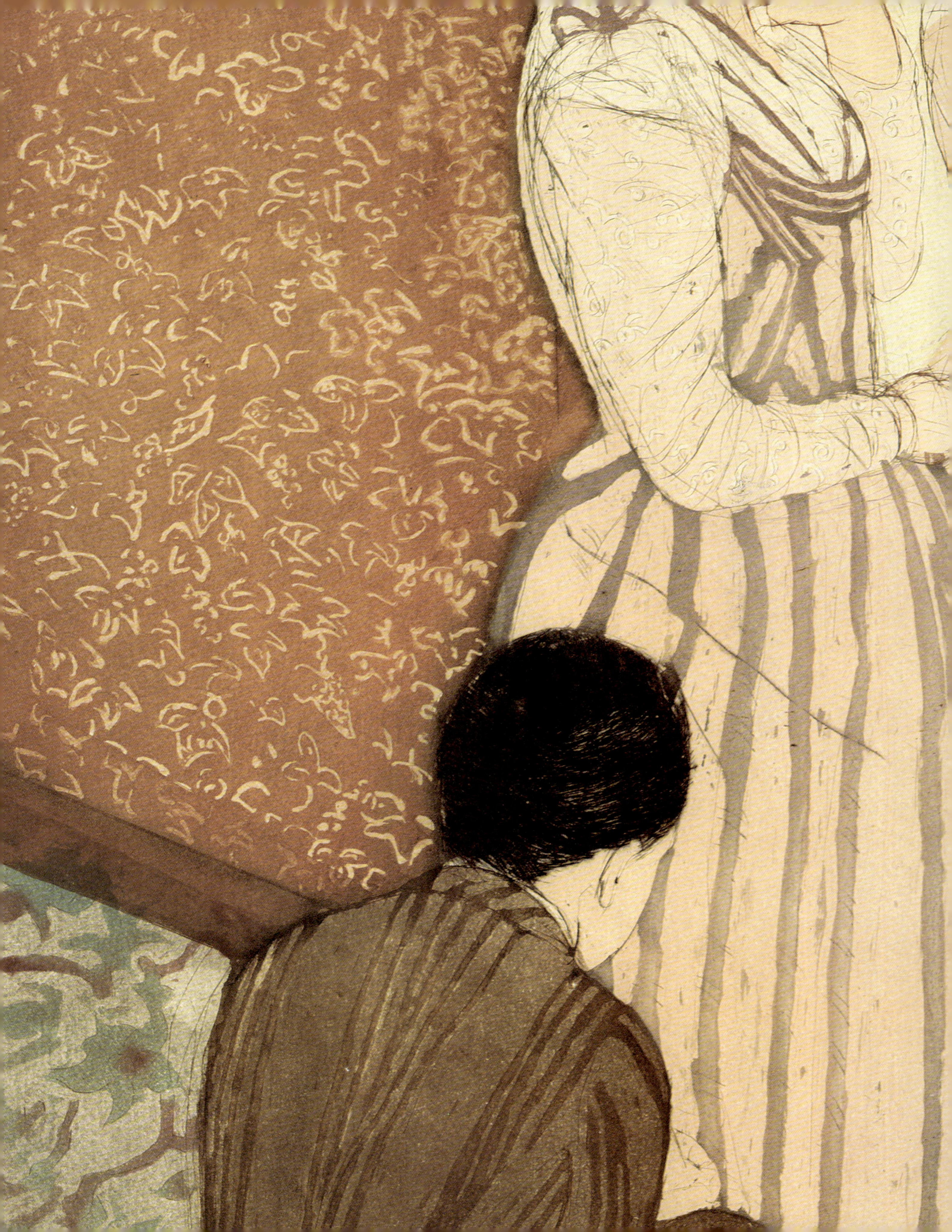

The Prints of Mary Cassatt – Experimentation and Virtuosity

Mary Cassatt's prints are a central part of her artistic legacy. She is one of a small number of major artists who seems to have intuitively and completely understood the special character and unique possibilities of working on copper. This collection of prints and drawings, acquired by Ambroise Vollard directly from the artist and augmented by him with a few choice impressions from major early collections, is extraordinary in its breadth and in the number of aesthetic revelations it provides. There are beautiful examples of Cassatt's early prints, many of which were done in a studio that Degas set up for himself and his artist friends. Included is a stunning group of proofs and final states of what is recognized as her greatest contribution to the history of printmaking—the set of ten color prints inspired by the immensely influential 1890 exhibition in Paris of Japanese woodblock prints.

The particular thrill of viewing this collection is that these works have been preserved in portfolio since the time they were done, so that their immediacy and freshness have come down to us undiminished by the accidents of time.

As a young artist, Cassatt had rejected academic drawing as antithetical to her pictorial sensibility, and she was happy to embrace the anti-Salon ideals of the Impressionists. Her experimentation with the creative alchemy of etching led her to discover first the seductive atmosphere of soft-ground and aquatint and then the elegance of drypoint. In printmaking, there was no need for her to confront the expectations of conventional pictorial detail and completeness. She could concentrate all of her attention on capturing, with a few deft strokes, the facial expressions and the telling gestures of her models, while completing her image by the skillful manipulation of printing ink left on the surface of the plate, or with broad areas of color or pattern.

Cassatt's earliest significant prints were done in the studio of Edgar Degas, and later she set up her own press. Throughout her career, she did most of the printing herself, pulling proofs as she went along. It is an indication of the importance she attached to her many experiments in printmaking that she retained such a large body of this work in her collection, though she typically did not bother to meticulously document the stages or states of her work.

Edgar Degas (1834–1917)

Mary Cassatt at the Louvre: The Etruscan Gallery, 1879–1880

(Delteil 30; Adhémar 53; Reed & Shapiro 51)

Soft-ground etching, drypoint, aquatint, and etching, Reed and Shapiro's ninth (final) state, one of only about 25 known impressions of this state (of which an edition of 50 was intended), with the Atelier stamp (Lugt 657), on smooth, ivory laid oriental paper, with full margins, in good condition (some crinkling in the upper left margin corner, a narrow strip of old hinging tape along upper margin edge on the *verso*)

Plate: 27 × 23.7 cm   10⅝ × 9⅜ in.
Sheet: 35.7 × 26.9 cm   14⅛ × 10⅝ in.

All the preceding states of this work, on which Degas lavished such careful attention, are known in mostly only one or two proofs. In this elegant representation of his famous American protégée and colleague, Degas achieved a level of refinement in the balance between the techniques of etching, drypoint and aquatint seldom equaled since the time of Goya.

A fashionably turned-out Mary Cassatt contemplates a sarcophagus, while her companion, probably her sister Lydia, reads from a guidebook.

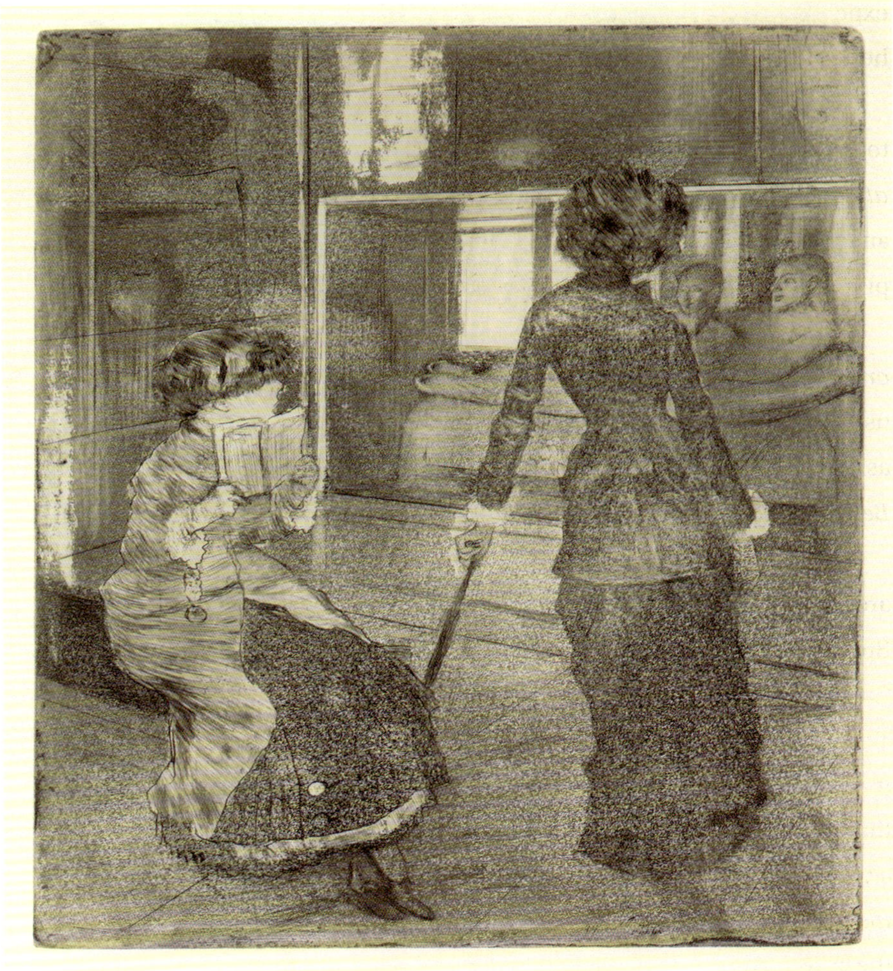

Because most of her prints were not done with a view to publication, they were printed in few examples and are extremely rare. The "studio collection," as it has come down to us today, spans Cassatt's artistic career as a printmaker. It includes eleven prints known only in the present impression,[1] fourteen previously unknown states of prints,[2] and several unique color variants.

A key work from her early period, 1879–1880, is *In the Opera Box (No. 3)* (pp. 28–29: Breeskin 22), done in Degas's studio and intended as Cassatt's contribution to *Le Jour et la nuit*, a publication project conceived by Degas but never brought to fruition. This image shows the influence of Degas in the composition and choice of subject. Yet, even at this early date, we see personal characteristics that anticipate her later color prints in the way she has transformed a three-dimensional scene into a two-dimensional composition, impressionistically justified here by the flattening effect of a brightly lit subject in a darkened theater. The preceding works in this catalogue show the artist experimenting with the manipulation of tonal values and working towards her final resolution of the composition.

It is a tribute to his respect for Cassatt that Degas's intended contribution to *Le Jour et la nuit* was the soft-ground, drypoint and aquatint, *Mary Cassatt at the Louvre: The Etruscan Gallery*, which is one of his most carefully studied and meticulously executed compositions. (A fine impression of this work purchased by Vollard from the Degas estate sale is included in this exhibition.)

Some examples of Cassatt's early use of aquatint, such as *Mlle Luguet Seated on a Couch* (p. 35: Breeskin 49), show a romantic homage to Goya's virtuosic use of contrasting areas of aquatint grain. Others elegantly exploit this medium as a compositional device for flattening and abstracting pictorial space, as in *Before the Fireplace (No. 1)* (p. 38: Breeskin 64).

To appreciate the way in which Cassatt's distinctive strengths as a draftsman are revealed in her drypoints, one has only to look at *Baby's Back* (pp. 54–55: Breeskin 128), the second in the famous series of twelve drypoint subjects that Cassatt exhibited at the 1890 *Peintres-Graveurs* exhibition held at Durand-Ruel. This print is essentially adapted from a pastel, *At the Window* (BrCR 179), now in the Musée d'Orsay, Paris. In comparing the two, one can see immediately that the artist completely restudied the expressions and gestures, and produced a work of art more elegant in line and more sharply characterized. As in so many of her prints, Cassatt exploited the elimination of irrelevant details of the surrounding space to distill an image of universal appeal.

The "studio collection" includes numerous discoveries of previously unknown states of rare and unpublished prints, e.g., *Portrait Sketch of Mme M…*; *Mimi Seated, Wearing a Sleeveless Dress*; *On the Balcony* (pp. 48–49: Breeskin 114, 115, and 120); and *Mother Berthe Holding Her Child* (p. 52: Breeskin 126); as well as extraordinary sequences of states, such as those for *The Mandolin Player* (pp. 57–59: Breeskin 130) and *Reflection* (pp. 60–61: Breeskin 131), which also include two previously unrecorded states. The unique print, *Sketch for "The Bath"* (p. 75: Breeskin 142+), one of the works Cassatt executed directly before her series of ten color prints, is as close as one can get to a true sketch on copper and vividly illustrates the way in which the medium can be used to enhance the completeness and communicative power of a spontaneously rendered scene.

Among the set of ten great color prints, the series of impressions of *The Bath* (pp. 76–79: Breeskin 143) gives some idea of the serious exploration the artist went through in refining the devices that she would use throughout this series for allocating the compositional elements among her printing plates. Within this group too there are unique and/or newly discovered states (see

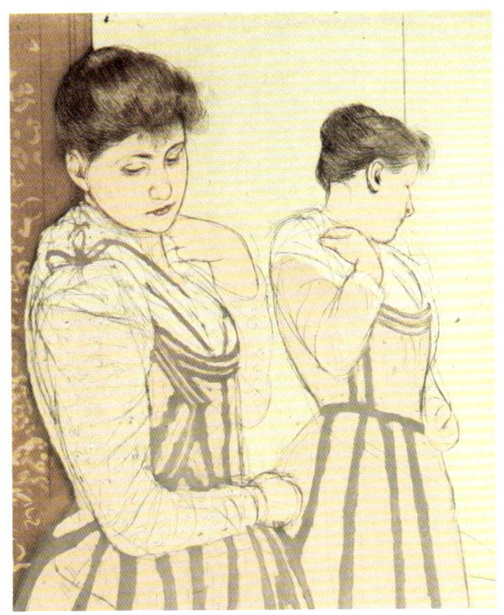

The Fitting
Proof of a previously unknown state, before Mathews and Shapiro's sixth state of seven, showing an area of aquatint grain on the reflection of the sleeve
[Detail of illustration on page 88]

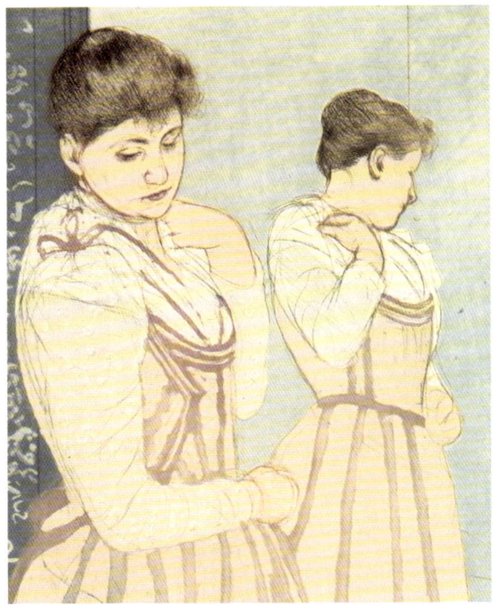

The Fitting
Color variant of the final state, showing the aquatint grain on the reflection of the sleeve replaced by diagonal drypoint shading
[Detail of illustration on page 89]

The Bath, pp. 76–79: Breeskin 143; *The Lamp*, p. 80: Breeskin 144; and *The Fitting*, pp. 86–90: Breeskin 147); and in the case of *The Fitting*, not only do we have new states and variant proofs, but these differences and discoveries greatly add to our appreciation of the range of Cassatt's aesthetic experiments with choice and harmony of colors. (See details of the penultimate and final states.) The impression of *The Fitting* with the patterned wall printed in russet-brown surprises the viewer in its fresh intensity, while the predominately blue hues in the final state are dazzling and unexpected. No one who knows her color prints could have expected to find such a radical experimental combination in an impression of the final state. In the end, however, the artist, perhaps influenced by the hundred-year-old examples of Utamaro's prints she had so much admired (see Mathews and Shapiro, p. 65), reverted to a more subdued color balance for the usual printing of the final state. (Since Cassatt inked the plates individually and slightly differently for each impression, no two impressions are exactly alike.)

But even those works in this collection that are closer to familiar color combinations are surprising in the intensity and freshness of their color: the hot rose of the dress in *The Omnibus* (pp. 82–83: Breeskin 145), the deep blue of *Woman Bathing* (pp. 90–91: Breeskin 148), the exceptionally strong, powdery blue background in *Mother's Kiss* (pp. 92–93: Breeskin 149), the effect of which has been likened to the mica dusted on the surface of a Japanese woodblock print.

Though conceived as a set, this remarkable series of works shows a wide range of approaches to composition, from the classical pyramid of *The Bath*, with its generalized background, to those showing the flattened, diagonal space of a Japanese print.

Between 1893 and 1897, Cassatt executed several more color prints, a few of which directly explore the free application of printing inks to unetched areas of the copper plate. Very little of the color work in *The Banjo Lesson* (pp. 98–99: Breeskin 156) is etched on the plate, but is instead freely applied in a monotype fashion; and the unique color variant of *Peasant Mother and Child* (pp. 104–105: Breeskin 159) shows the artist using monotype in a painterly way to extend her composition. The richness of this collection is again evident in the newly discovered early state of *The Banjo Lesson* and in the four impressions, including new states and variants, of *Gathering Fruit* (pp. 100–101: Breeskin 157), as well as in the first and beautiful final state impressions of *Feeding the Ducks* (pp. 102–103: Breeskin 158), and the differently inked impressions of *By the Pond* and *Under the Horse-Chestnut Tree* (pp. 108–109: Breeskin 161 and 162).

The prints from the last period of her work, from the end of the nineteenth century through the first decade of the twentieth, are represented here in exceptionally fine impressions of several well-known subjects (*Margo Leaning against Her Mother*; *Reine and Margot Seated on a Sofa, No. 2*; and *The Crocheting Lesson*, pp. 114–117: Breeskin 175, 177, and 178), and in several rare and unique examples, including the early impression of *Margot Wearing a Bonnet, No. 1* (p. 118: Breeskin 179). Included in this part of the catalogue is the only known impression of *Katharine Kelso Cassatt* (p. 122: Breeskin 198+), which Breeskin had mistakenly dated to ca. 1905, but which clearly belongs in the context of her earlier work.

In one way or another, almost every work in this collection provides us with aesthetic surprises and delights, and enriches our understanding of the artist's creative process. The "studio collection" as it now stands is unparalleled in private hands and indeed is barely matched by the finest museum collections.

MARC ROSEN and SUSAN PINSKY
Marc Rosen Fine Art, Ltd., New York City

NOTES

1. The eleven subjects in the "studio collection" that are unique impressions are: *Sewing by Lamplight, Head of Margaret Sloane (No. 2), Sketch for "The Bath," Two Heads: One Upside Down, Heads of Two Little Girls, Reine and Blond Baby with a Cat, Margot in a Poke Bonnet, Katharine Kelso Cassatt, Denise in Profile to Right with a Hand Mirror, Woman Trying on a Necklace before a Mirror,* and *Heads of Denise and Child* (Breeskin 71+, 92+, 142+, 154+, 167+, 177+, 184+, 198+, 208+, 216+ and 218+).

   In addition, the only known impression of *Seated under an Umbrella* (Breeskin 55) is included in this collection, and a number of other prints in this group are apparently only the second known impression of prints recorded by Breeskin as surviving in a unique impression.
2. The fourteen previously unknown states are for the following subjects: *Mrs. Cassatt Reading to her Grandchildren (No. 2), Portrait Sketch of Mme M…., Mimi Seated, Wearing a Sleeveless Dress, On the Balcony, Mother Berthe Holding Her Child, Reflection, The Mirror, The Lamp, The Fitting, Blanche without Her Hat, The Banjo Lesson,* and *Gathering Fruit* (Breeskin 59, 114, 115, 120 126, 131 [two states], 136, 144, 147 [two states], 154, 156, and 157), for which the final example in this collection is also a unique variant. This list does not include examples of unique inking or unique color combinations.

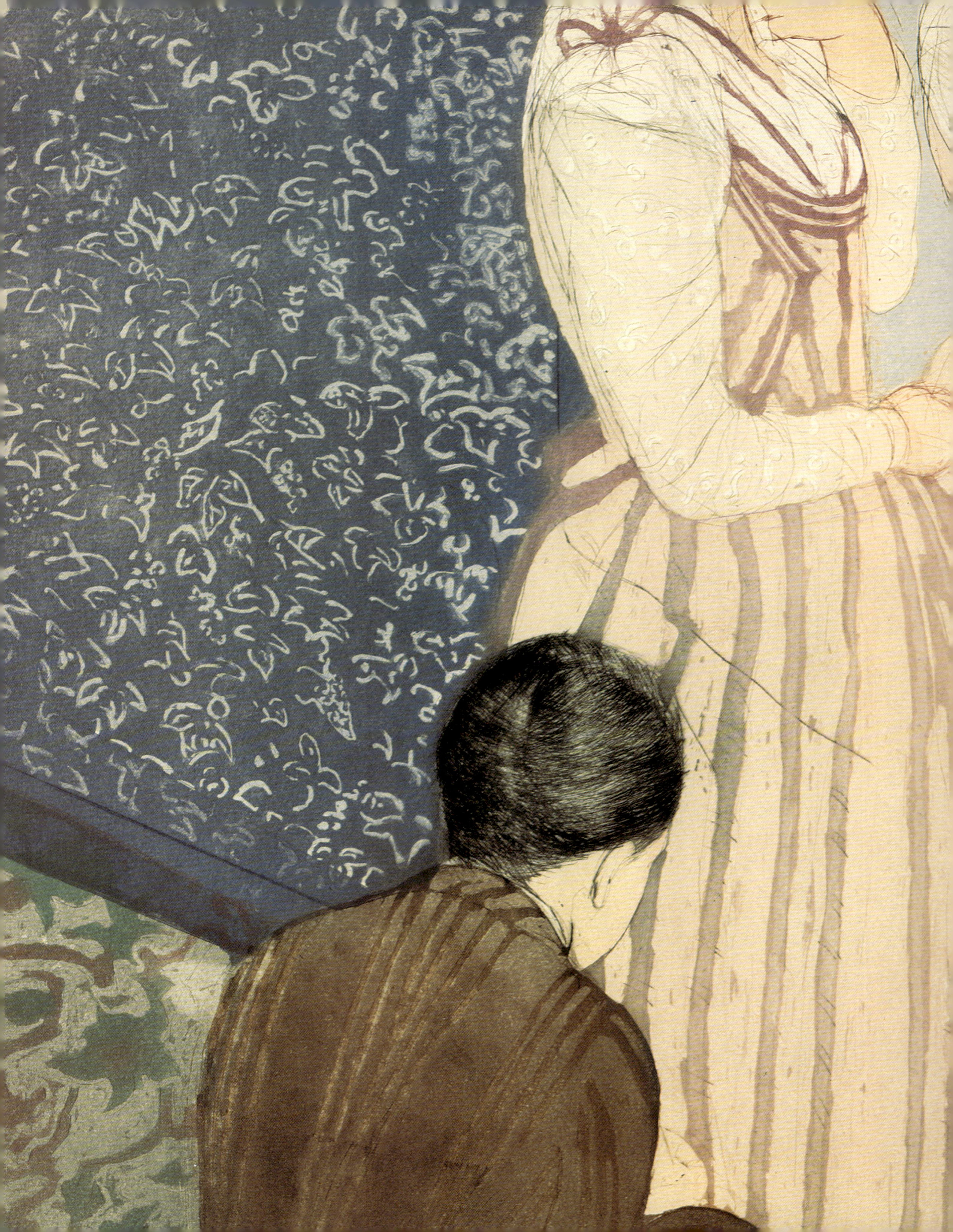

NOTES ON THE USE OF THE CATALOGUE

As the essayists in this catalogue have noted, the presentation of a collection of this magnitude provides us with much new information and many exciting avenues for future investigation. This volume supplements the pioneering scholarship of Adelyn Dohme Breeskin, complements the catalogue prepared by Nancy Mowll Mathews and Barbara Stern Shapiro for the 1989 exhibition *Mary Cassatt: The Color Prints,* and draws on the ongoing research of the Mary Cassatt Catalogue Raisonné Committee.

The titles of works used here are those found in Breeskin's catalogues of Cassatt's oeuvre. Where alternate titles are conventionally used, or where recent scholarship has identified titles originally used by the artist, these are given in brackets.

Because a comprehensive review of the dating of Cassatt's work is still pending, for convenience the Breeskin catalogue number order has been retained. Dates given following the titles are the dates of execution as proposed by Breeskin with the exception of those re-dated by Mathews and Shapiro. Where more recent dating of individual prints has come to our attention, those dates are included in brackets. It should be noted that such re-dating of individual prints may likely lead to a re-examination and re-dating of related works.

Citations for drawings and other original works of art published in Breeskin's catalogue raisonné of paintings, pastels, watercolors, and drawings are abbreviated as **BrCR** and citations for works recorded in the catalogue of Cassatt's graphic art are referred to simply as **Breeskin**.

For each print, we have placed a descriptive text on the same page as the corresponding illustration. When this has not been possible, the reader is referred to the location of the illustration. For the drawings, we have additionally provided the **BrCR** number, directly under the illustration.

All print measurements are given for plate and sheet size, height before width, in centimeters and in inches. The drawing measurements are for the fold marks that represent the field in which the artist worked, as well as the full sheet size.

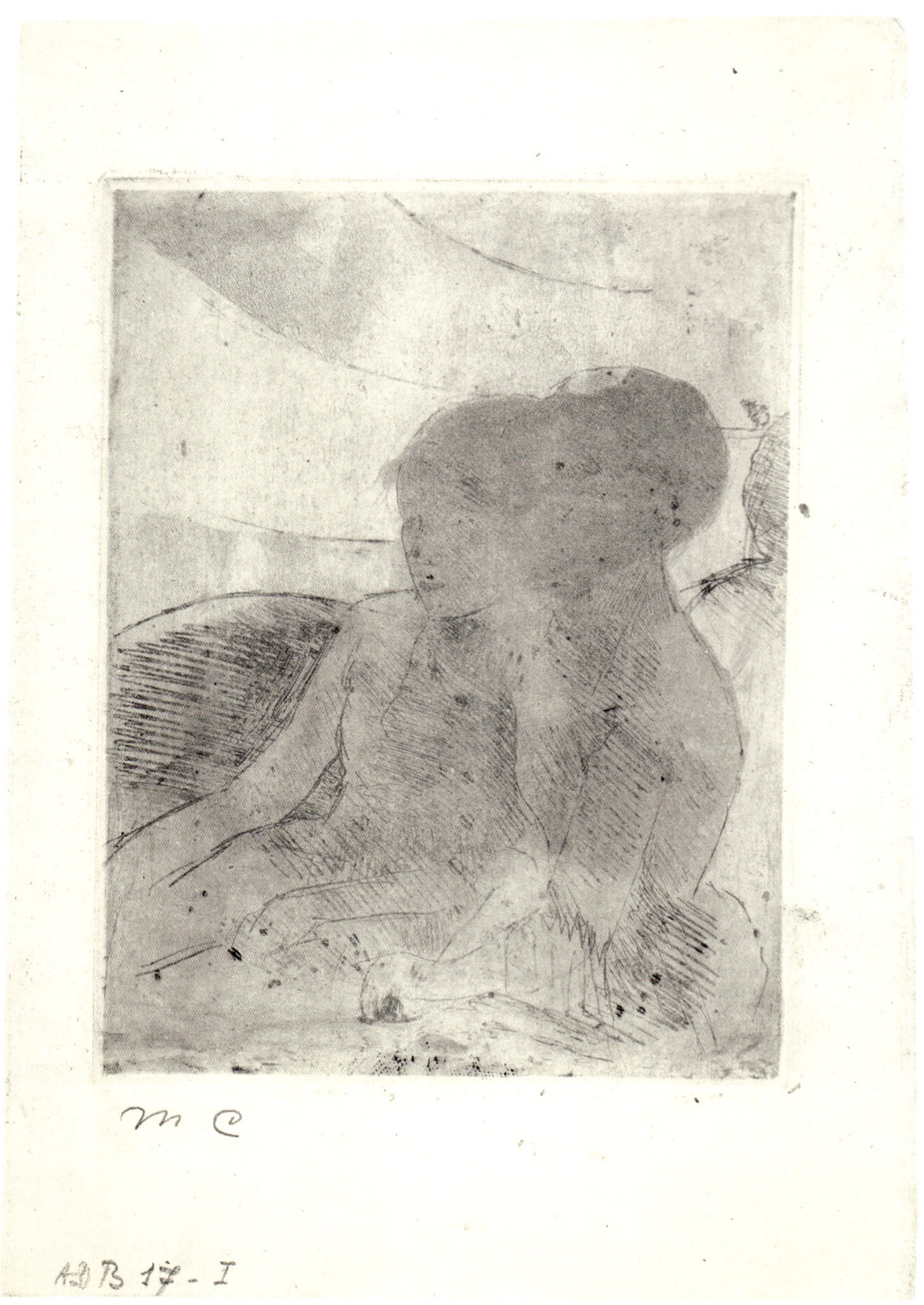

Two Ladies in a Loge, Facing Left (No. 2), ca. 1882 [1879–1880]

Breeskin 17

Soft-ground and aquatint, Breeskin's second state of four, initialed *M C,* on laid paper, the full sheet, in good condition apart from minor, tan handling stains at lower right

Plate: 21 × 15.7 cm 8¼ × 6⅛ in.
Sheet: 29.7 × 20.5 cm 11⅝ × 8⅛ in.

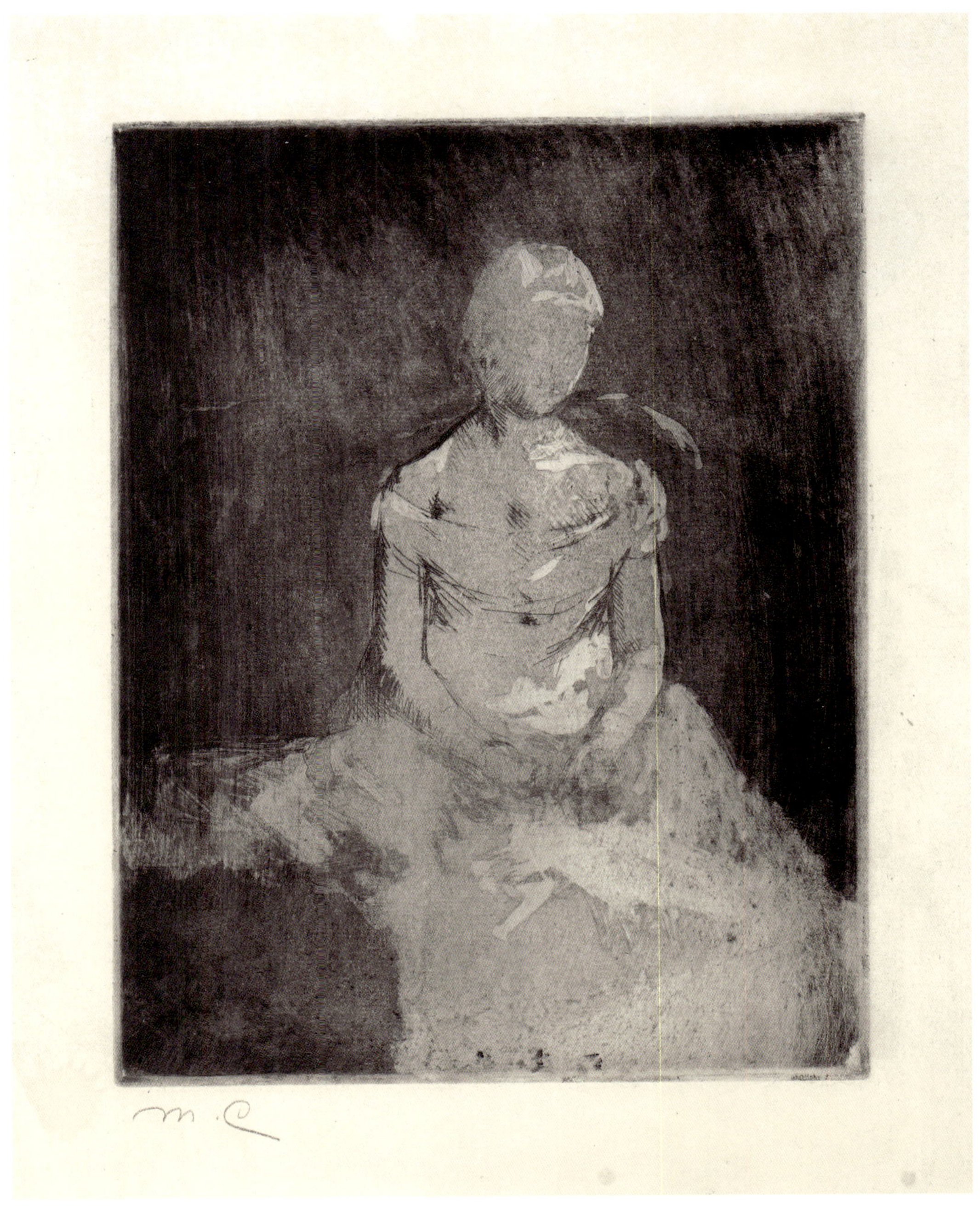

The Bouquet, ca. 1880

Breeskin 19

Soft-ground and aquatint, first state of three, initialed *M. C*, a trial proof with exceptionally strong, directionally wiped plate tone in the background enveloping the dimly lit figure in dark space, on Van Gelder laid paper, the full sheet, except lower right corner lacking, and with stains, creases, and small tears in the margins, annotated *before 1 state*

Plate: 28.5 × 21.7 cm 11¼ × 8½ in.
Sheet: 47.5 × 31.5 cm 18⅝ × 12⅜ in.

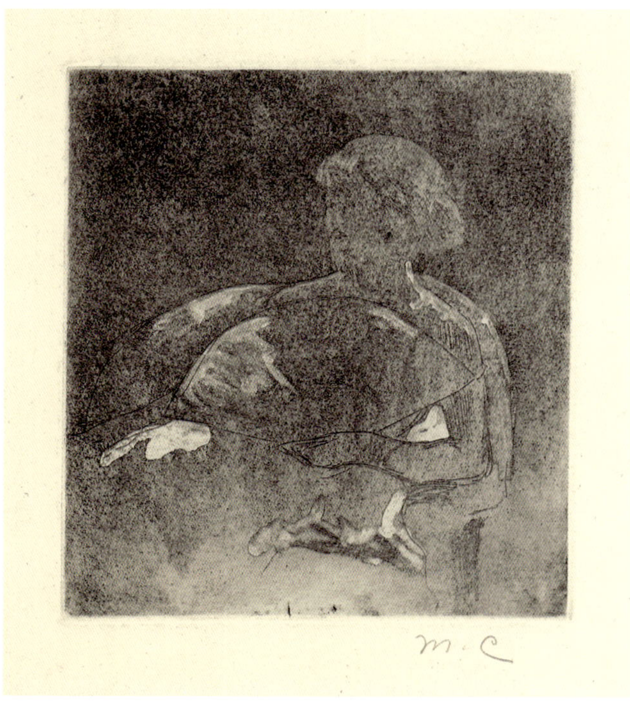

In the Opera Box (No. 1), ca. 1880

Breeskin 20

Soft-ground and etching, initialed *M. C*, on laid paper with a proprietary watermark, the full sheet, in good condition (soft crease across top left margin corner), annotated *A*

Plate: 21.7 × 19.5 cm 8½ × 7⅝ in.
Sheet: 39 × 29.1 cm 15⅜ × 11½ in.

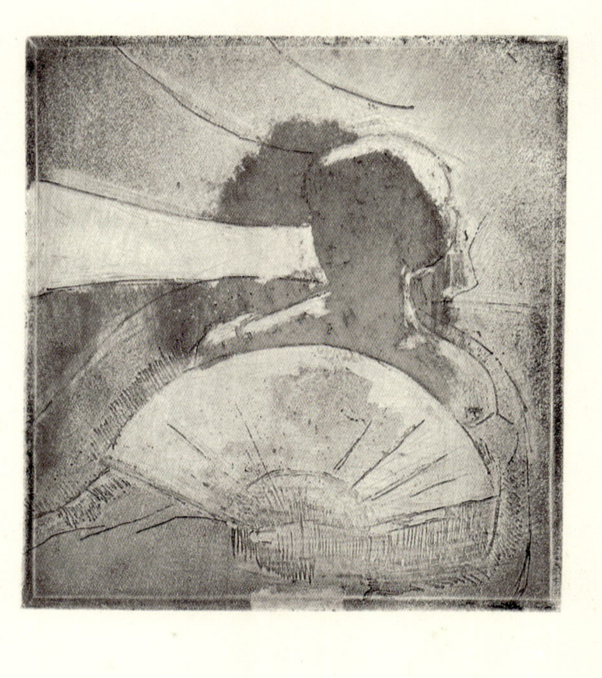

In the Opera Box (No. 3) [Femme au Théâtre], 1879–1880

Breeskin 22

Soft-ground, aquatint and etching, third state of four, on heavy, white, wove paper, the full sheet (smaller margins at sides), foxing, essentially visible only in margins

Plate: 20.6 × 18.9 cm 8⅛ × 7½ in.
Sheet: 31.3 × 22.6 cm 12¼ × 8⅞ in.

PROVENANCE
Edgar Degas (sale, 6 November 1918, stamp, Lugt 657)

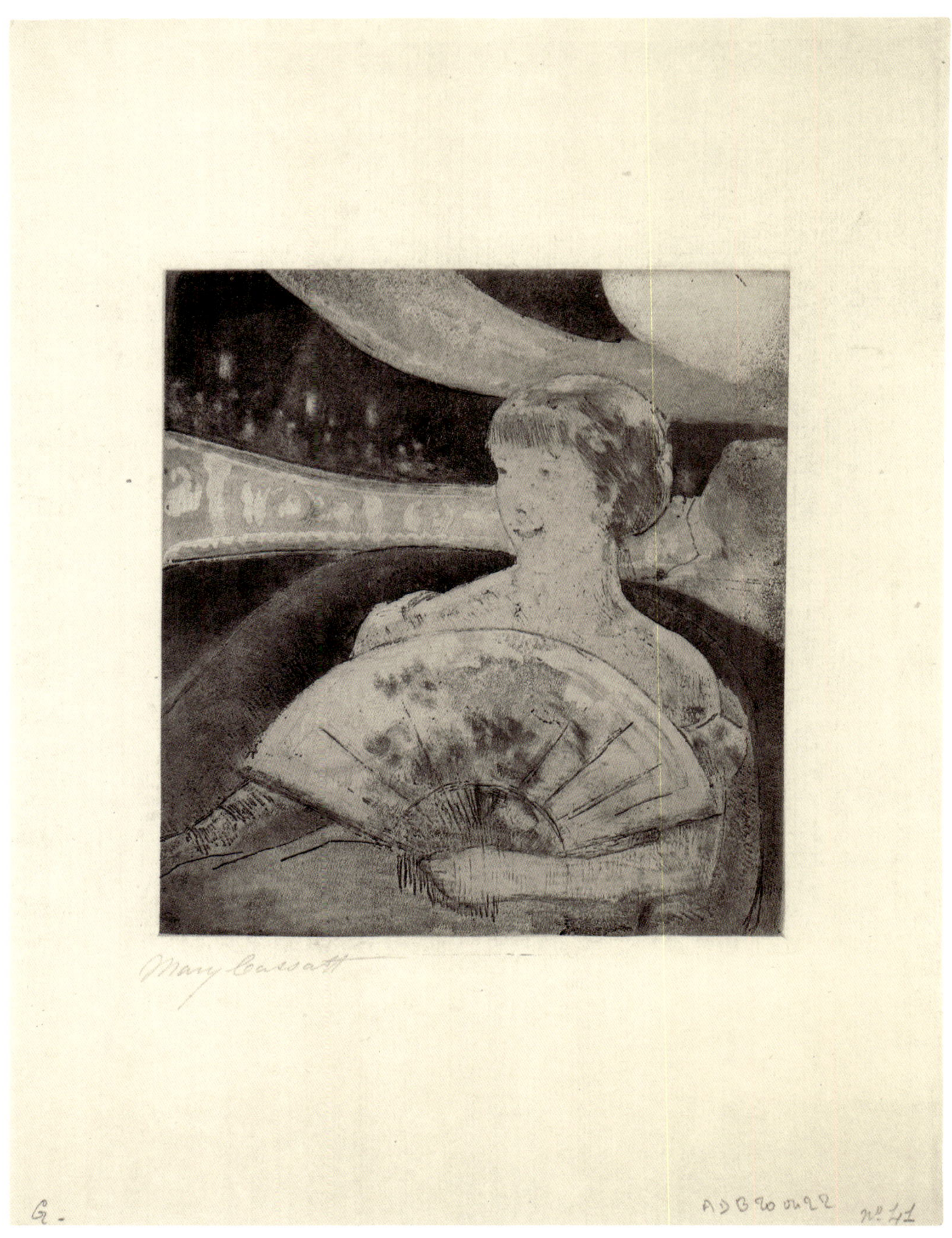

In the Opera Box (No. 3)
[Femme au Théâtre], 1879–1880

Breeskin 22

Soft-ground, aquatint, and etching, fourth state of four, signed in full, from the edition of 50, intended for publication in *Le Jour et la nuit,* on laid Japan paper, the full sheet, in good condition

Plate: 20.9 × 18.8 cm   8¼ × 7⅜ in.
Sheet: 35.7 × 26.8 cm   14 × 10⅝ in.

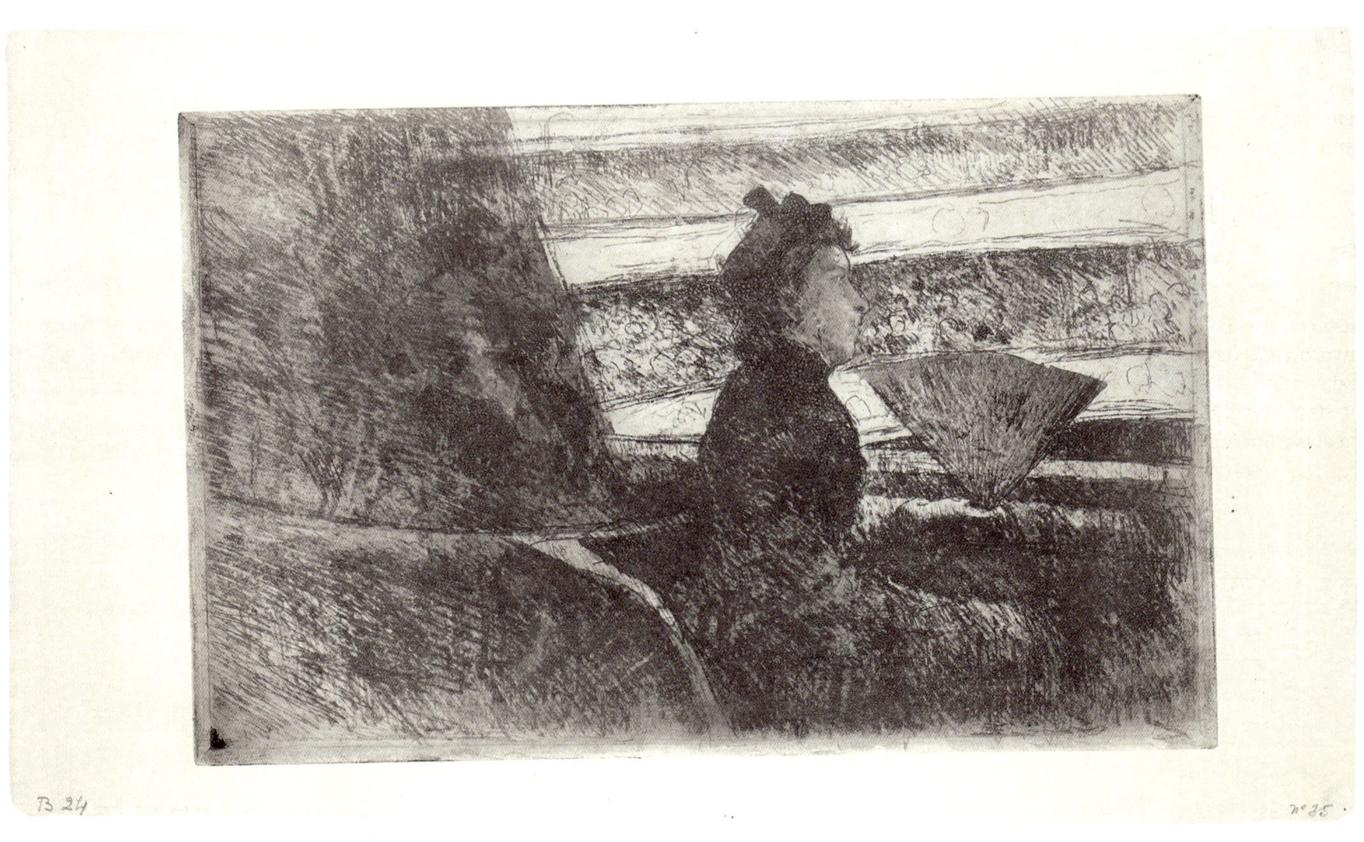

Lady in Black, in a Loge, Facing Right [Au Spectacle],
ca. 1880 [1879–1880]

Breeskin 24

Soft-ground, third state of three, on laid paper with VanderLey watermark, the full sheet, in good condition

Plate: 19.5 × 29.6 cm 7⅝ × 11⅝ in.
Sheet: 23.9 × 39 cm 9⅜ × 15⅜ in.

George Moore, ca. 1880

Breeskin 27

Soft-ground, first state of two, printed with plate tone, on thin, wove (China) paper, with large, irregular margins, some inherent irregularity in paper

Plate: 22.2 × 13.9 cm 8¾ × 5½ in.
Sheet: 34.5 × 31 cm 13½ × 12¼ in.

PROVENANCE
Edgar Degas (sale, 6 November 1918, stamp, Lugt 657)

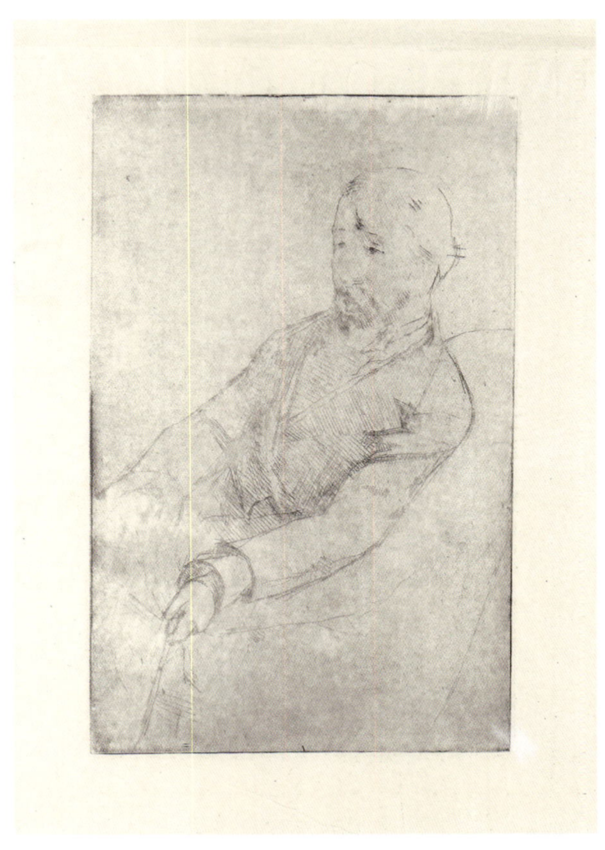

George Moore, ca. 1880

Breeskin 27

Soft-ground and aquatint, second state of two, on laid paper, the full sheet, in good condition, but with pale light-stain, mat-stain on verso, and inherent thin spot at center

Plate: 22.1 × 13.9 cm 8¾ × 5½ in.
Sheet: 29.4 × 20.4 cm 11½ × 8 in.

PROVENANCE
Edgar Degas (sale, 6 November 1918, stamp, Lugt 657)

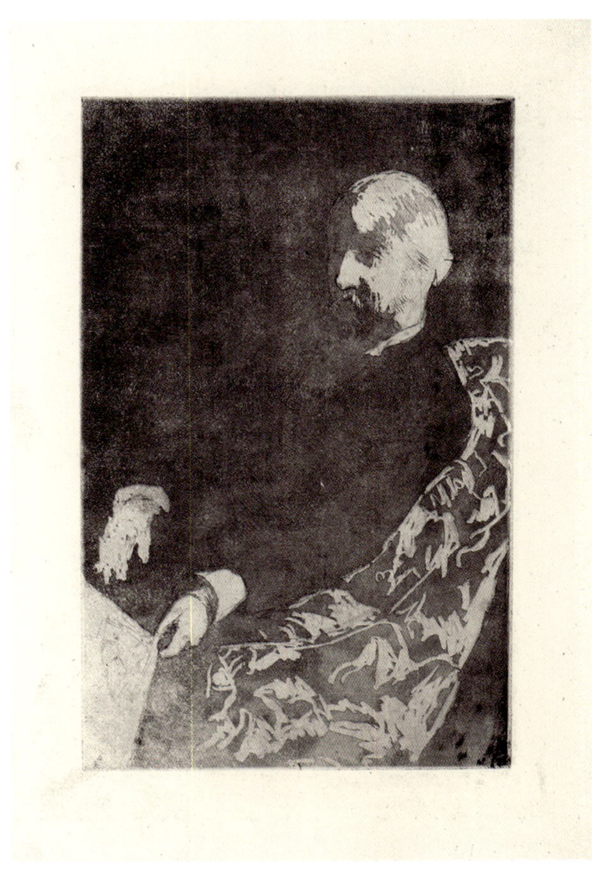

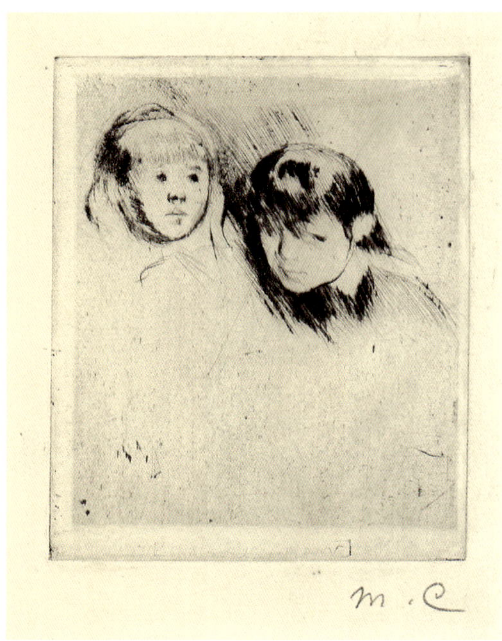

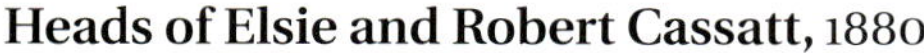

Heads of Elsie and Robert Cassatt, 1880

Breeskin 38

Drypoint, an extraordinary early proof of the second state of two, with powerful accents of burr and plate tone, initialed *M. C,* on Van Gelder laid paper, the full sheet, in good condition (minor soiling at edges)

Plate: 12.3 × 9.9 cm 4⅞ × 3⅞ in.
Sheet: 27.5 × 18.5 cm 10¾ × 7¼ in.

EXHIBITION
The Graphic Art of Mary Cassatt, Museum of Graphic Art and Smithsonian Institution, traveling exhibition, 1967–1968, no. 8, ill. (catalogue by Adelyn D. Breeskin)

Heads of Elsie and Robert Cassatt, 1880

Breeskin 38

Drypoint, second state of two, on Van Gelder laid paper, the full sheet, in good condition

Plate: 12.2 × 9.9 cm 4⅞ × 3⅞ in.
Sheet: 27.5 × 18.7 cm 10¾ × 7⅜ in.

[Not illustrated]

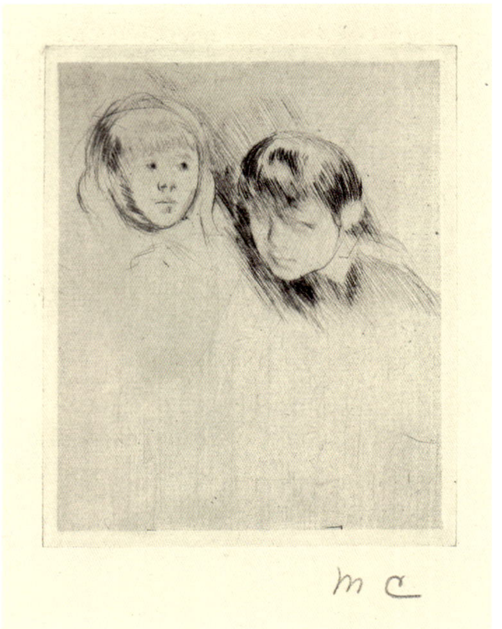

Heads of Elsie and Robert Cassatt, 1880

Breeskin 38

Drypoint, second state of two, initialed *M. C,* on Van Gelder laid paper, with margins, in good condition except top right margin corner folded back

Plate: 12.4 × 9.9 cm 4⅞ × 3⅞ in.
Sheet: 24.8 × 18.1 cm 9¾ × 7⅛ in.

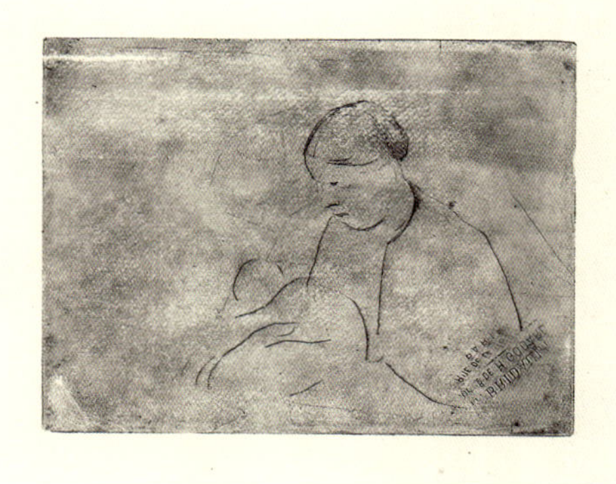

Outline Sketch of a Mother and Baby, ca. 1880

Breeskin 41

Drypoint, printed with plate tone, on laid paper with part of a Fortuna watermark, with margins, in good condition

Plate: 11.9 × 15.7 cm 4⅝ × 6⅛ in.
Sheet: 18.1 × 21 cm 7⅛ × 8¼ in.

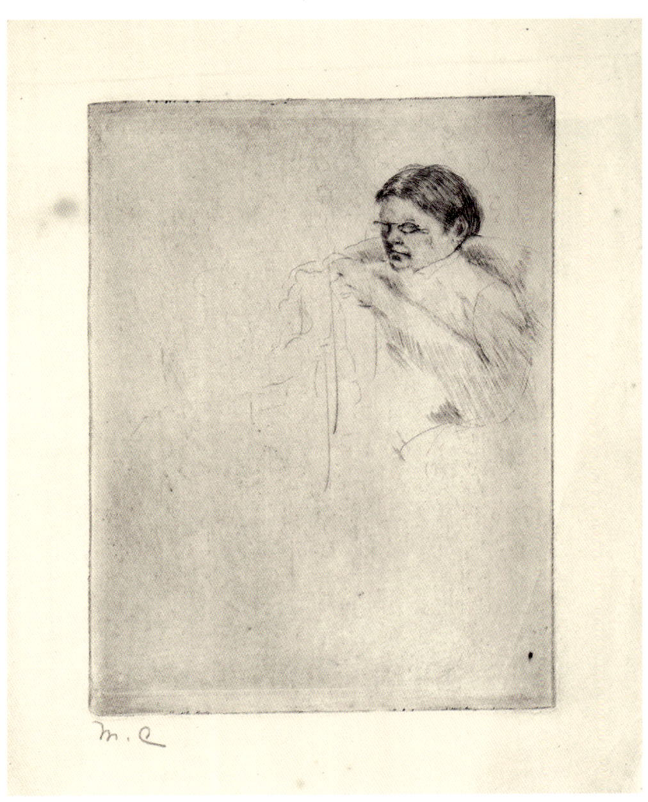

Mrs. Cassatt Sewing, ca. 1881

Breeskin 44

Etching and drypoint, printed with atmospheric plate tone, initialed *M. C,* on Van Gelder laid paper, with margins, a few creases in margins, and one across the lower right corner of the subject, a few stains in margins

Plate: 21.3 × 15.7 cm 8⅜ × 6⅛ in.
Sheet: 28.6 × 22 cm 11¼ × 8⅝ in.

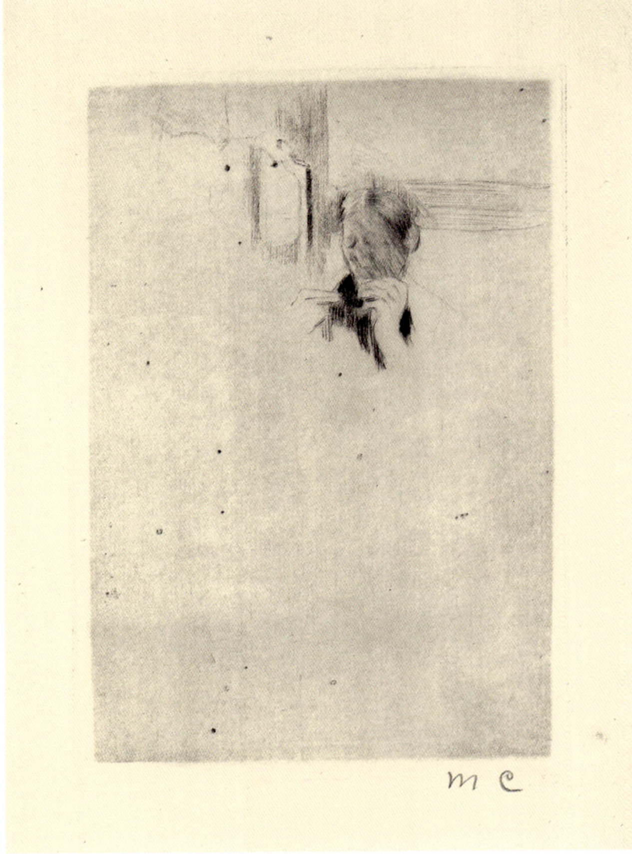

Mrs. Cassatt Threading a Needle, ca. 1881

Breeskin 45

Drypoint, printed with plate tone, initialed *M. C,* on Van Gelder laid paper, the full sheet, in good condition

Plate: 23.5 × 15.8 cm 9¼ × 6¼ in.
Sheet: 29.8 × 21.3 cm 11¾ × 8⅜ in.

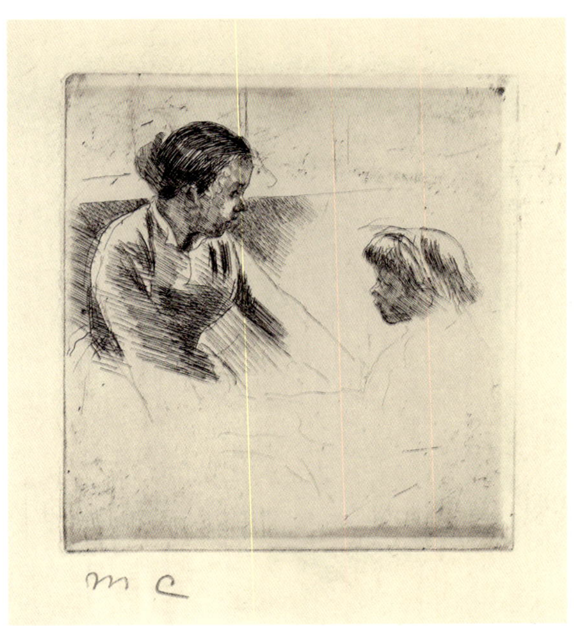

Susan and Child Facing Each Other, ca. 1883

Breeskin 46

Etching, printed with plate tone, initialed *M. C,* on Van Gelder laid paper, the full sheet, in good condition

Plate: 13.8 × 12.7 cm 5⅜ × 5 in.
Sheet: 27.8 × 18.7 cm 11 × 7⅜ in.

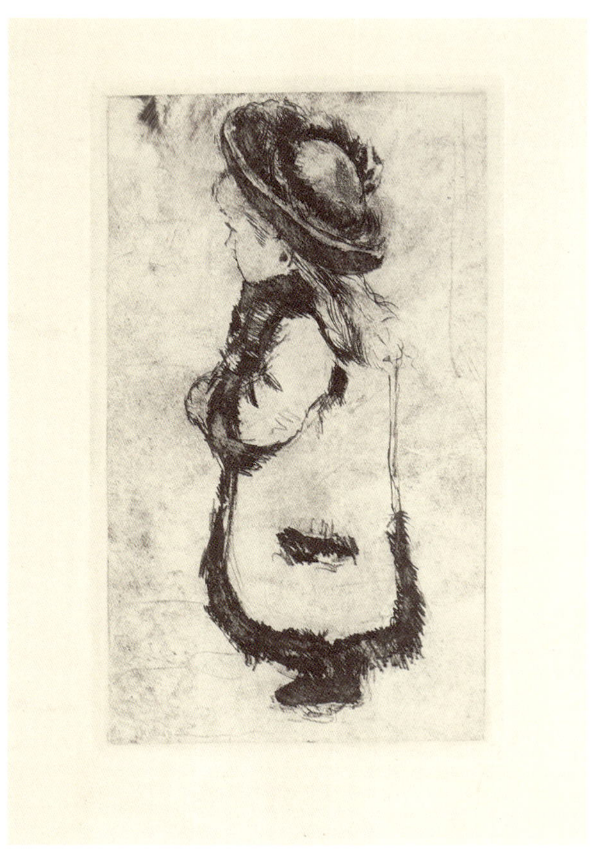

Mlle Luguet in a Coat and Hat, ca. 1883

Breeskin 48

Soft-ground, Breeskin's first state of two, on stiff, white Japan paper, with margins, in good condition apart from slight thin spots in top edge *verso*, minor crease in the lower right corner

Plate: 21.7 × 12.8 cm   8½ × 5 in.
Sheet: 31.6 × 22.5 cm   12½ × 8⅞ in.

A trial proof exists before Breeskin's first state.

PROVENANCE
Alexis Rouart [1839–1911] (violet stamp, *recto* and *verso*, variant of Lugt 2187a). Rouart was an industrialist who assembled a large and distinguished collection of the art of his day.

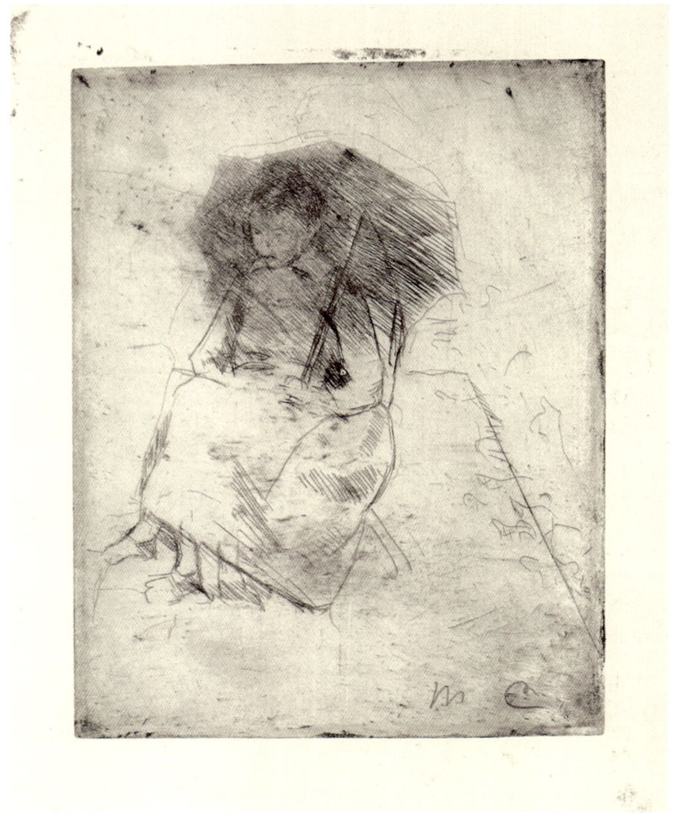

Seated under an Umbrella, ca. 1883

Breeskin 55

Etching and drypoint, only state, initialed *M. C* within the subject, printed in brown-black ink, on VanderLey laid paper, the full sheet, in good condition

Plate: 16.8 × 12.8 cm   6⅝ × 5 in.
Sheet: 23.9 × 19.5 cm   9⅜ × 7⅝ in.

Breeskin illustrates this impression and cites no others.

Mlle Luguet Seated on a Couch, ca. 1883

Breeskin 49

Soft-ground and aquatint, first state of two, initialed *M. C*, an exceptionally fine impression, with the work on the dress rich and strong, and the two aquatint grains in the background clearly differentiated, on sturdy wove paper, the full sheet, in good condition apart from minor soiling and scattered light brown spots in margins, a few stray bits of pastel offset on *verso*, and a bit of blue pastel (?) in the image at lower right, annotated *HP./Epr. d'état*

Plate: 21.9 × 14.1 cm 8⅝ × 5½ in.
Sheet: 35.9 × 27.7 cm 14⅛ × 10⅞ in.

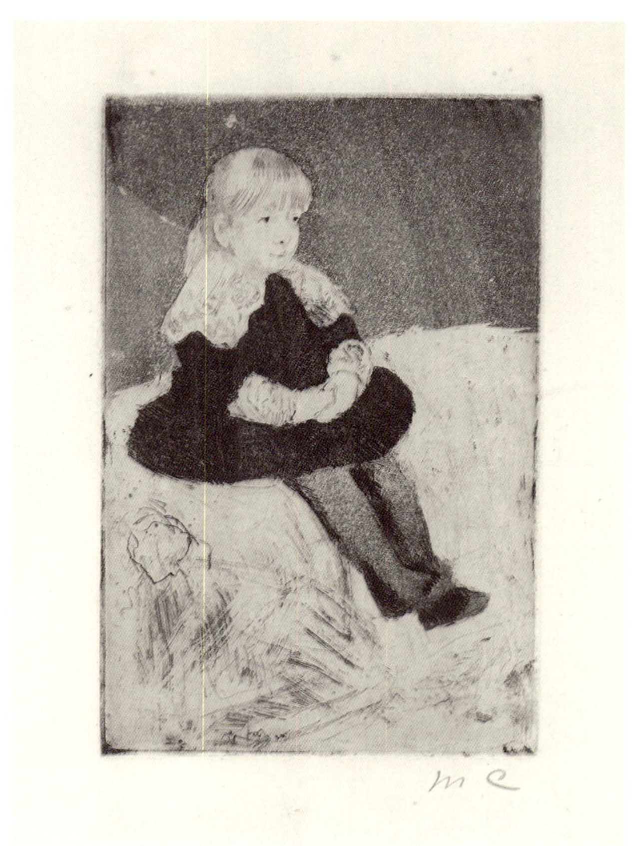

Mlle Luguet Seated on a Couch, ca. 1883

Breeskin 49

Soft-ground and aquatint, a fine impression of the first state of two, on laid paper, with full margins, in good condition apart from foxing, mainly in the margins

Plate: 21.7 × 14.2 cm 8½ × 5⅝ in.
Sheet: 30.7 × 21.8 cm 12⅛ × 8⅝ in.

PROVENANCE

Roger Marx [1859–1913] (black stamp lower right corner, *recto*, Lugt 2229), renowned and influential art critic, whose collection of beautifully chosen prints was particularly rich in the works of Mary Cassatt.

Emile Laffon [1868–1931] (blue stamp, *verso*, Lugt 877a)

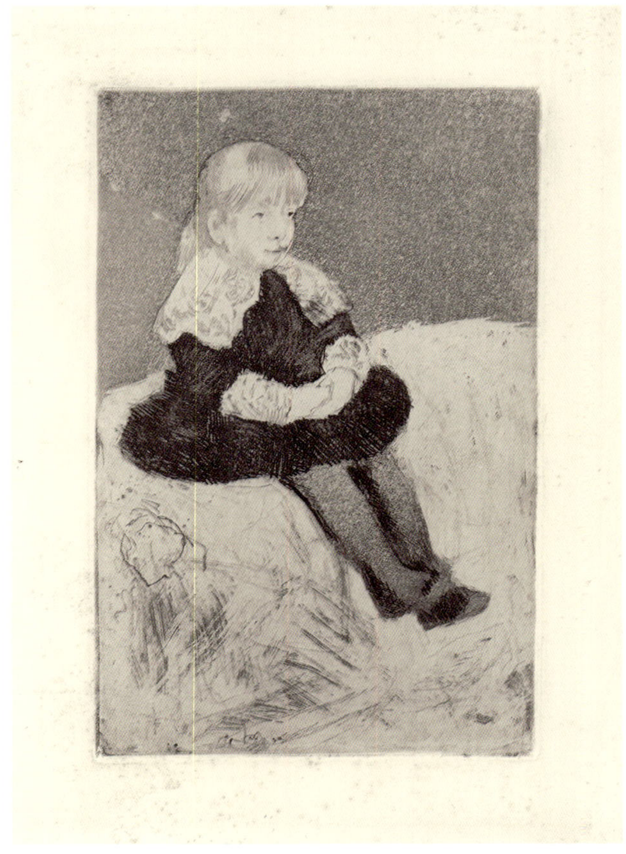

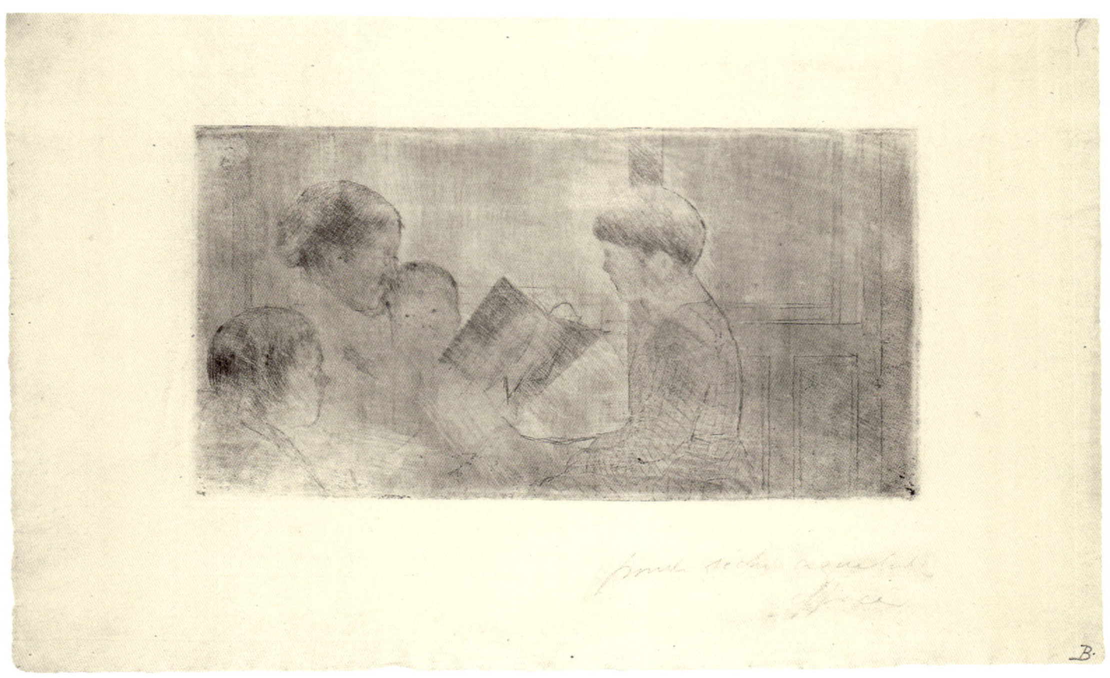

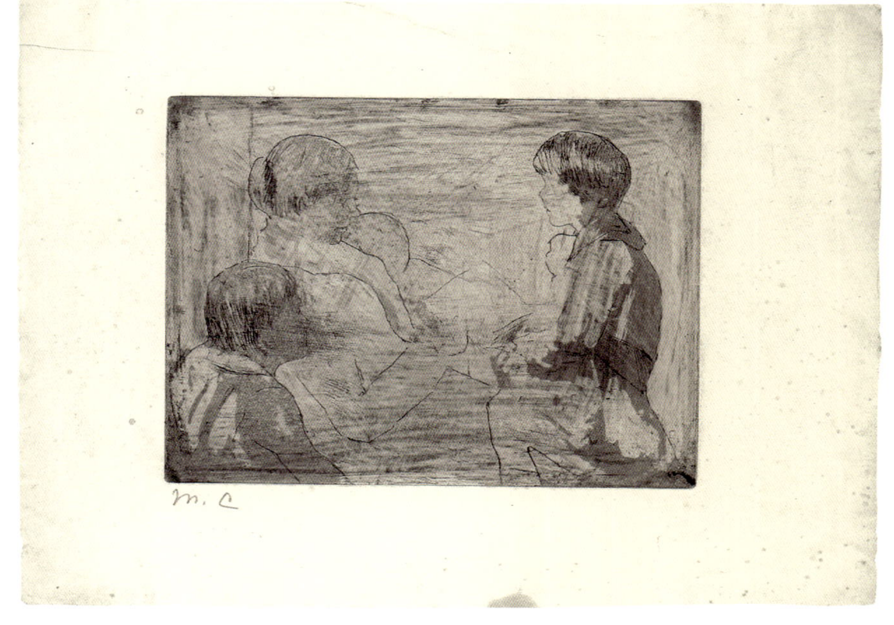

Mrs. Cassatt Reading to Her Grandchildren (No. 1), ca. 1880

Breeskin 58

Soft-ground, with drypoint and aquatint, third state of three, on Van Gelder laid paper, the full sheet, in good condition apart from slight soiling in the margins, with a notation in the lower margin, *pointe sèche effacé*

Plate: 15.7 × 30.2 cm   6¼ × 11⅞ in.
Sheet: 27.5 × 44.8 cm   10¾ × 17⅝ in.

Mrs. Cassatt Reading to Her Grandchildren (No. 2), ca. 1880

Breeskin 59

Soft-ground, with aquatint and roulette, a state undescribed by Breeskin, initialed *M. C,* on Arches laid paper, with full margins, somewhat crinkled, foxing mainly in the margins

Plate: 16.7 × 22.3 cm   6½ × 8¾ in.
Sheet: 26.2 × 36 cm   10¼ × 14¼ in.

Lydia Reading, Turned toward Right, ca. 1881

Breeskin 63

Soft-ground and aquatint, initialed *M. C,* first state of two, or an intermediate state, between Breeskin's first and second states, with the aquatint grain, but before the burnishing to define folds in the drapery, on wove paper, the full sheet, in good condition apart from slight soiling in the margins, and two creases across the lower right margin

Plate: 17.9 × 11.2 cm   7 × 4¾ in.
Sheet: 27.4 × 18 cm   10¾ × 7⅛ in.

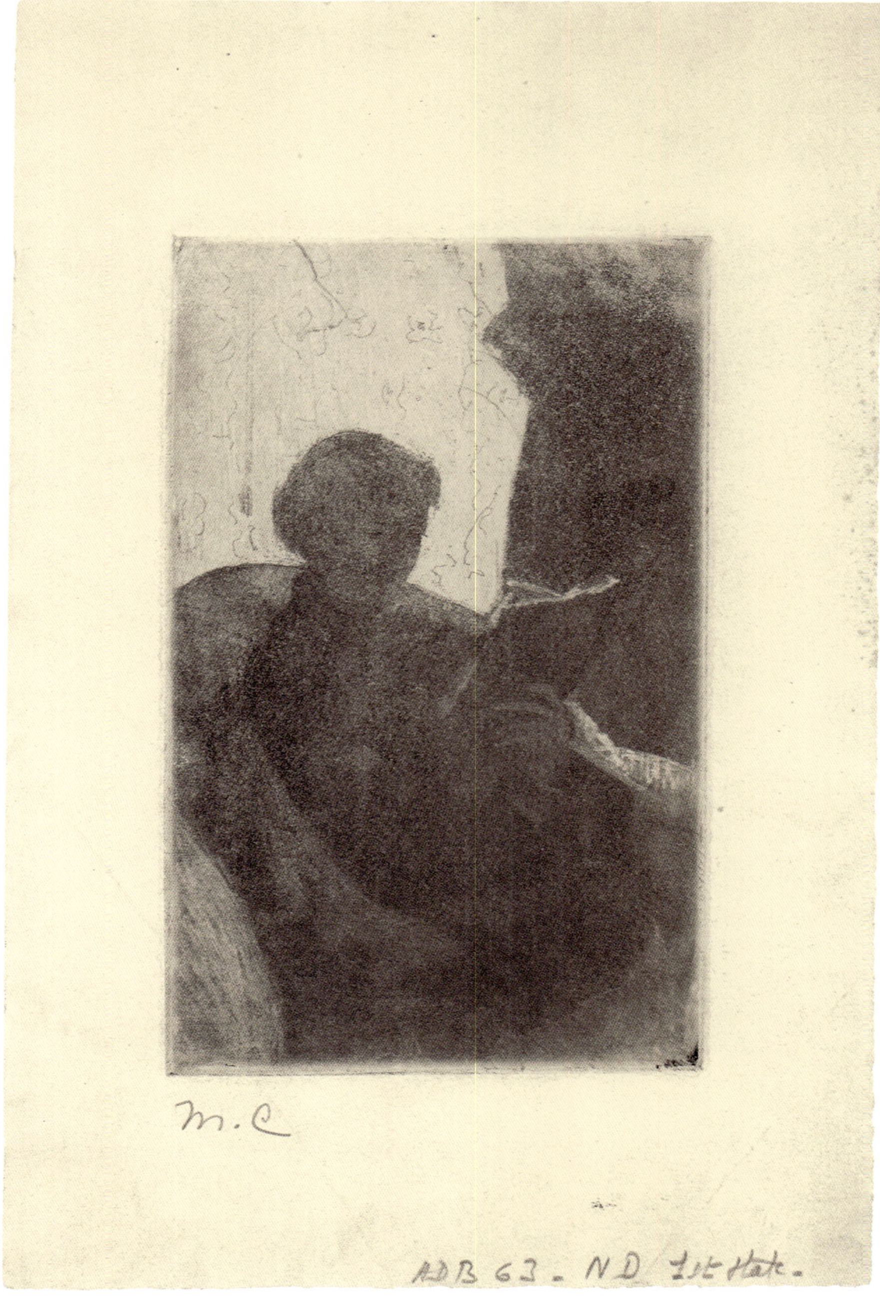

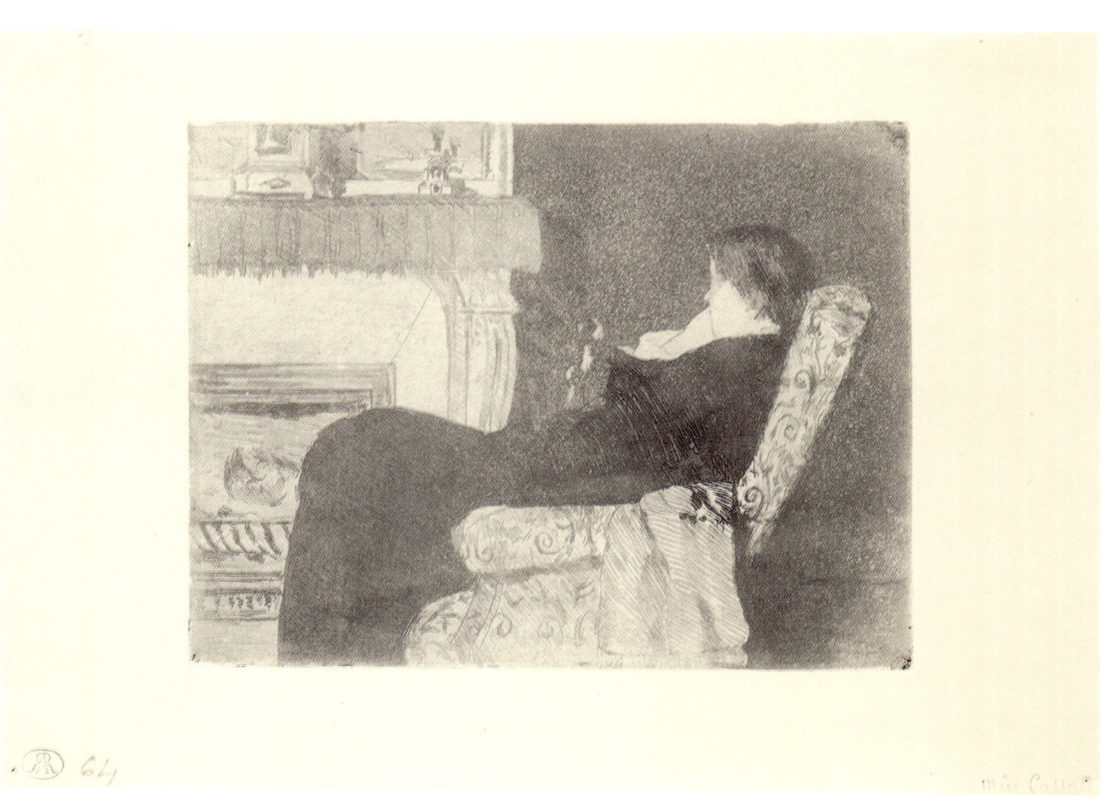

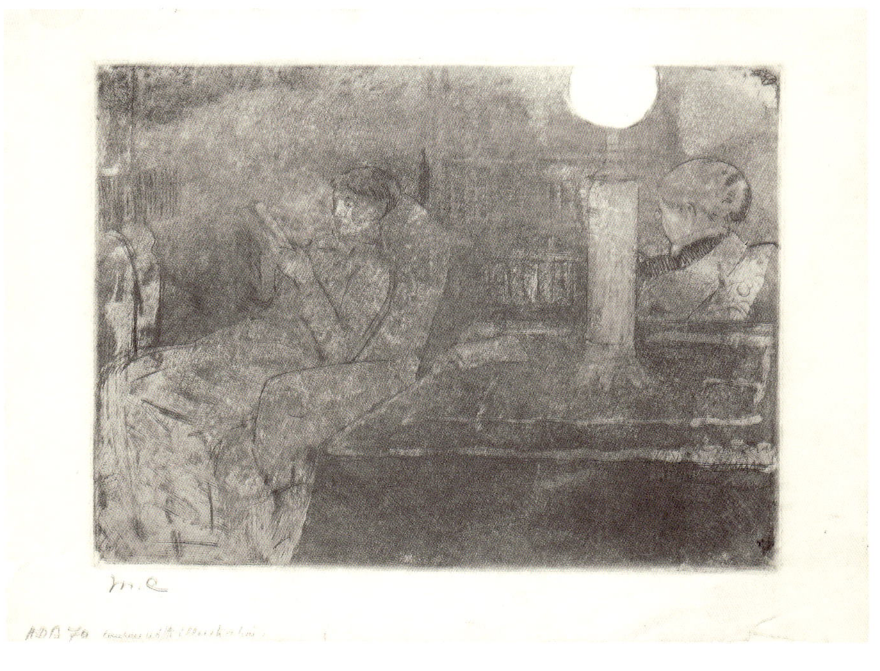

Before the Fireplace (No. 1) [Au Coin de feu],
ca. 1882 [1879–1880]

Breeskin 64

Soft ground and aquatint, third state of three, on stiff Japan paper, the full sheet, in good condition apart from a few soft creases in the margins

Plate: 16.3 × 20.9 cm 6⅜ × 8¼ in.
Sheet: 22.5 × 31.7 cm 8⅞ × 12½ in.

Mrs. Cassatt and Lydia in the Library, 1882

Breeskin 70

Soft-ground and aquatint, Breeskin's first state of two, before the additional highlights on the faces and changes in the work on the table, on sturdy wove paper, with margins, a few creases, nicks and some soiling in the margins, including a bit of dark red paint at the top left edge

Plate: 21.7 × 28.7 cm 8½ × 11¼ in.
Sheet: 27.2 × 36 cm 10¾ × 14⅛ in.

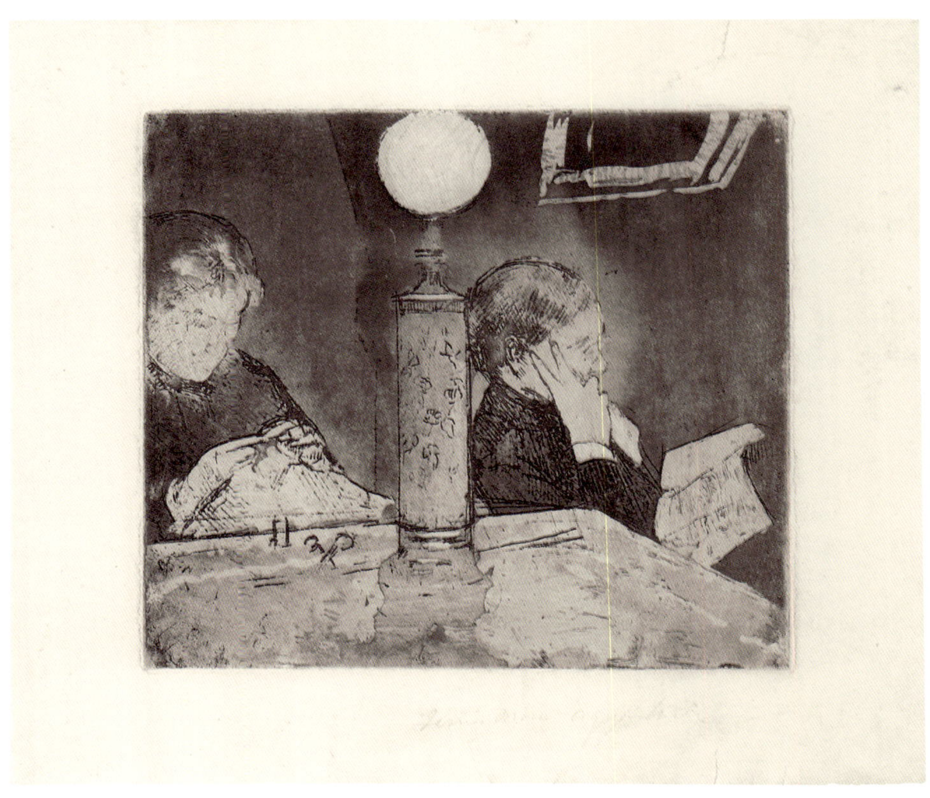

Under the Lamp [Le Soir], ca. 1882 [1879–1880]

Breeskin 71

Soft-ground and aquatint, second state of two, on sturdy wove paper, the full sheet, a few tears, creases, and slight soiling in the margins, some surface scuffs in subject

Plate: 19.6 × 22 cm 7¾ × 8¾ in.
Sheet: 26.7 × 30.9 cm 10½ × 12⅛ in.

Breeskin notes that Cassatt commented in connection with this work, "That is what teaches one to draw!"

Sewing by Lamplight, ca. 1882

Breeskin 71+

Soft-ground and aquatint, initialed *M. C,* printed in dark brown ink, on Van Gelder laid paper, the full sheet, in good condition

Plate: 19.7 × 15 cm 7¾ × 5⅞
Sheet: 30.7 × 22.5 cm 12⅛ × 8⅞ in.

This is the only known impression of this work, illustrated by Breeskin.

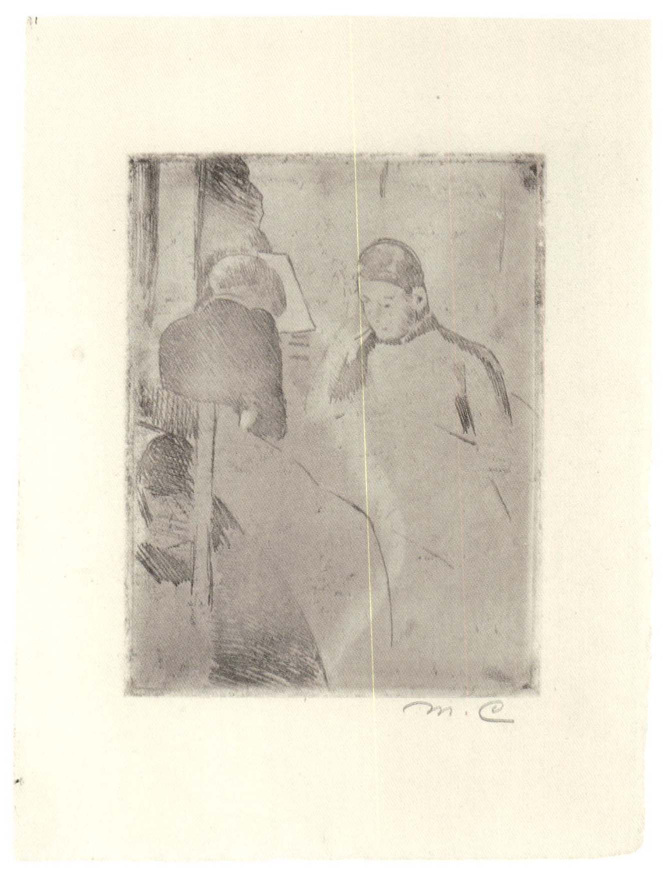

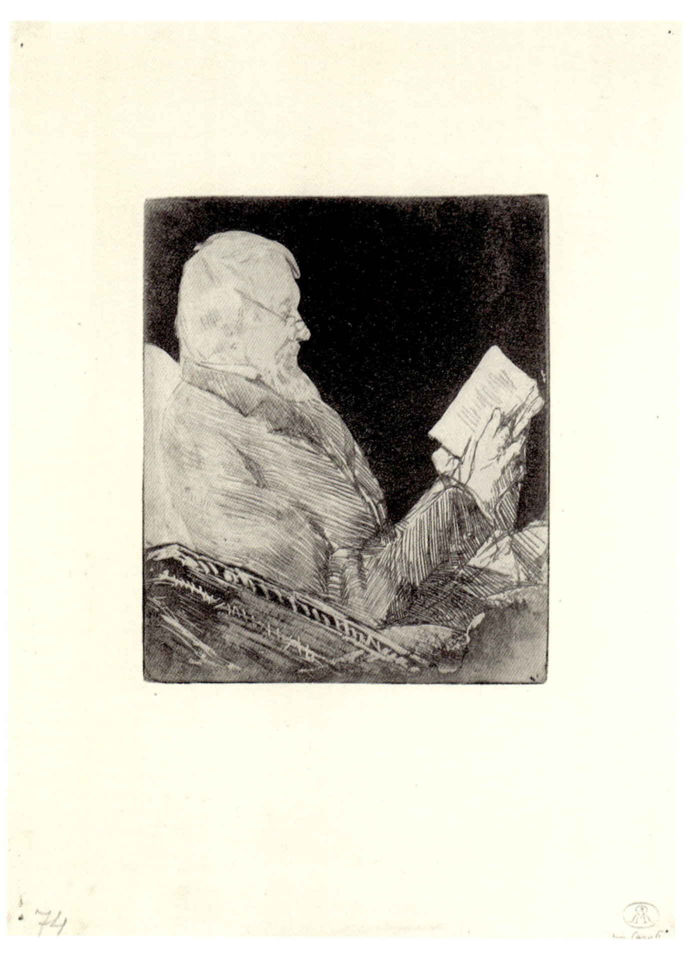

Mr. Cassatt Reading, ca. 1882

Breeskin 74

Soft-ground, with soft-ground texture and aquatint, on stiff, white Japan paper, the full sheet, in good condition (pinholes at corners and minor soiling)

Plate: 16.7 × 13.6 cm   6½ × 5⅜
Sheet: 31.6 × 22.6 cm   12½ × 8⅞ in.

PROVENANCE
Alexis Rouart [1839–1911] (violet stamp, *recto* and *verso*, variant of Lugt 2187a)

Interior: On the Sofa,
ca. 1883 [ca. 1880]

Breeskin 76

Soft-ground, with soft-ground texture, initialed *M. C,* on sturdy, wove paper, the full sheet, some foxing and creases, including one broken through in the top left corner of subject

Plate: 14.3 × 21.6 cm   5⅝ × 8½ in.
Sheet: 18 × 27.5 cm   7⅛ × 11¾ in.

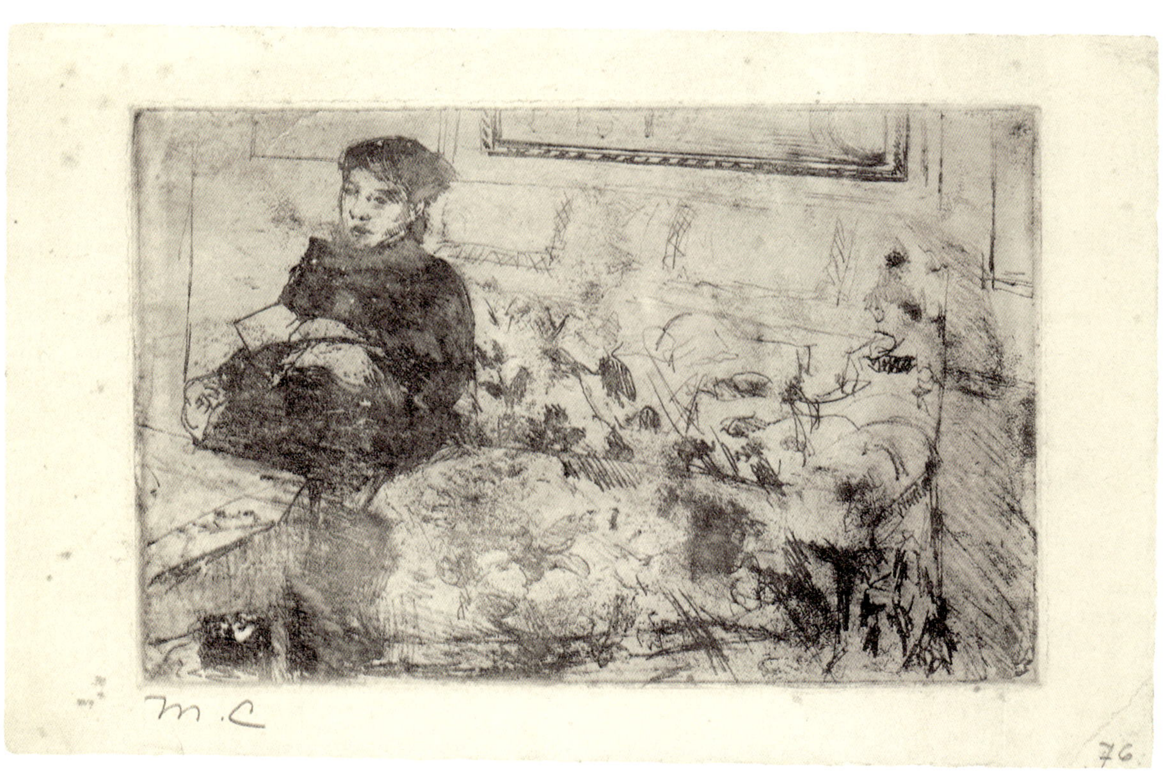

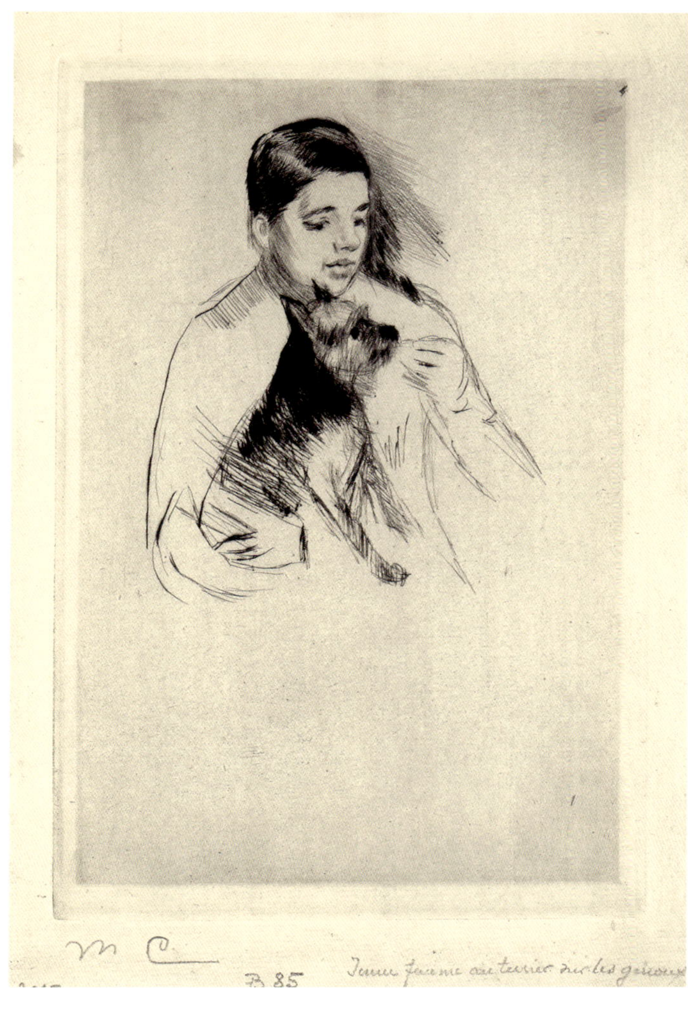

Mathilde Feeding a Dog (No. 1),
ca. 1884

Breeskin 85

Drypoint, printed with strong burr and plate tone, initialed *M. C,* on Van Gelder laid paper, the full sheet, in good condition apart from two slight stains at sheet edges

Plate: 23.7 × 15.9 cm 9⅜ × 6¼ in.
Sheet: 27.8 × 18.8 cm 10⅞ × 7⅜ in.

Mathilde Feeding a Dog (No. 2),
ca. 1884

Breeskin 86

Soft-ground and aquatint, signed in full, probably from the edition of nine, printed by Delâtre for the artist in 1923, on grey-blue laid paper with a bunch of grapes watermark, with large margins, in good condition (almost imperceptible light-stain)

Plate: 11.9 × 80 cm 4¾ × 3⅛ in.
Sheet: 25.2 × 20.2 cm 10 × 8 in.

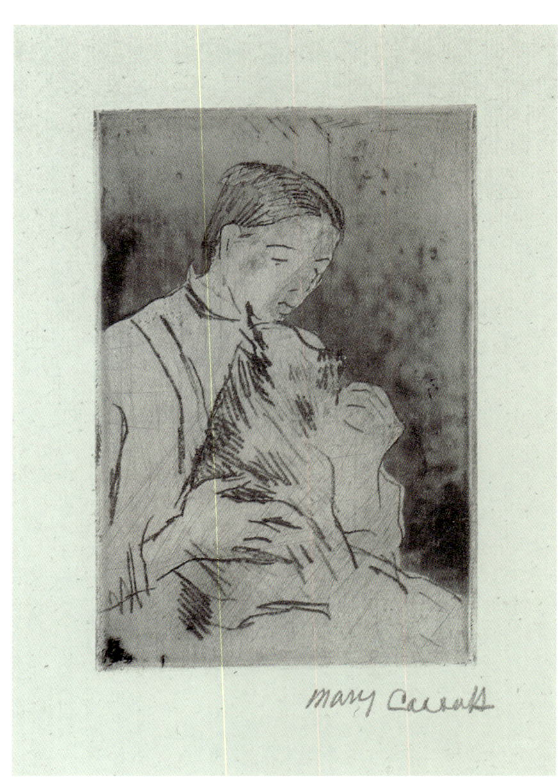

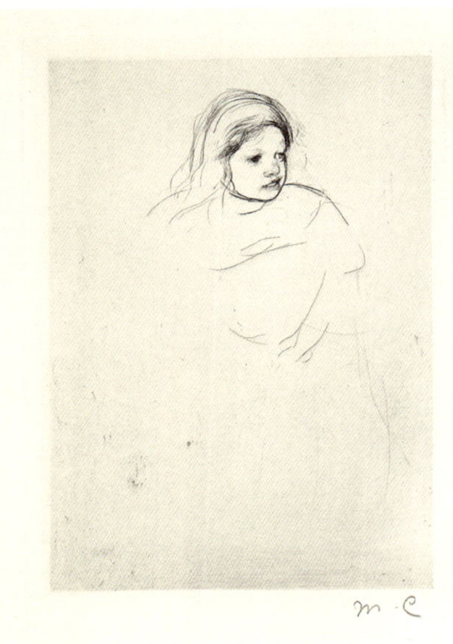

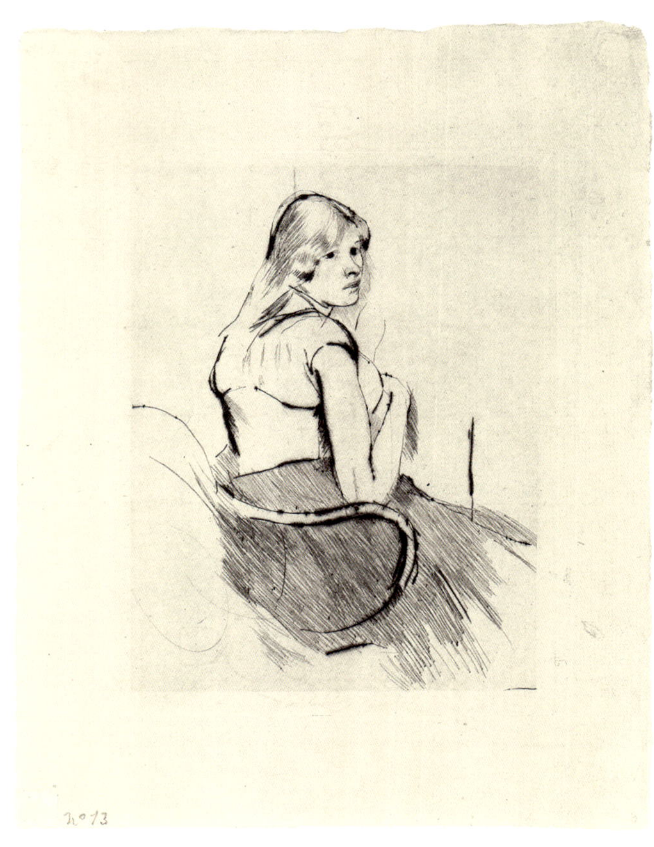

Head of Margaret Sloane (No. 2), ca. 1893

Breeskin 92+

Drypoint, printed with plate tone, initialed *M. C,* on wove paper, the full sheet, in good condition apart from minor soiling

Plate: 17.7 × 12.8 cm 7 × 5 in.
Sheet: 38.2 × 28.3 cm 15⅛ × 11⅛ in.

This is the only known impression of this work, illustrated by Breeskin.

En Déshabillé, ca. 1889

Breeskin 95

Drypoint, with strong burr and delicate plate tone, on fine, Van Gelder laid paper, with a post horn and shield watermark, the full sheet, in good condition apart from a small hinging defect in top right corner, and slight darkening of paper tone

Plate: 18.1 × 13.9 cm 7⅛ × 5½ in.
Sheet: 25.8 × 20 cm 10¼ × 7⅞ in.

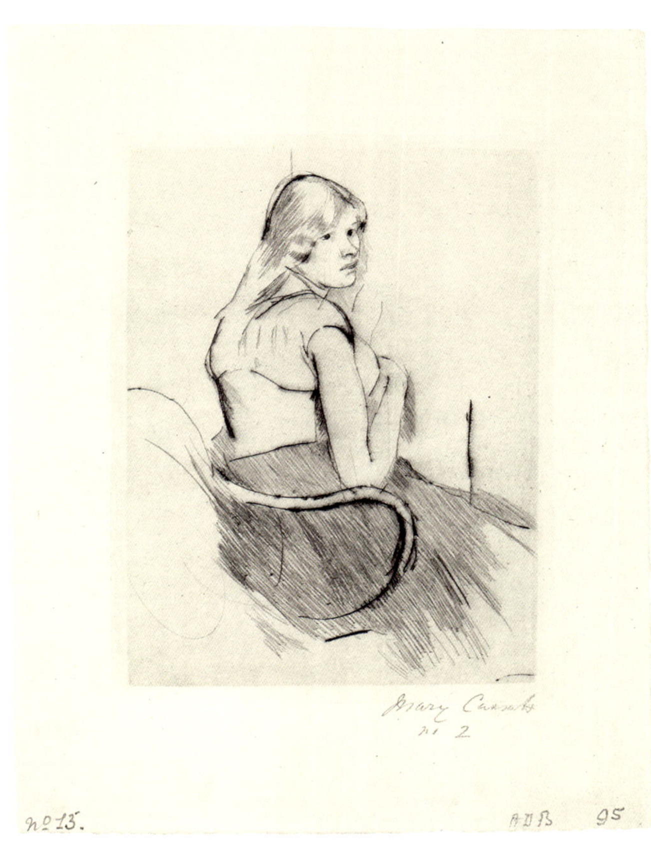

En Déshabillé, ca. 1889

Breeskin 95

Drypoint, with strong burr and plate tone, signed in full and inscribed *no. 2,* on fine, Van Gelder laid paper, with a post horn and shield watermark, the full sheet, in good condition

Plate: 18.3 × 13.9 cm 7⅛ × 5½ in.
Sheet: 25.9 × 20.1 cm 10¼ × 7⅞ in.

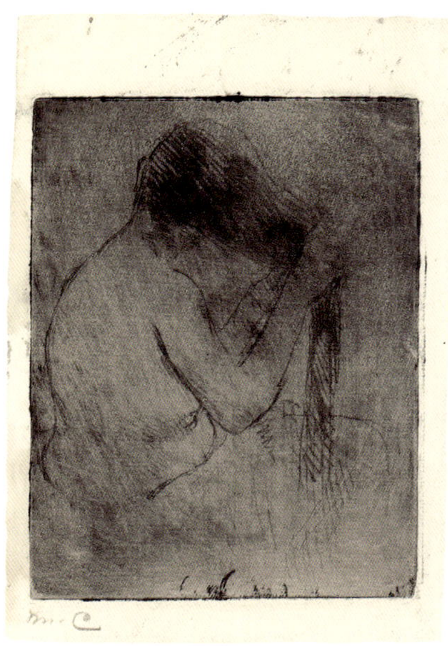

Back View of Draped Model Arranging Her Hair, ca. 1889 [ca. 1880?]

Breeskin 96

Soft-ground, with aquatint, printed with very strong, monotype inking, initialed *M. C*, on laid paper with irregular, small margins, paint stains in the left edge and less noticeably at lower center

Plate: 14.6 × 11 cm 5¾ × 4¼ in.
Sheet: 18.3 × 12.6 cm 7¼ × 4⅞ in.

Described by Breeskin as first state of two, but possibly only more richly inked than the "second state" example in the Metropolitan Museum of Art, New York.

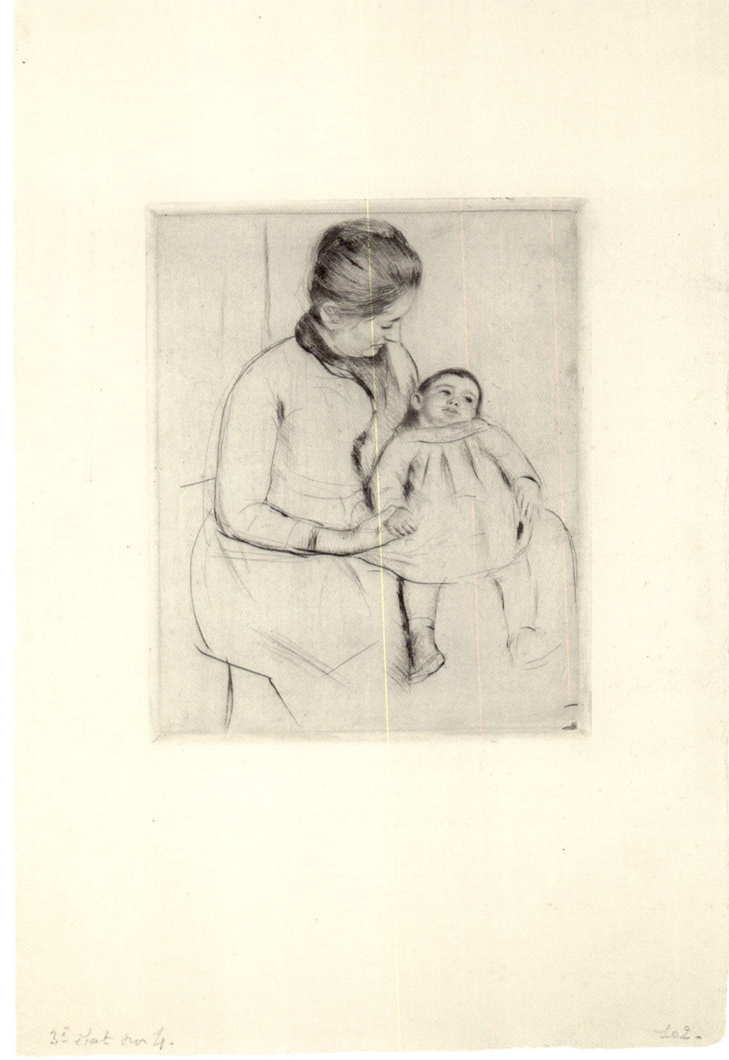

Solicitude, ca. 1889

Breeskin 102

Drypoint, third state of four, printed in dark brown ink, on laid paper with a watermark of crossed scepters surmounted by a crown, the full sheet, in good condition

Plate: 18.8 × 14.9 cm 7⅜ × 5⅞ in.
Sheet: 36.6 × 24.1 cm 14⅜ × 9½ in.

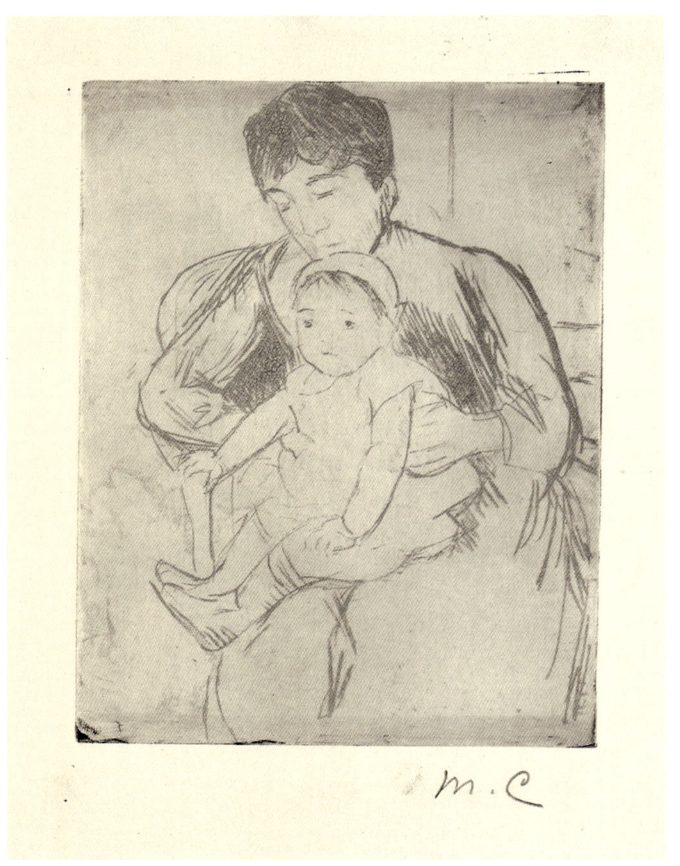

Preparing Bill for an Outing,
ca. 1889

Breeskin 106

Soft-ground, first state of two, initialed *M C,* printed in olive-brown ink, on laid paper with a shield watermark, the full sheet, in good condition, annotated *E.* in lower left corner

Plate: 16.3 × 12.5 cm   6½ × 5 in.
Sheet: 31.6 × 23.8 cm   12⅜ × 9⅜ in.

Preparing Bill for an Outing,
ca. 1889

Breeskin 106

Soft-ground, first state of two, initialed *M. C,* printed in olive-brown ink, on laid Japan paper, the full sheet (large, hand-cut piece), in good condition apart from a few pale finger smudges of ink and paint oil, annotated in lower left corner, *A*

Plate: 16.4 × 12.6 cm   6½ × 5 in.
Sheet: 32.2 × 25 cm   12⅝ × 9⅞ in.

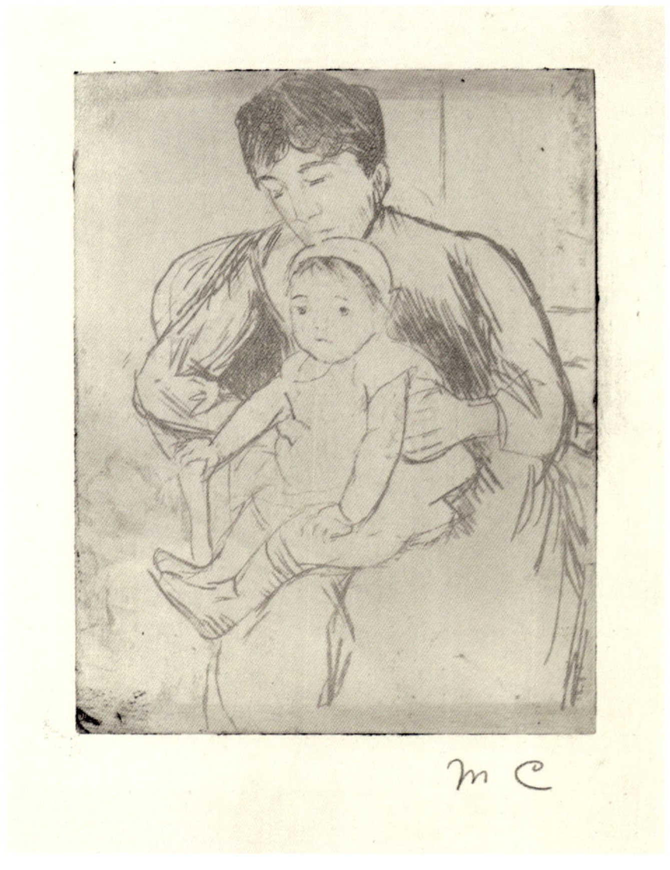

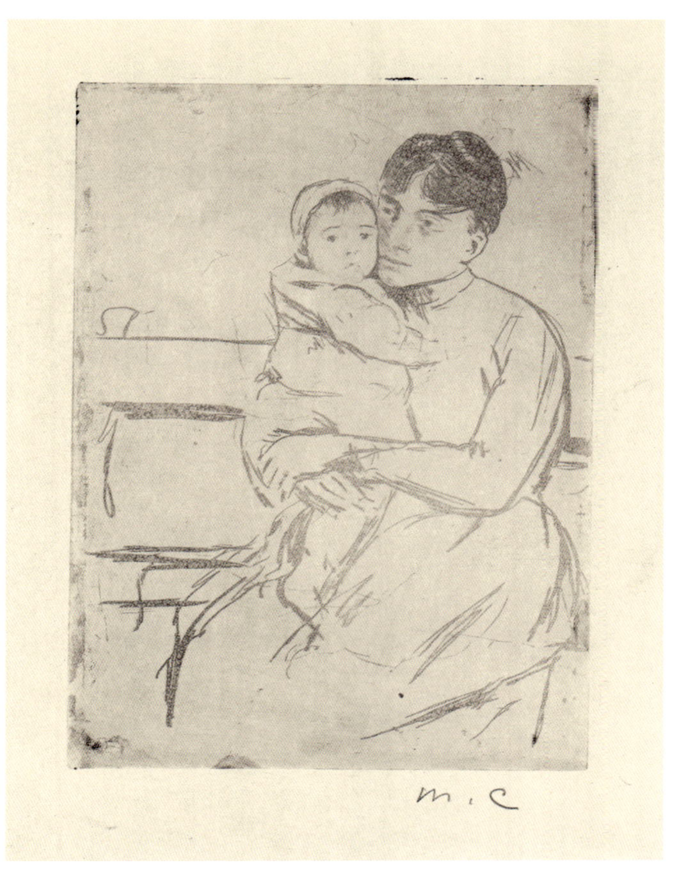

On the Bench, 1889–1890

Breeskin 107

Soft-ground, initialed *M. C,* printed in dark brown ink, on VanderLey laid paper, the full sheet, in good condition, annotated *C.* in lower left corner

Plate: 18.8 × 13.8 cm 7⅜ × 5⅜ in.
Sheet: 39 × 23.3 cm 15⅜ × 9⅛ in.

On the Bench, 1889–1890

Breeskin 107

Soft-ground, initialed *M. C,* printed in olive-brown ink, on laid Japan paper, the full sheet, in good condition, annotated *B.* in lower left corner

Plate: 18.9 × 14 cm 7½ × 5½ in.
Sheet: 32.6 × 25.1 cm 12¾ × 9⅞ in.

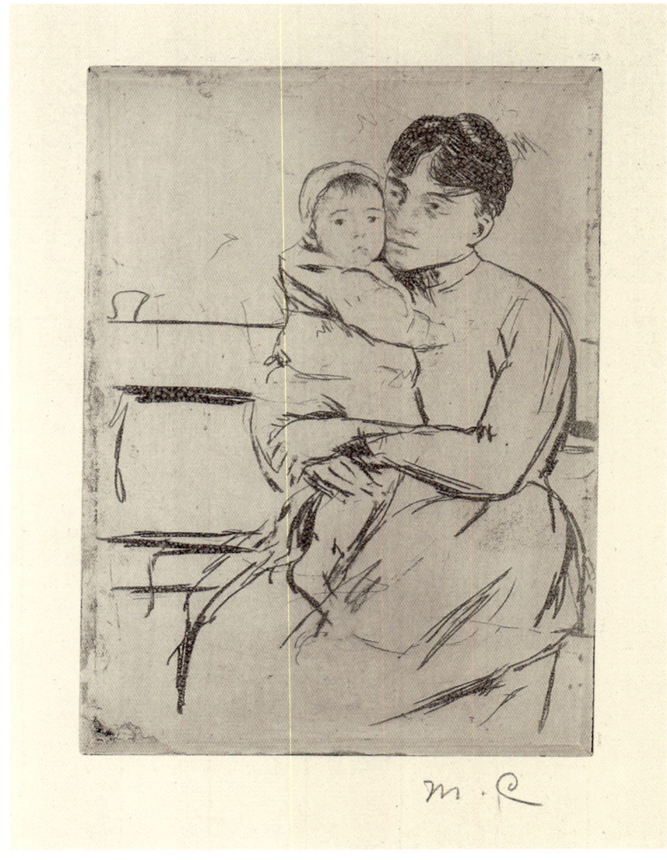

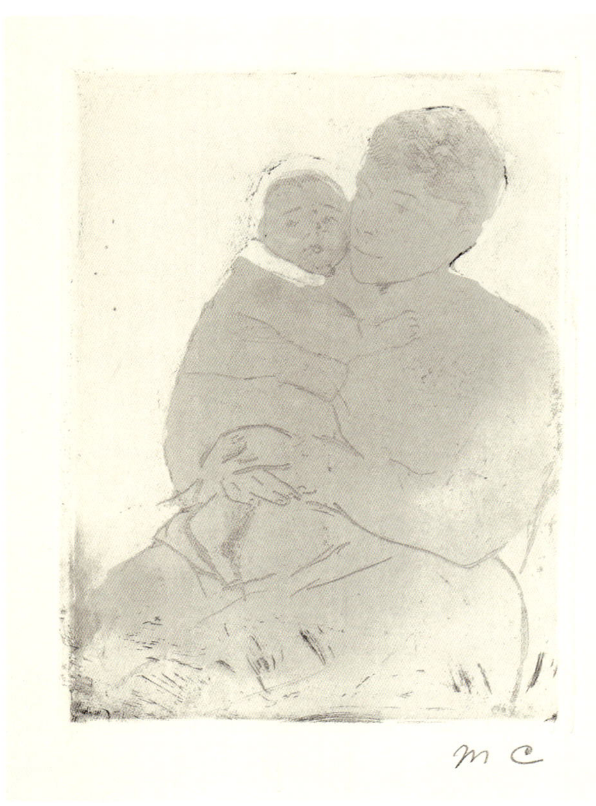

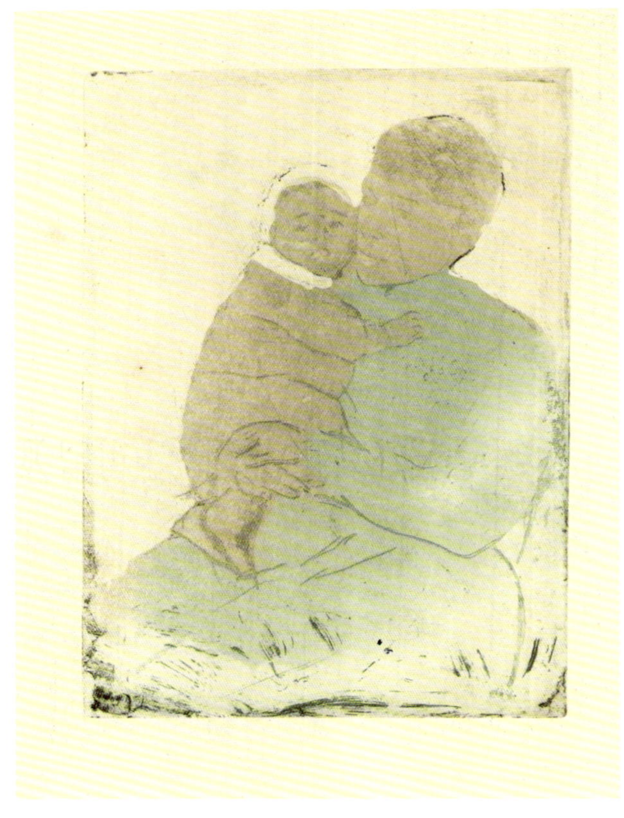

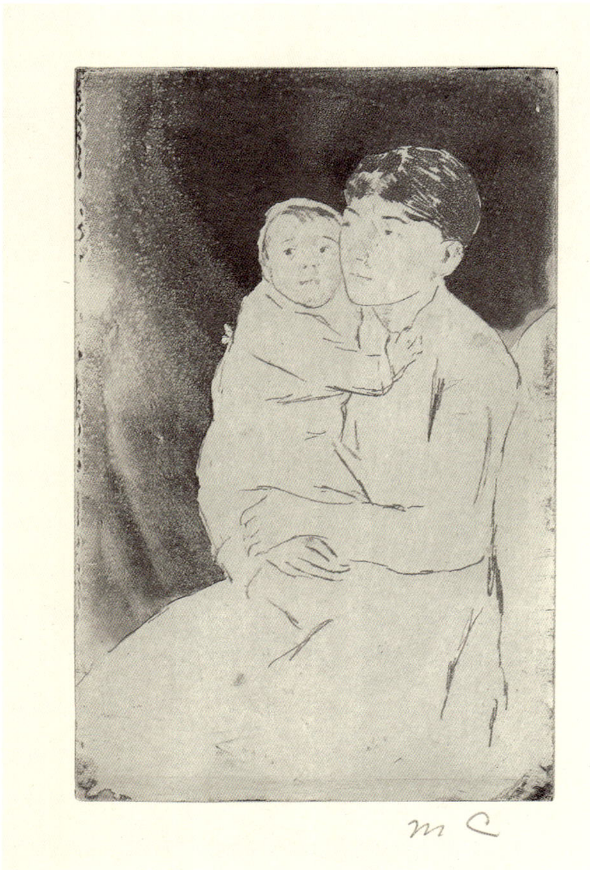

Nurse and Baby Bill (No. 1),
ca. 1889–1890

Breeskin 108; Mathews/Shapiro 2

Soft-ground and aquatint, fourth state of four, initialed *M. C*, printed in grey-brown ink, on sturdy wove paper, the full sheet, in good condition, annotated *A.* in lower left corner

Plate: 18.8 × 13.9 cm   7⅜ × 5½ in.
Sheet: 38.2 × 28.2 cm   15 × 11⅛ in.

See note to following.

Nurse and Baby Bill (No. 1),
ca. 1889–1890

Breeskin 108; Mathews/Shapiro 2

Soft-ground and aquatint, fourth state of four, printed in green, olive-brown, and rose (for the lips), on laid paper with watermark ANDERLEY, the full sheet, in good condition apart from a few specks of foxing, annotated *B* in lower left corner

Plate: 18.8 × 13.7 cm   7⅜ × 5⅜ in.
Sheet: 35.5 × 21 cm   14 × 8¼ in.

Mathews and Shapiro cited only one known impression of this state, printed in similar colors (Museum of Fine Arts, Boston).

Nurse and Baby Bill (No. 2), ca. 1889–1890

Breeskin 109; Mathews/Shapiro 1

Soft-ground and aquatint, second state of two, initialed *M C,* printed in dark brown ink, on laid Japan paper, the full sheet, in good condition, annotated *A.* in lower left corner

Plate: 21.8 × 14 cm   8⅝ × 5½ in.
Sheet: 32.2 × 25.2 cm   12⅝ × 9⅞ in.

[See illustration on facing page, lower left]

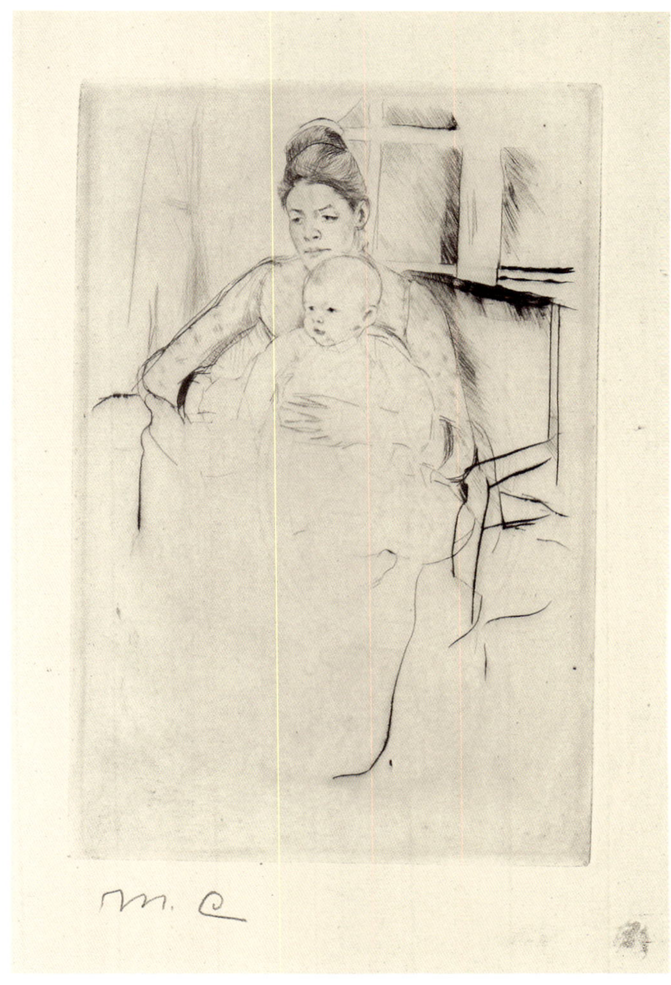

Baby's Lullaby, ca. 1887

Breeskin 110

Drypoint, first state of two, initialed *M C,* printed in black ink, on fine, laid paper with fragment of letters watermark, the full sheet, in good condition (a fox mark in left margin)

Plate: 16 × 16 cm   6¼ × 6¼ in.
Sheet: 27.9 × 22.6 cm   11 × 8⅞ in.

The other impression of this state noted by Breeskin is in the Avery Collection (New York Public Library).

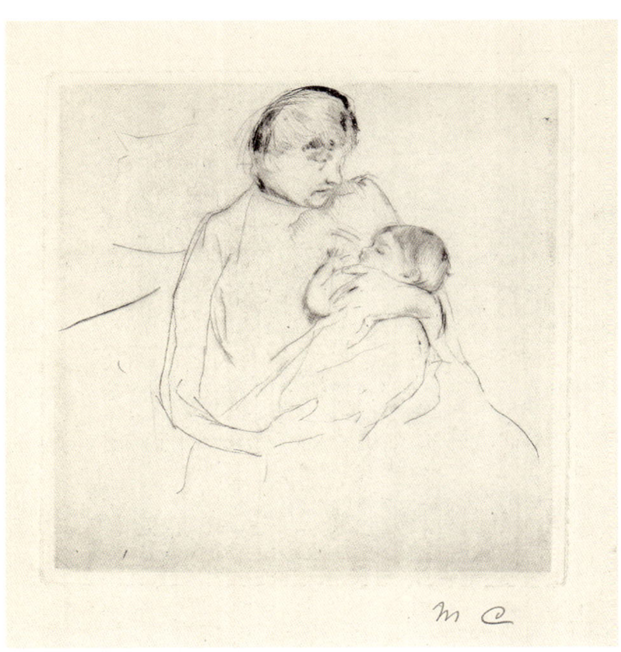

Mrs. Gardner Cassatt and Her Baby Seated near a Window, ca. 1887

Breeskin 112

Drypoint, initialed *M. C,* printed in black ink, on fine, laid paper with a Pro Patria watermark, the full sheet, in good condition (a slight handling crease, a small, inherent hole, associated with the watermark, in the sheet at lower center)

Plate: 21.3 × 13.8 cm   8⅜ × 5⅜ in.
Sheet: 35.9 × 20.9 cm   14⅛ × 8¼ in.

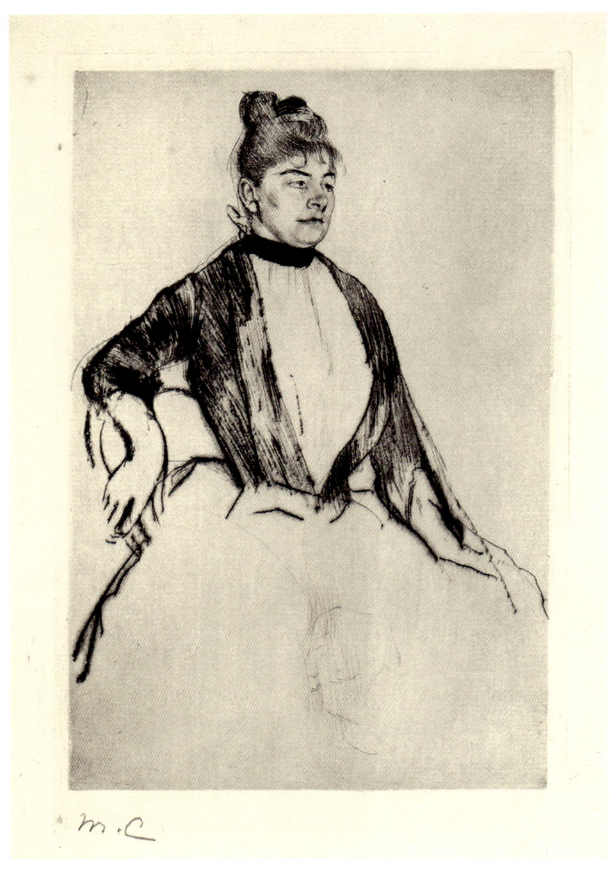

Mimi Seated, Wearing a Sleeveless Dress, ca. 1889

Breeskin 115

Drypoint, an extremely fine impression of a previously unknown and probably unique first state, before Breeskin's "only known state," signed in full, printed in black ink with plate tone, clean-wiped at the edges, on Van Gelder laid paper, the full sheet, in good condition apart from slight discoloration (bits of stamp hinging in the right edge)

Plate: 22.8 × 15.9 cm 9 × 6¼ in.
Sheet: 43 × 30.5 cm 17 × 12 in.

In this state, there are fewer lines defining the folds of the skirt, and less shading, while the fresh drypoint gives the face a more vivid expression. Cassatt noted on the impression of the second state in the Avery Collection (NYPL): "Only three proofs taken and plate then destroyed."

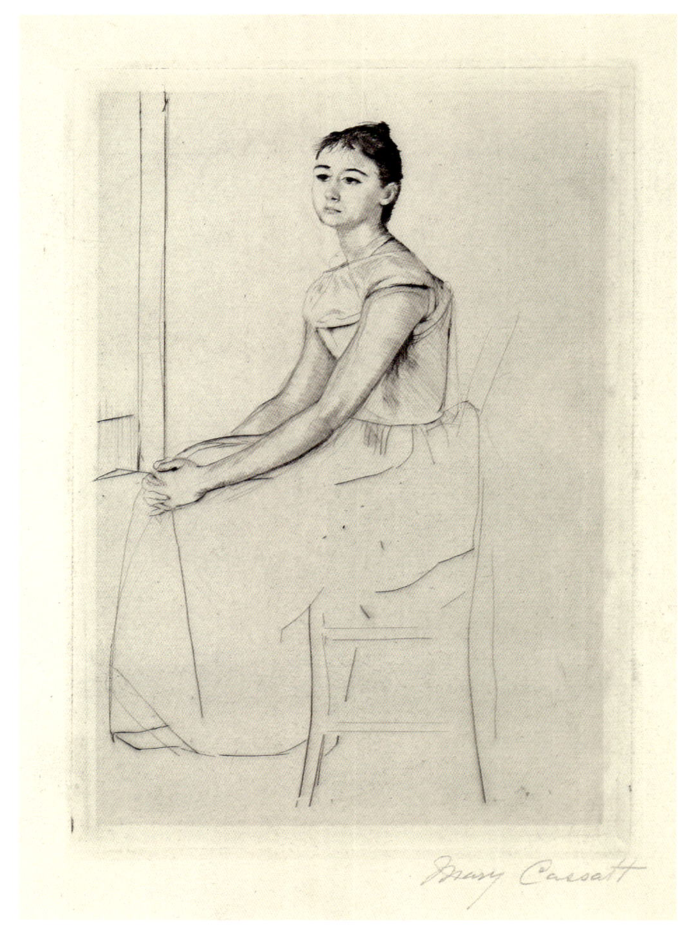

Portrait Sketch of Mme M..., ca. 1889

Breeskin 114

Drypoint, a previously unknown and probably unique second state, with the figure completed, and the chair and dress more fully developed (a scratched out sketch of a head at lower center), initialed *M. C* across the platemark at lower left, printed in black ink, with powerful burr, and plate tone to provide spatial atmosphere, wiped clean at the edges, on sturdy, laid paper (Van Gelder?), the full sheet, in good condition (a few specks of foxing, and a bit of paint at the upper edge at left)

Plate: 22.6 × 14.5 cm 8⅞ × 5⅝ in.
Sheet: 27 × 17.8 cm 10⅝ × 7 in.

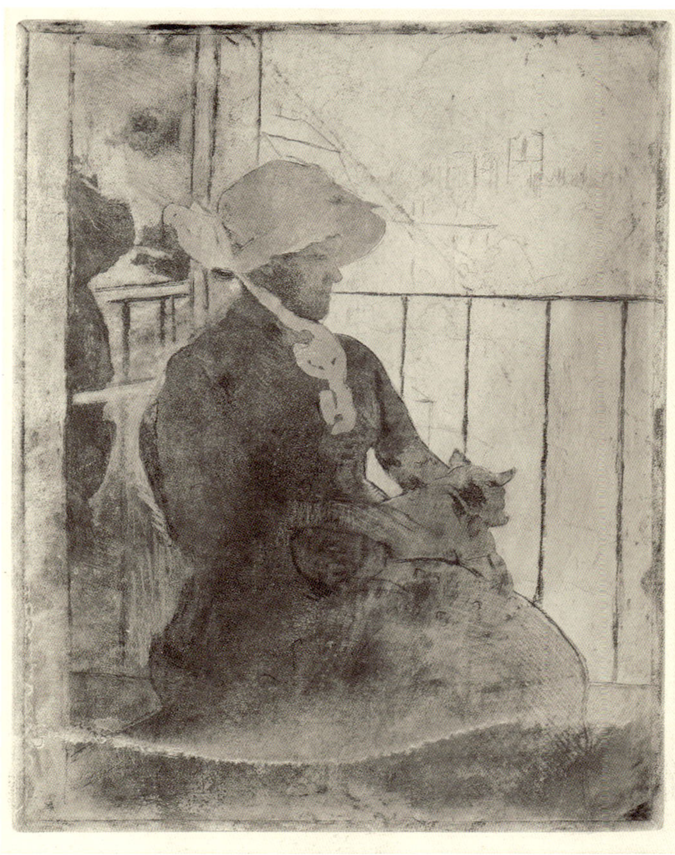

The French Screen, ca. 1889

Breeskin 121

Soft-ground, only state, initialed *M. C,* on Van Gelder laid paper, the full sheet, in good condition

Plate: 16.9 × 11.9 cm 6⅝ × 4⅝ in.
Sheet: 25.2 × 18.2 cm 9⅞ × 7⅛ in.

On the Balcony, ca. 1889

Breeskin 120

Soft-ground and aquatint, apparently a previously unrecorded state between Breeskin's second and third, with greater definition of details, added grain, and burnishing to separate the woman's back from the reflection at left, before the details of the face, hat, scarf, and dog were obscured by an overall grain, printed in brown ink, on laid paper with watermark, BLACONS, and number 31, the full sheet, in good condition except mat stained

Plate: 27.8 × 21.8 cm 11 × 8⅝ in.
Sheet: 31.4 × 23.9 cm 12⅜ × 9⅜ in.

A probably unique proof of this state. Of the previous state, Breeskin records only the impression in the Cincinnati Art Museum, which is illustrated in Museum of Graphic Art, no. 31.

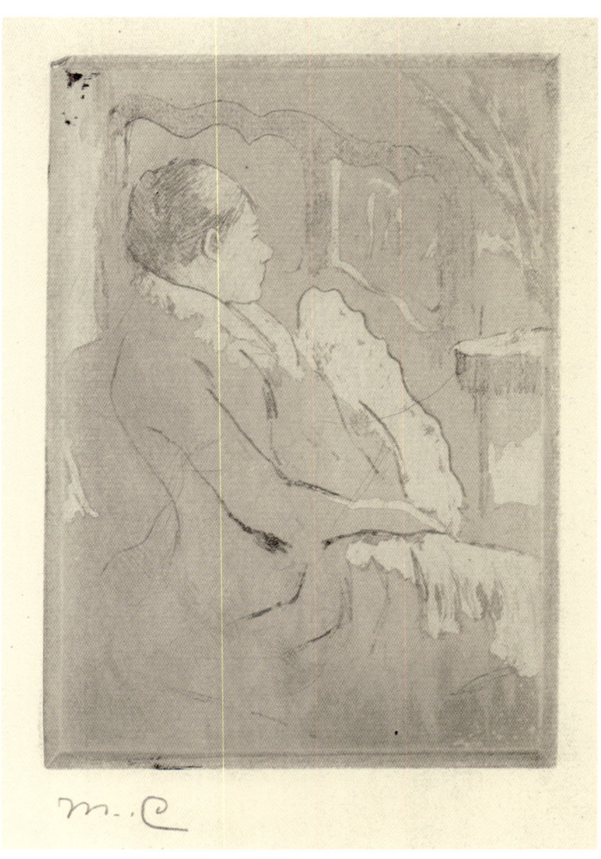

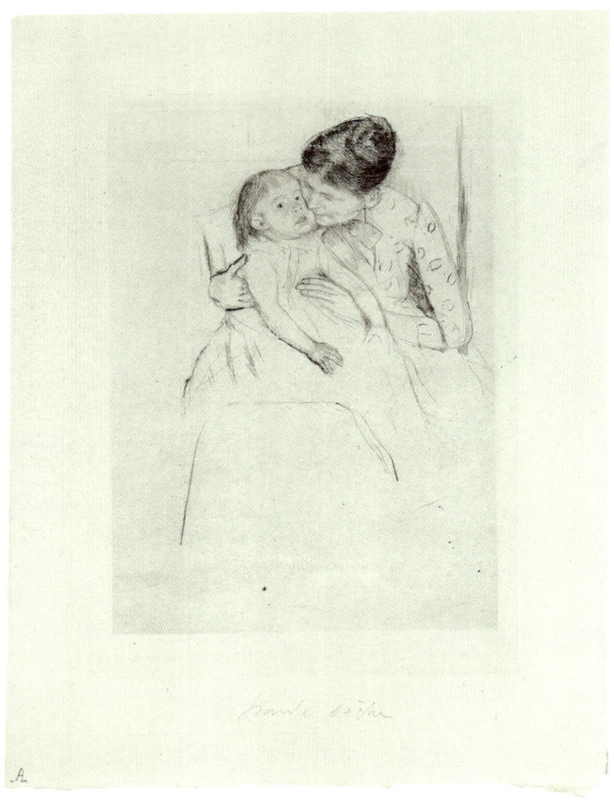

The Sick Child (No. 3), ca. 1889

Breeskin 125

Drypoint, first state of two, printed in gritty black ink, with plate tone, wiped clean at the edges, on Van Gelder laid paper, the full sheet, in good condition, annotated *A* in the lower left corner

Plate: 22.7 × 16.7 cm   8⅞ × 6½ in.
Sheet: ca. 30 × 22.5 cm   11¾ × 8⅞ in.

The Sick Child (No. 3), ca. 1889

Breeskin 125

Drypoint, first state of two, printed in gritty black ink, with light plate tone, wiped clean at the edges, on Van Gelder laid paper, the full sheet, in good condition, annotated *C* in the lower right corner

Plate: 22.7 × 16.7 cm   8⅞ × 6½ in.
Sheet: 30 × 22 cm   11¾ × 8⅝ in.

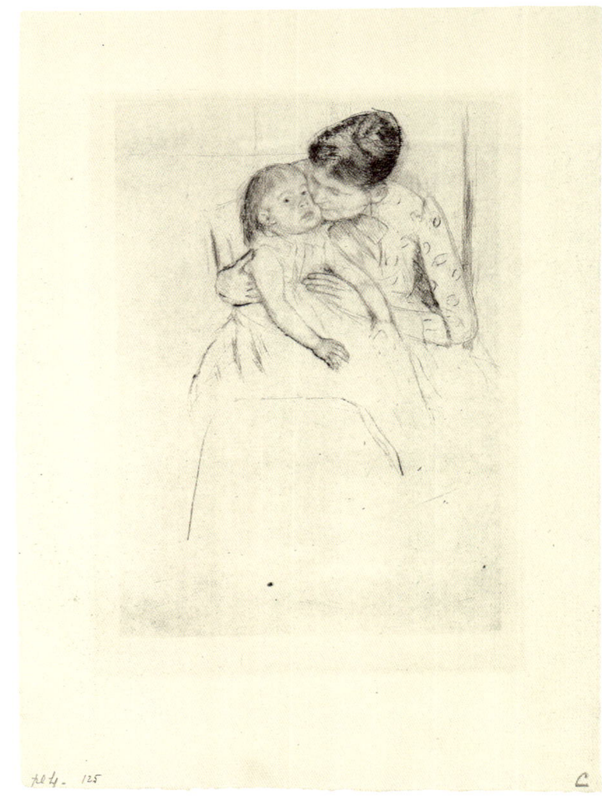

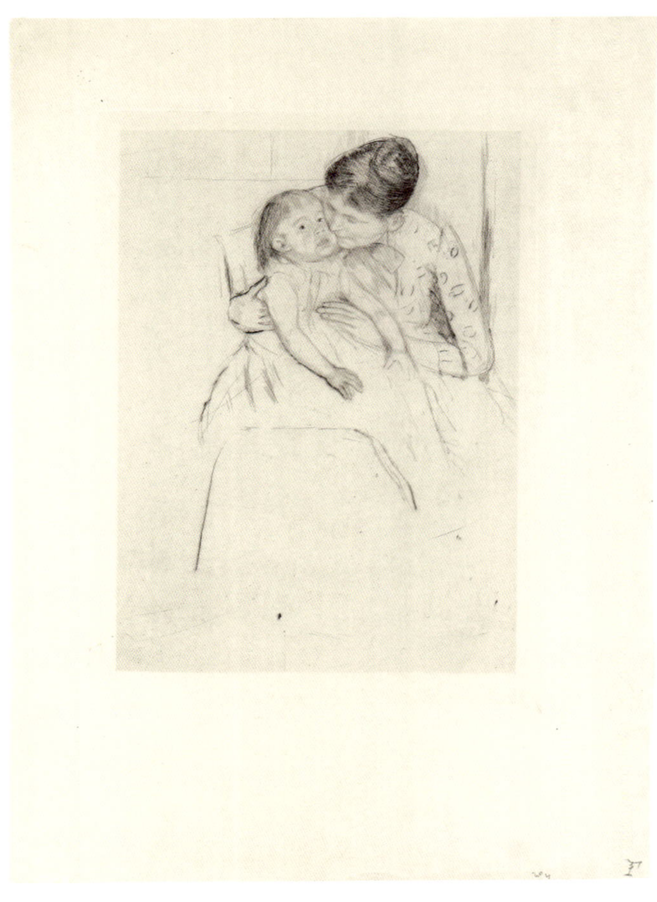

The Sick Child (No. 3), ca. 1889

Breeskin 125

Drypoint, first state of two, printed in brown ink, with manipulated plate tone, on Van Gelder laid paper, the full sheet, in good condition

Plate: 22.7 × 16.7 cm 8⅞ × 6½ in.
Sheet: 31.3 × 21.6 cm 12⅜ × 8½ in.

The Sick Child (No. 3), ca. 1889

Breeskin 125

Drypoint, first state of two, a fine impression, printed in black ink, with plate tone, wiped clean at the edges, on sturdy, Japan wove paper, the full sheet, in good condition (minor soiling in margins), annotated *F* in the lower right corner, and *no 4* in the lower edge

Plate: 22.7 × 16.7 cm 8⅞ × 6½ in.
Sheet: 32.6 × 23.7 cm 12¾ × 9¼ in.

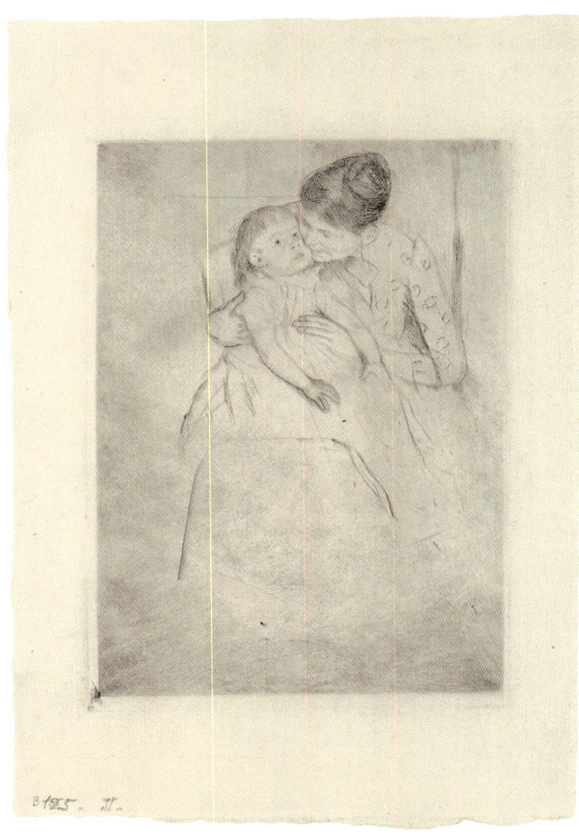

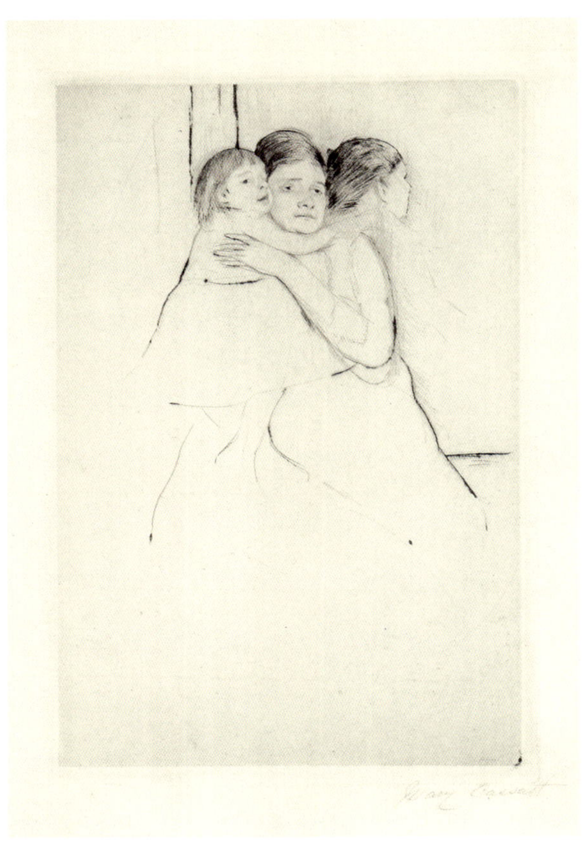

Mother Berthe Holding Her Child,
ca. 1889

Breeskin 126

Drypoint, Breeskin's second state, signed in full, printed in black ink, with even plate tone, wiped clean at the bevel, on white laid paper with a fleur-de-lys in shield watermark, the full sheet, in good condition apart from slight soiling

Plate: 23.6 × 15.9 cm 9¼ × 6¼ in.
Sheet: 28 × 22.8 cm 11 × 9 in.

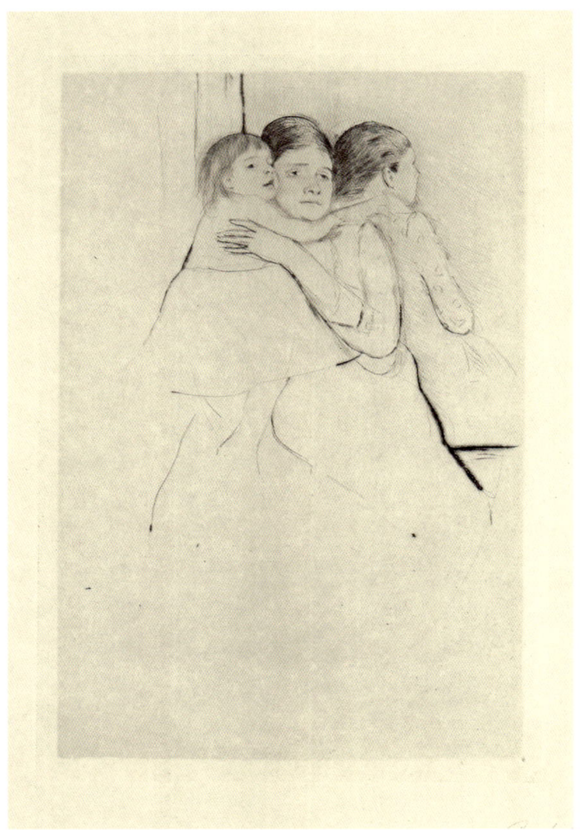

Mother Berthe Holding Her Child,
ca. 1889

Breeskin 126

Drypoint, a previously unrecorded third state, signed in full and inscribed, *No. 2*, printed in black ink with exceptionally strong burr and even plate tone, clean wiped at the edges, on warm-toned, sturdy, Japan wove paper, the full sheet, in good condition apart from a minor stain at lower edge

Plate: 23.6 × 15.9 cm 9¼ × 6¼ in.
Sheet: 34.6 × 25.7 cm 13⅝ × 10⅛ in.

A further state, unrecorded by Breeskin and after her second, in which the artist has added the mother's arm with patterned sleeve to the reflection in the mirror. Another impression of this state is in the Metropolitan Museum of Art, New York.

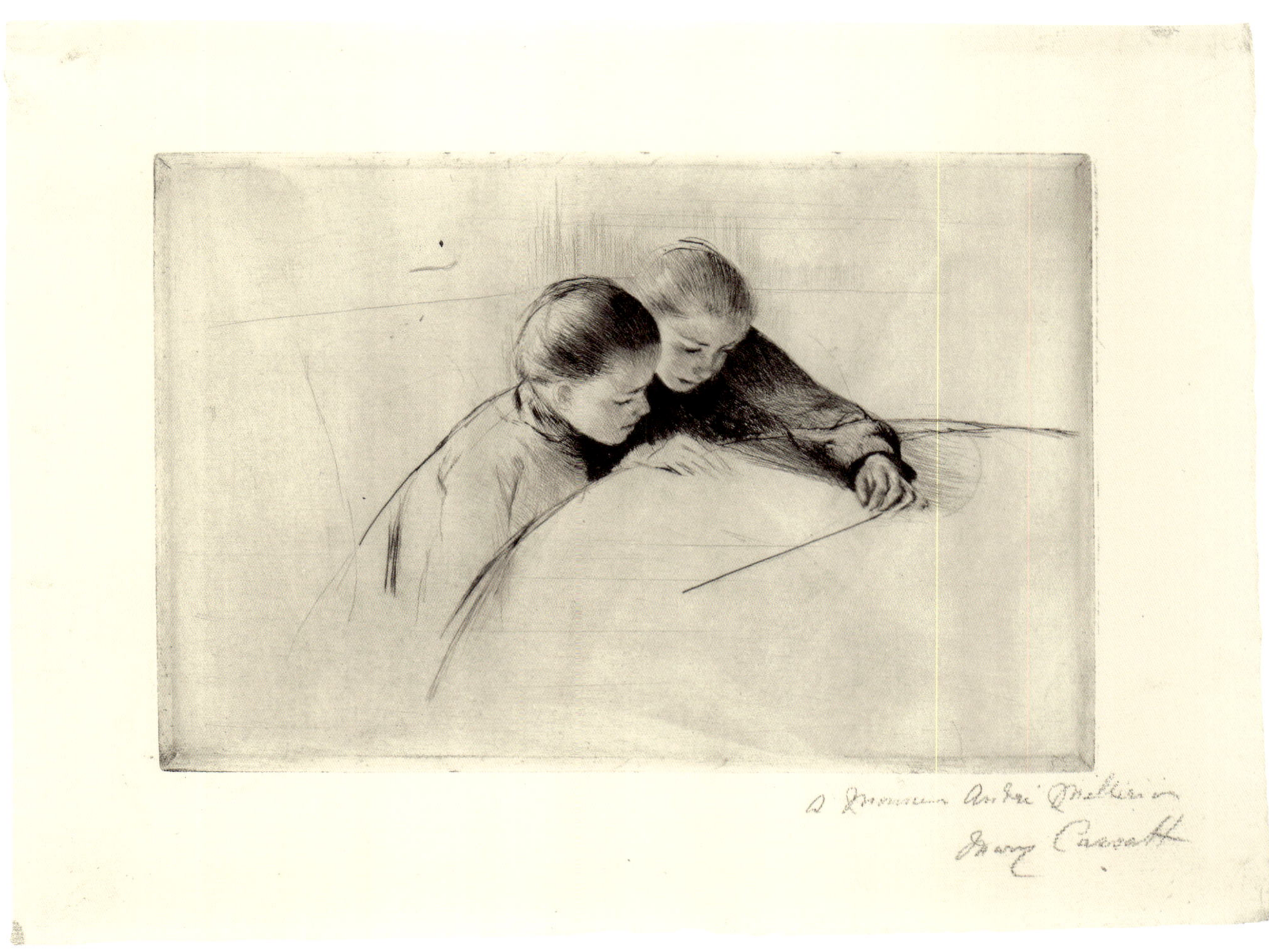

The Map [The Lesson], 1889–1890

Breeskin 127

Drypoint, third state of three, signed in full, with dedication, *à Monsieur André Mellerio*, with the artist's blue initial stamp in the lower right plate corner (Lugt 604), a fine impression, printed in dark brown ink, with strong burr and plate tone, on white, laid paper, the full sheet, in good condition apart from a small water stain at lower right, visible only on *verso*

Plate: 15.9 × 23.1 cm 6¼ × 9⅛ in.
Sheet: 23.5 × 31.1 cm 9¼ × 12¼ in.

The first in a series of 12 drypoints (Breeskin 127–138), each printed in an edition of 25 in the final state, which were exhibited by Durand-Ruel in 1890.

PROVENANCE
André Mellerio (black stamp *verso*, Lugt 153a), art critic, musician, connoisseur, author of many books and articles on art, including the standard catalogue raisonné of the prints of Odilon Redon, and collector primarily of prints by major artists of his day, as well as lithographic incunabula.

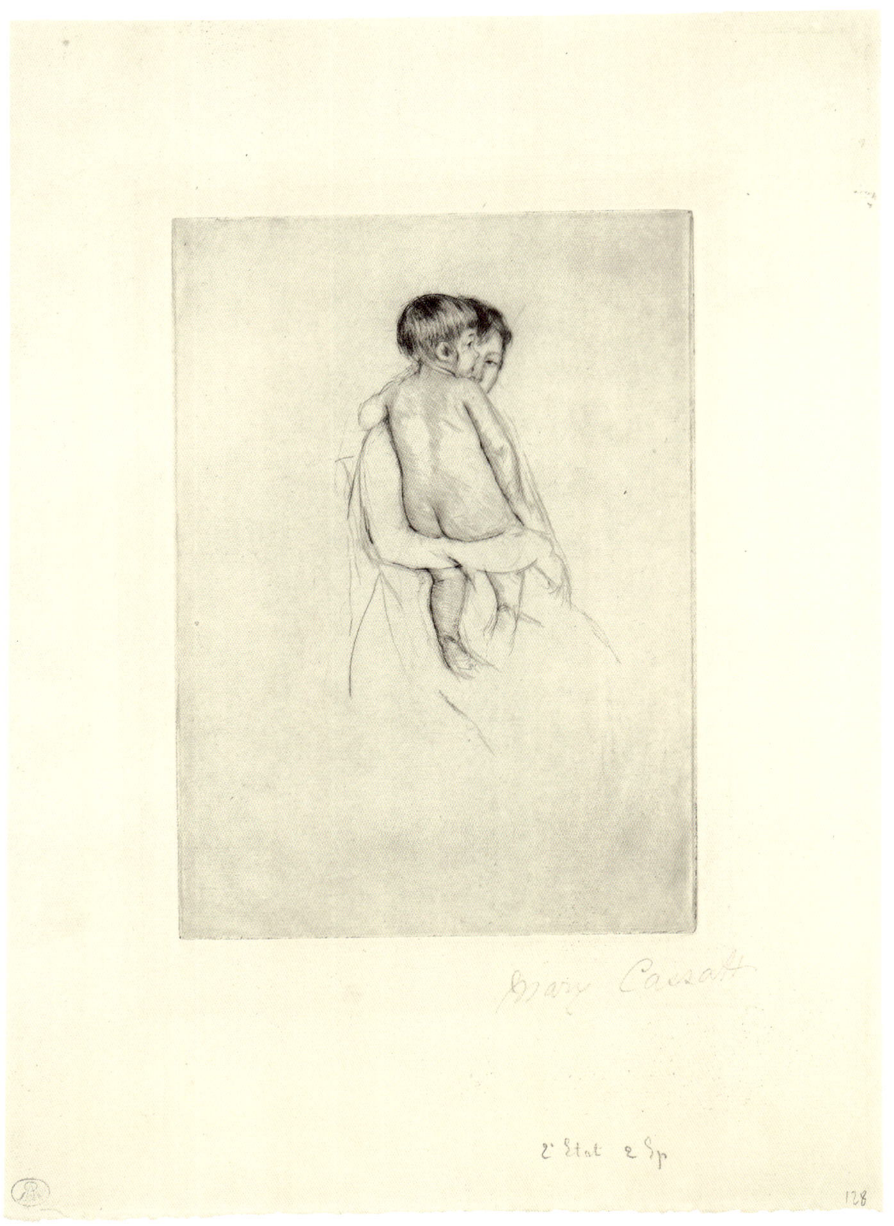

Baby's Back [Mother and Child], 1889–1890

Breeskin 128

Drypoint, second state of three, signed in full, annotated *2 Etat 2 Ep*, printed in black ink, with the fresh drypoint work adding lively accents to the expressions and definition of the figures, on Van Gelder laid paper, the full sheet, in good condition apart from very slight mat stain, and speckles of foxing in the margins

Plate: 23.4 × 16.4 cm   9¼ × 6½ in.
Sheet: 38.8 × 27.6 cm   15¼ × 10⅞ in.

One of the series of 12 drypoints exhibited by Durand-Ruel in 1890.

PROVENANCE

Alexis Rouart [1839–1911] (violet stamp, *recto*, variant of Lugt 2187a)

Pierre Demany [b. 1887] (purple stamp, *verso*, Lugt 780b), whose collection was distinguished by its range and quality.

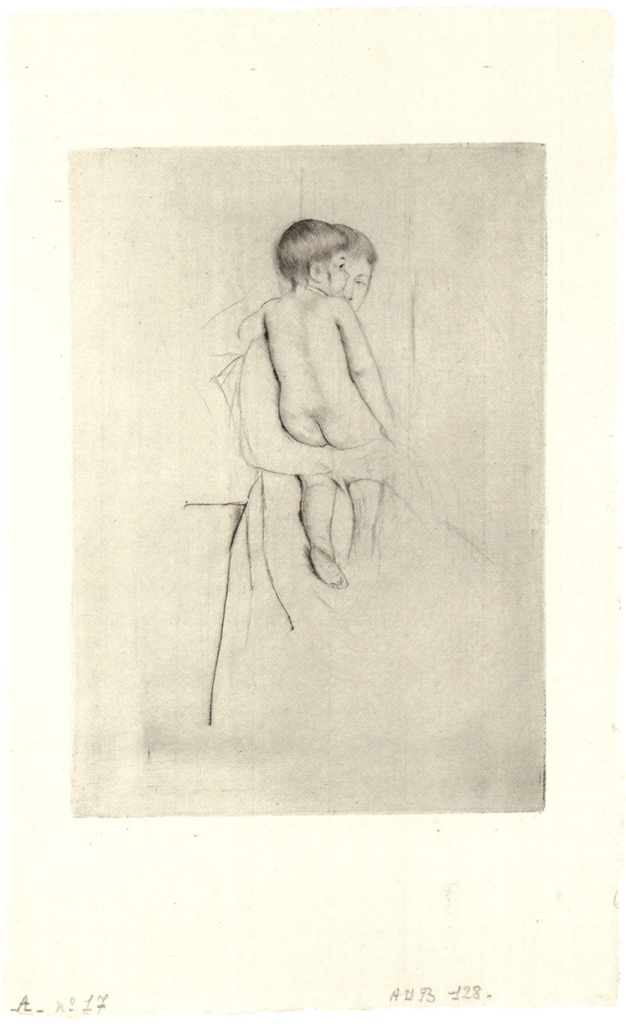

Baby's Back [Mother and Child],
1889–1890

Breeskin 128

Drypoint, third state of three, a particularly fine impression of this state, printed in rich, warm brown ink, with burr and plate tone, on laid paper with a Pro Patria watermark, the full sheet, in good condition (a bit of stray blue ink at lower left, apparently dating from the time of printing), annotated *A.* in the lower left corner

Plate: 23.3 × 16.2 cm 9¼ × 6⅜ in.
Sheet: 35.1 × 21 cm 14⅞ × 8¼ in.

One of the series of 12 drypoints exhibited by Durand-Ruel in 1890.

Baby's Back [Mother and Child],
1889–1890

Breeskin 128

Drypoint, third state of three, printed in dark brown ink, with delicate plate tone, on laid paper with a Pro Patria watermark, the full sheet, in good condition apart from a speck of foxing upper center, annotated *C.* in the lower left corner

Plate: 23.3 × 16.3 cm 9¼ × 6⅜ in.
Sheet: 32.1 × 21.2 cm 12⅝ × 8⅜ in.

One of the series of 12 drypoints exhibited by Durand-Ruel in 1890.

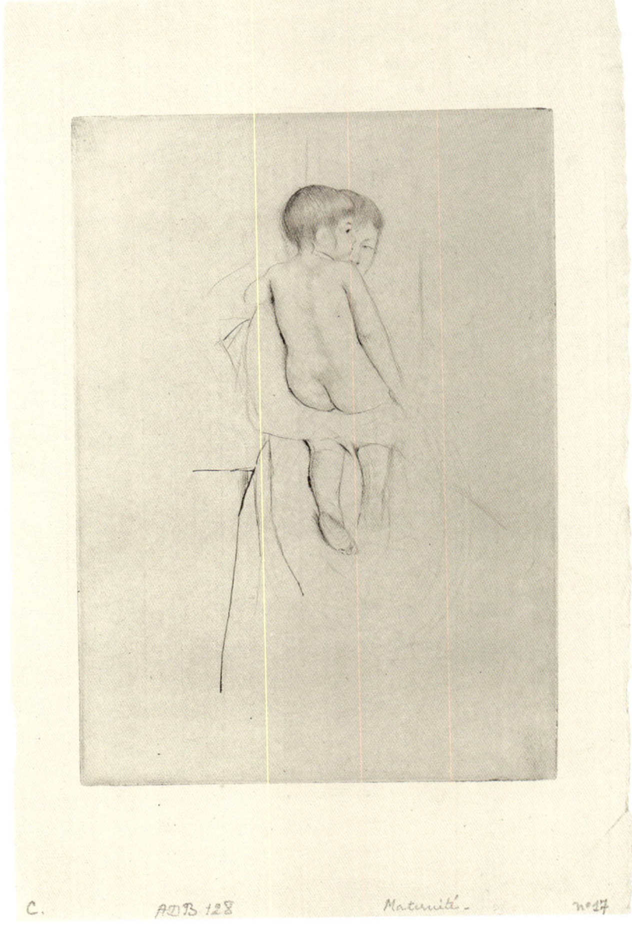

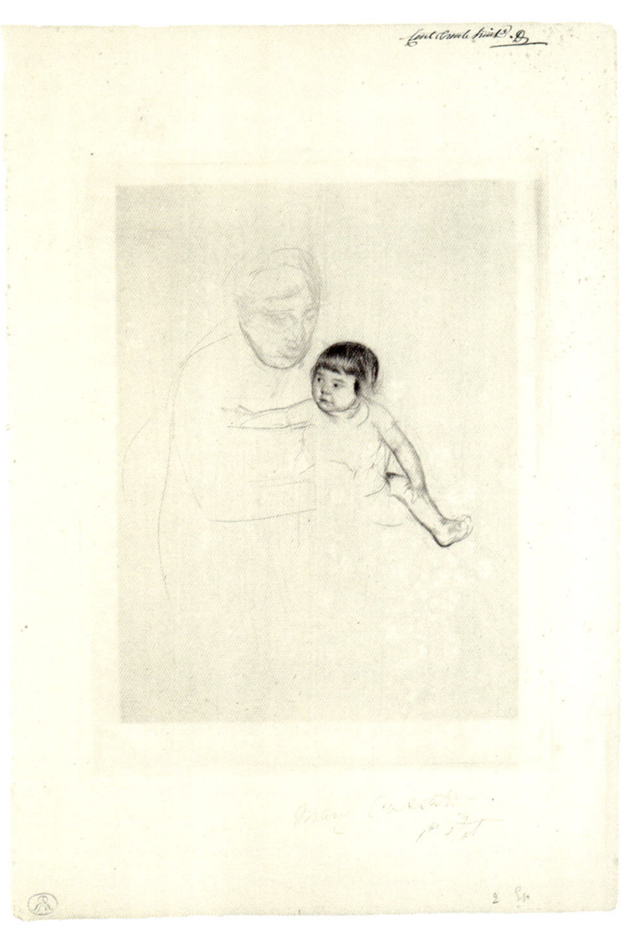

The Stocking, 1889–1890

Breeskin 129

Drypoint, fifth state of six, signed in full, with the artist's blue initial stamp in the lower right plate corner (Lugt 604), printed in dark brown ink, on laid paper with a shield watermark, the full sheet, in good condition apart from a soft diagonal crease running from the top edge at left just into the plate

Plate: 25.6 × 18.7 cm 10⅛ × 7⅜ in.
Sheet: 31.2 × 23.7 cm 12¼ × 9⅜ in.

One of the series of 12 drypoints exhibited by Durand-Ruel in 1890. Printed in an edition of 25.

PROVENANCE

Marcel Guérin [1873–1948] (Lugt 1872b), whose collection of modern prints was one of the most important ever assembled.

Marcel Mirault [1860–1929] (Lugt 1892a), noted for his fine collection of old master and modern prints.

The Stocking, 1889–1890

Breeskin 129

Drypoint, first state of six, signed in full, inscribed *1er Etat*, also annotated *2 Ep*, printed in black ink, with plate tone wiped clean at the edges, on an old sheet of ledger paper with an armorial watermark, the full sheet, in good condition apart from some faint light spotting in the image and foxing in the margin, particularly towards the upper right

Plate: 25.9 × 19 cm 10¼ × 7½ in.
Sheet: 37 × 24.9 cm 14½ × 9¾ in.

One of the series of 12 drypoints exhibited by Durand-Ruel in 1890.

The Avery Collection (NYPL) impression, which is the only other known impression of the first state, is printed on an almost identical sheet of old paper from the same ledger.

PROVENANCE

Alexis Rouart [1839–1911] (violet stamp, *recto*, variant of Lugt 2187a)

Pierre Demany [b. 1887] (purple stamp, *verso*, Lugt 780b), whose collection was distinguished by its range and quality.

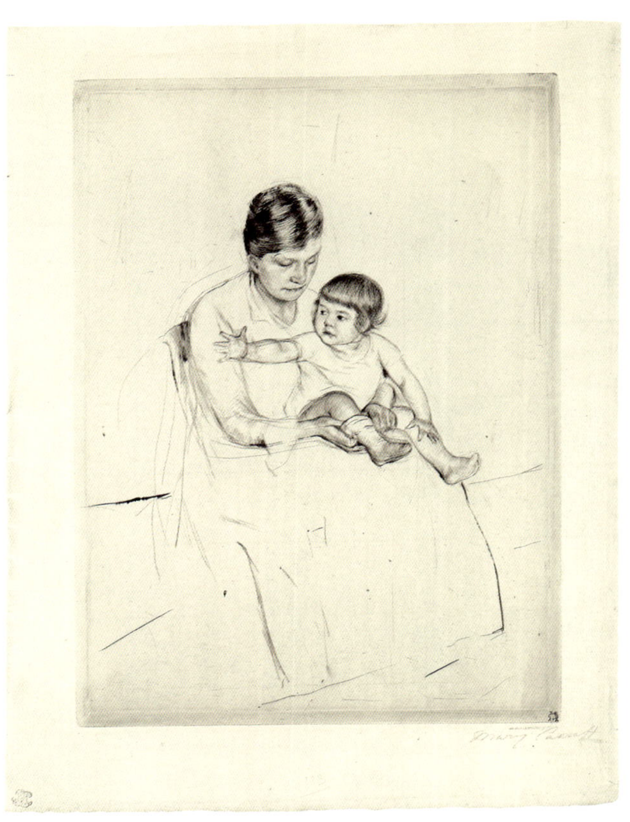

The Mandolin Player [The Mandoline], 1889–1890

Breeskin 130

Drypoint, second state of seven, signed in full, and with annotation, *1er Etat, 2 Ep,* printed in black ink with burr and strong plate tone, on warm-toned, laid paper with a Fortuna watermark, the full sheet, in good condition

Plate: 23.7 × 15.9 cm   9⅜ × 6¼ in.
Sheet: 44 × 27.7 cm   17¼ × 10⅞ in.

One of the series of 12 drypoints exhibited by Durand-Ruel in 1890.

PROVENANCE
Alexis Rouart [1839–1911] (violet stamp, *recto,* variant of Lugt 2187a)

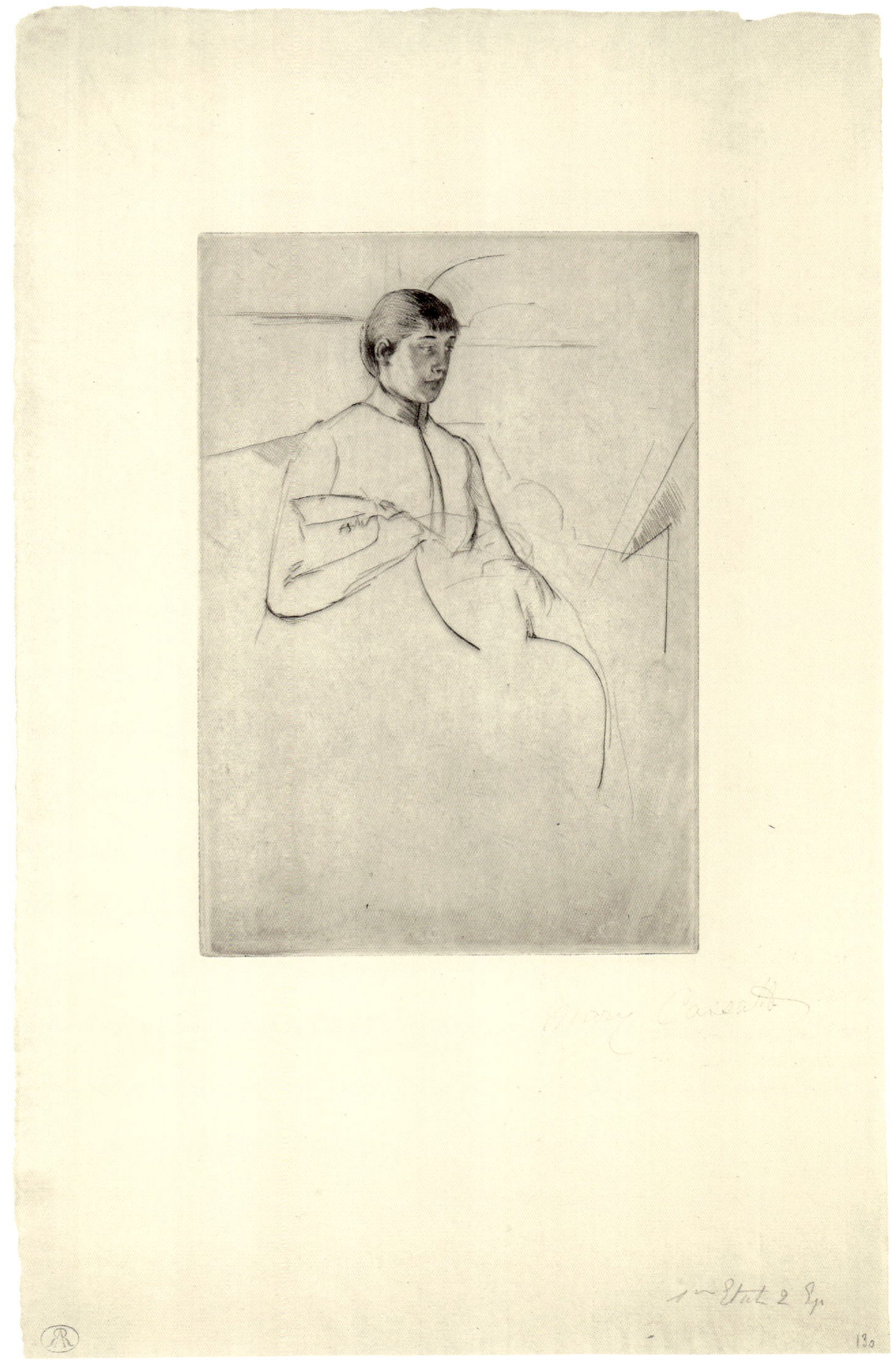

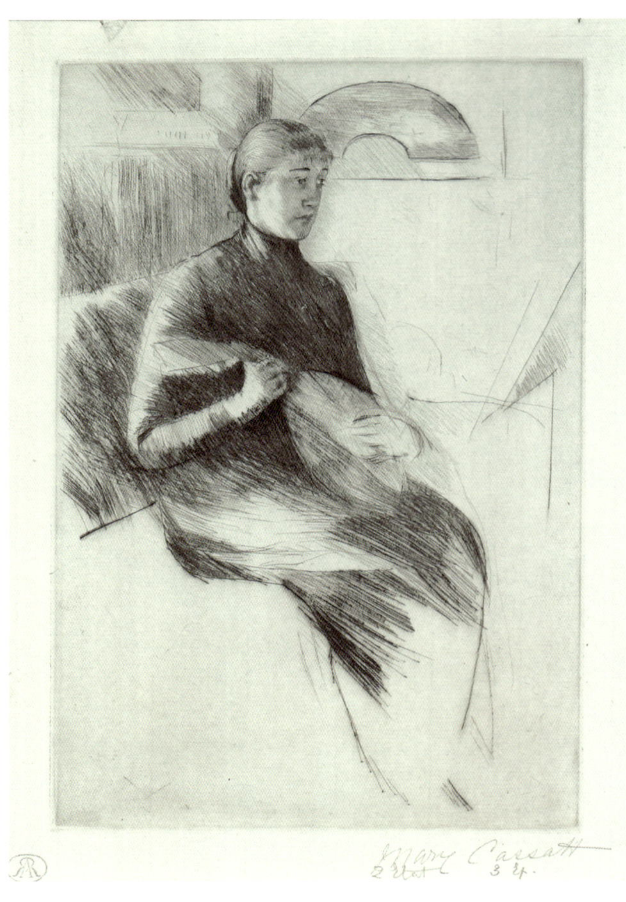

The Mandolin Player [The Mandoline], 1889–1890

Breeskin 130

Drypoint, fifth state of seven, printed in black ink, with burr and plate tone, on buff, laid paper with Van Gelder watermark, the full sheet, in good condition apart from speckled foxing, mainly in the right margin and a little into plate area, and a small blue stain in the lower margin at left, annotated *A.* at lower center

Plate: 23.8 × 16 cm 9⅜ × 6¼ in.
Sheet: 44.7 × 28.2 cm 17⅝ × 11⅛ in.

One of the series of 12 drypoints exhibited by Durand-Ruel in 1890.

The Mandolin Player [The Mandoline], 1889–1890

Breeskin 130

Drypoint, fourth state of seven, signed in full, and with annotation, *2 Etat 3 Ep.*, printed in dark brown ink, with light plate tone, on pale, blue-green, laid paper, with small margins, in good condition apart from two small nicks at top edge, and a bit of reflective matter in left margin and in plate edge

Plate: 23.6 × 15.9 cm 9⅜ × 6¼ in.
Sheet: 26.4 × 20 cm 10⅜ × 7⅞ in.

One of the series of 12 drypoints exhibited by Durand-Ruel in 1890.

PROVENANCE
Alexis Rouart [1839–1911] (violet stamp, *recto*, variant of Lugt 2187a)

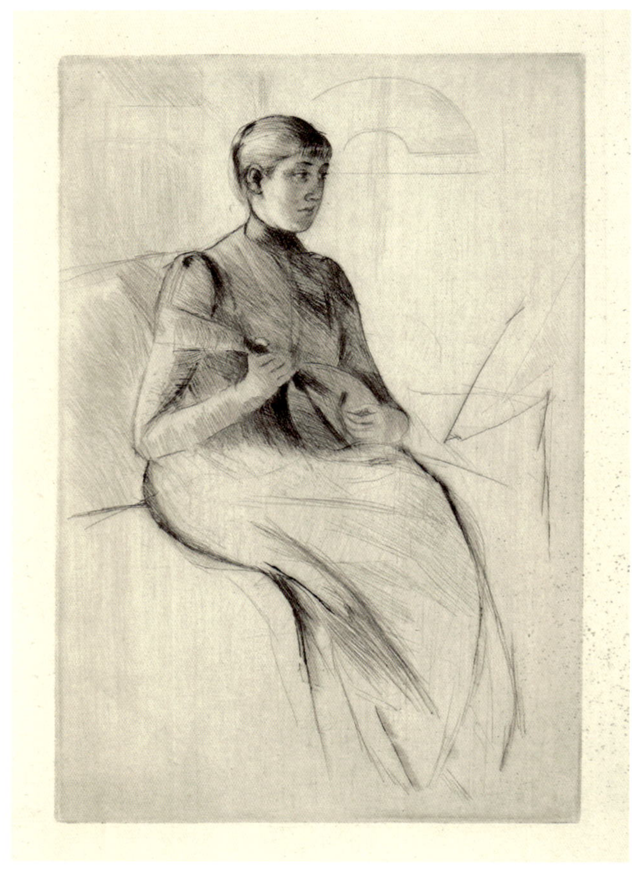

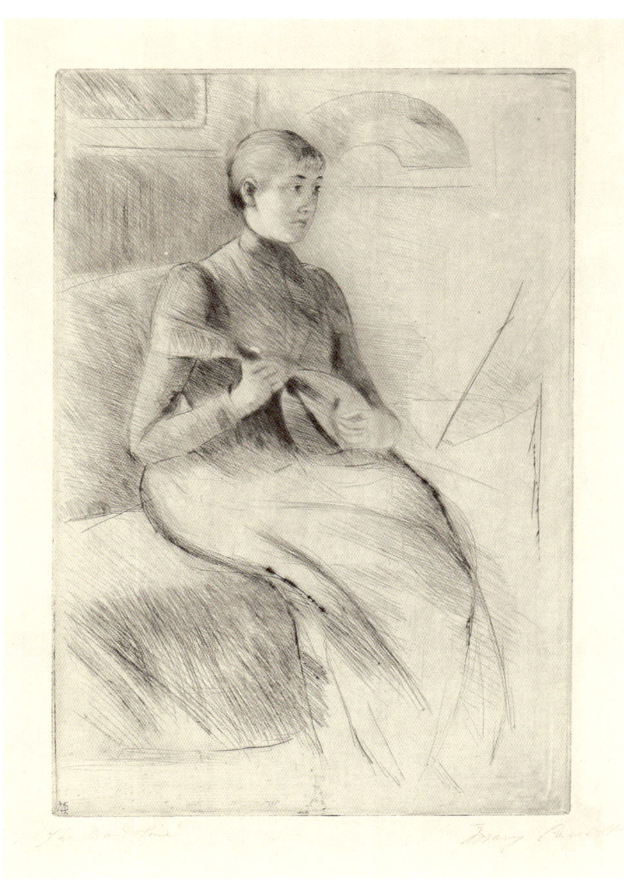

The Mandolin Player
[The Mandoline], 1889–1890

Breeskin 130

Drypoint, seventh state of seven, a trial proof, printed in russet-brown ink, with plate tone, on laid paper with a Pro Patria watermark, the full sheet, in good condition, annotated *B*

Plate: 23.5 × 15.7 cm   9¼ × 6¼ in.
Sheet: 35.3 × 20.6 cm   13⅞ × 8⅛ in.

One of the series of 12 drypoints exhibited by Durand-Ruel in 1890.

The Mandolin Player
[The Mandoline], 1889–1890

Breeskin 130

Drypoint, seventh state of seven, signed in full, and titled by the artist, *The Mandoline,* with the artist's blue initial stamp in the lower left plate corner (Lugt 604), from the edition of 25, printed in black ink, with a veil of plate tone, on laid Japan paper, the full sheet, in good condition apart from slight handling creases, and a few pale fox marks

Plate: 23.7 × 16 cm   9⅜ × 6¼ in.
Sheet: 32.3 × 25.1 cm   12¾ × 9⅞ in.

One of the series of 12 drypoints exhibited by Durand-Ruel in 1890.

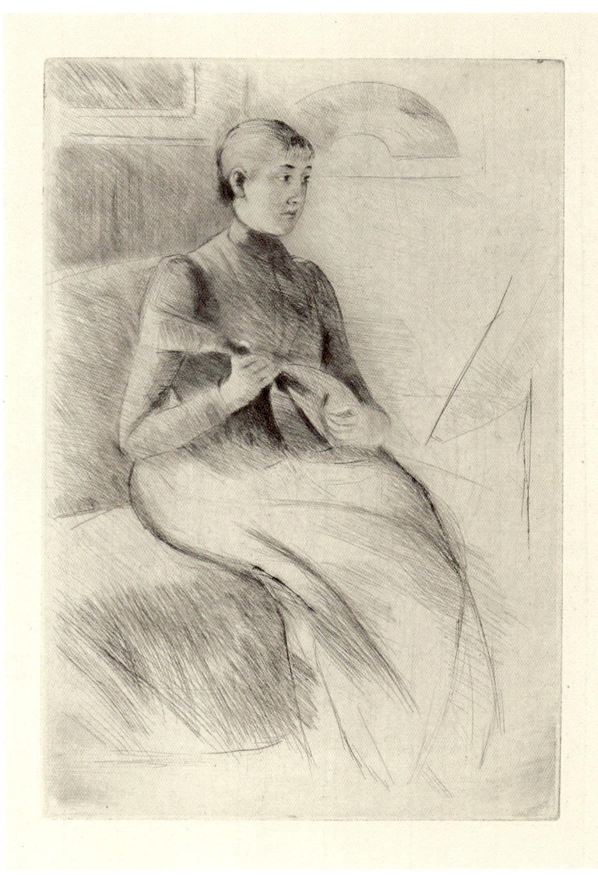

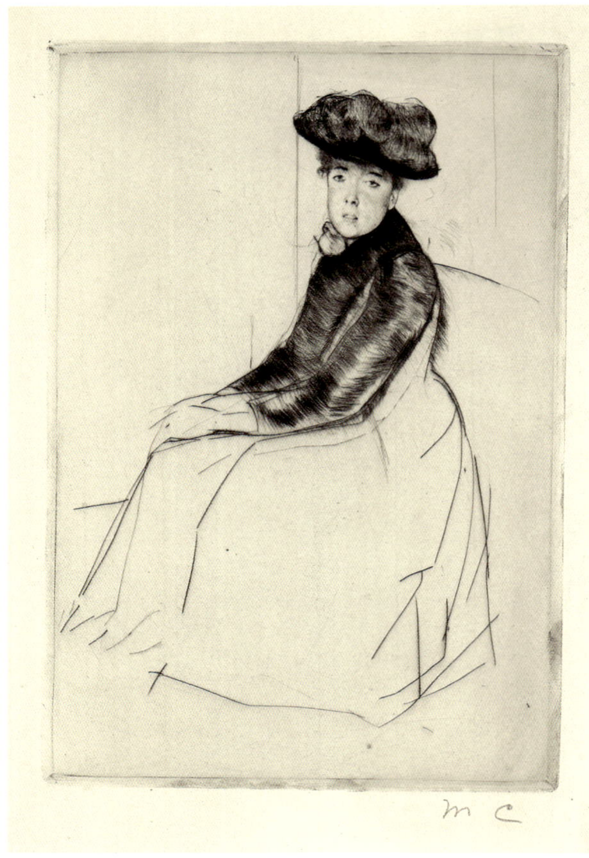

Reflection, 1889–1890

Breeskin 131, ca. 1890

Drypoint, a previously unrecorded state (Ia), between Breeskin's first and second of four, printed in warm, brown-black ink with varied tone, stronger at the edges, on blue laid paper with letters watermark, F ANDRIA/AL, the full sheet, in good condition apart from some foxing, mainly in the lower half of the lower margin, annotated *C.* in lower left corner

Plate: 26.3 × 17.7 cm 10⅜ × 6⅞ in.
Sheet: 40.5 × 26 cm 16 × 10¼ in.

One of the series of 12 drypoints exhibited by Durand-Ruel in 1890.

This state, possibly unique in this example, shows added work on the skirt and shoes and shadow behind the figure, etc., but is before the dog sketched against the skirt.

Reflection, 1889–1890

Breeskin 131

Drypoint, first state, initialed *M C,* printed in brown-black ink, on laid paper with Vanderley watermark, the full sheet, in good condition (slight darkening of paper and soft handling crease across top left corner), annotated *A.* and *Epr. d'état*

Plate: 26.1 × 17.6 cm 10¼ × 6⅞ in.
Sheet: 35 × 20.7 cm 13¾ × 8⅛ in.

One of the series of 12 drypoints exhibited by Durand-Ruel in 1890.

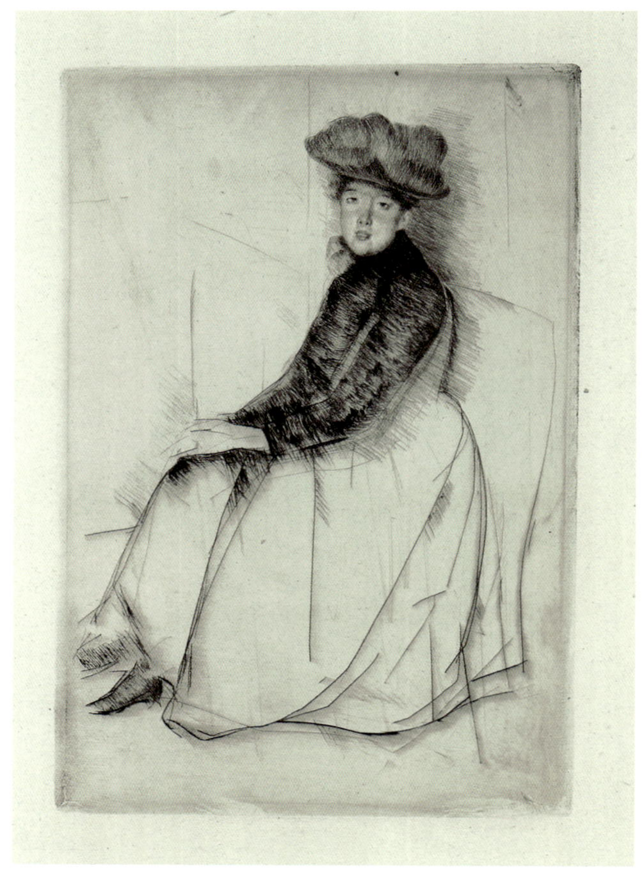

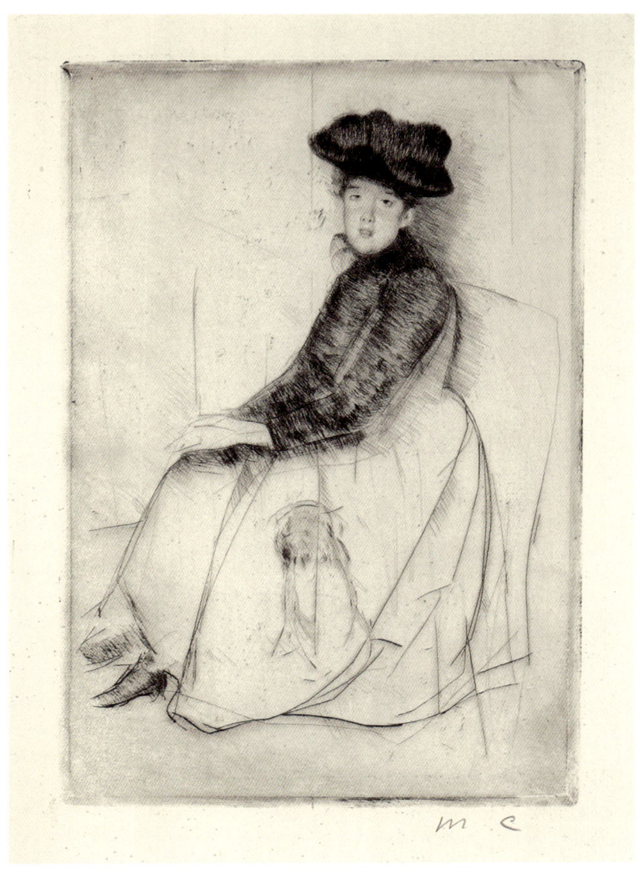

Reflection, 1889–1890

Breeskin 131

Drypoint, Breeskin's fourth (final) state, printed in brown-black ink, on laid paper with Vanderley watermark, the full sheet, in good condition apart from a few diagonal printer's creases at lower left, and a few others in the lower margin, annotated *E* in the lower left corner

Plate: 26.1 × 17.6 cm 10¼ × 6⅞ in.
Sheet: 35 × 20.7 cm 13¾ × 8⅛ in.

One of the series of 12 drypoints exhibited by Durand-Ruel in 1890.

Reflection, 1889–1890

Breeskin 131

Drypoint, a further previously unrecorded state (Ib) between Breeskin's first and second of four, initialed *MC*, printed in brown-black ink, with plate tone, stronger towards the edges and wiped a little cleaner on the skirt, on heavy laid paper with the crown of a Van Gelder watermark, the full sheet, in good condition apart from scattered speckles of foxing, hardly noticeable within plate area, annotated *D* in the lower left corner

Plate: 26.2 × 17.9 cm 10⅜ × 7 in.
Sheet: 32.3 × 24.4 cm 12¾ × 9⅝ in.

One of the series of 12 drypoints exhibited by Durand-Ruel in 1890.

In this state, possibly unique in this example, the dog has already been added, set against the skirt, but is more clearly defined than in Breeskin's second state, where its head and other details are slightly burnished; also, the artist has not yet redrawn the upper shoe in a higher position, as she will in Breeskin's second state.

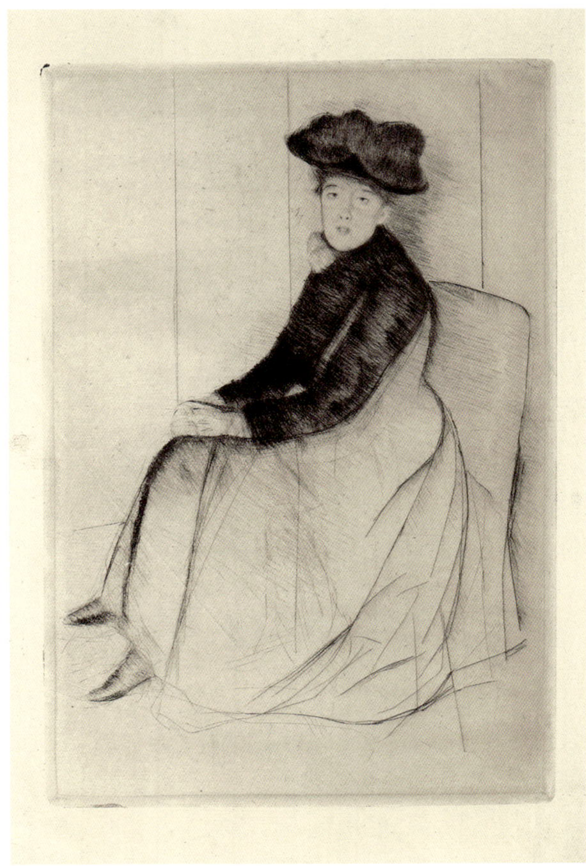

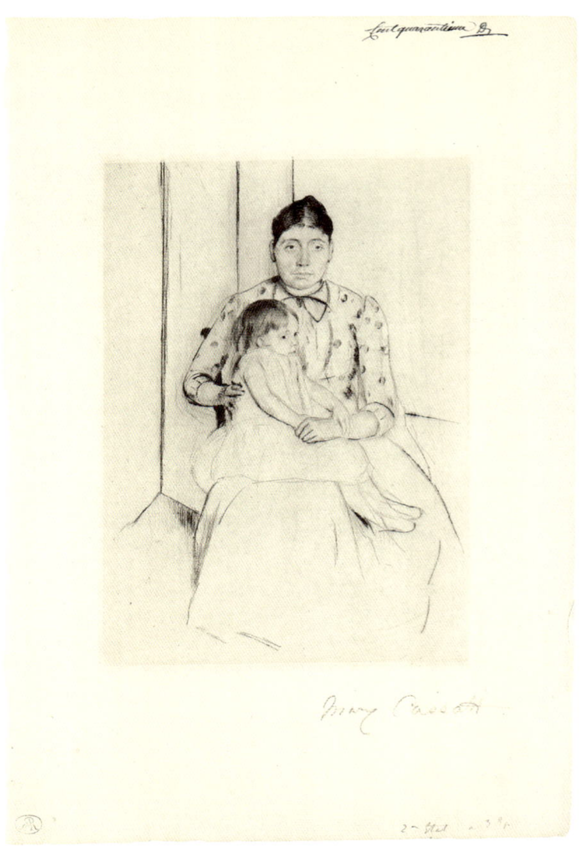

Repose [Resting], 1889–1890

Breeskin 132

Drypoint, fifth state of five, printed in black ink, on fine, handmade, wove paper, the full sheet, in good condition apart from a small tear and water stain in the lower edge, slight smudge above the molding at right, annotated *K.* in the lower left corner

Plate: 23.3 × 16.9 cm 9⅛ × 6⅝ in.
Sheet: 34.8 × 24.9 cm 13¾ × 9¾ in.

One of the series of 12 drypoints exhibited by Durand-Ruel in 1890.

Repose [Resting], 1889–1890

Breeskin 132

Drypoint, fourth state of five, signed in full, inscribed *2m Etat à 3 Ep,* printed in dark brown ink, with plate tone, wiped clean at the edges, on laid, 18th-century ledger paper with watermark, MOYRET . . . 1764 (from the same batch as Breeskin 129), the full sheet, in good condition apart from darkening of the paper and barely perceptible lighter spots in sheet within image

Plate: 23.4 × 16.9 cm 9¼ × 6⅝ in.
Sheet: 37 × 25 cm 14½ × 9⅞ in.

One of the series of 12 drypoints exhibited by Durand-Ruel in 1890.

PROVENANCE
Alexis Rouart [1839–1911] (violet stamp, *recto,* variant of Lugt 2187a)

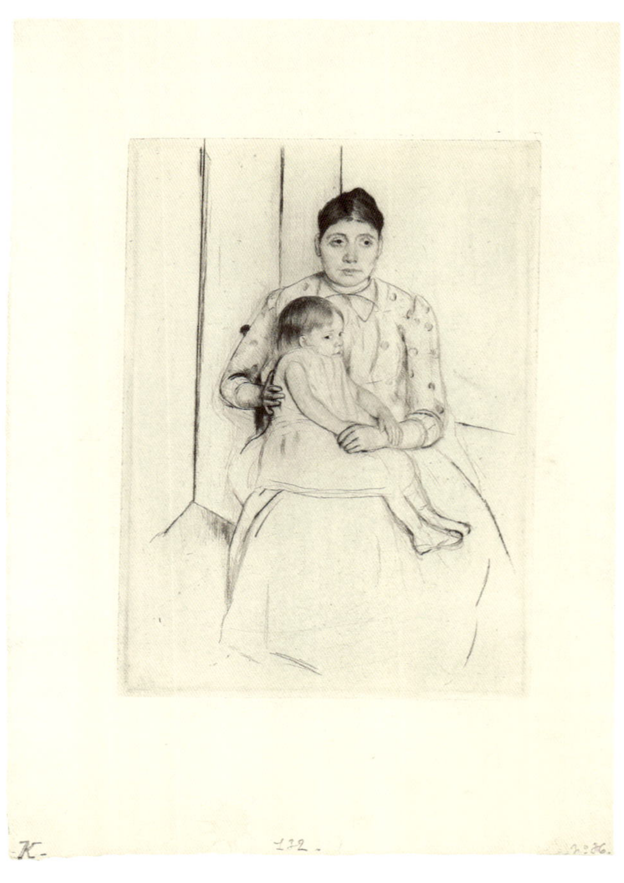

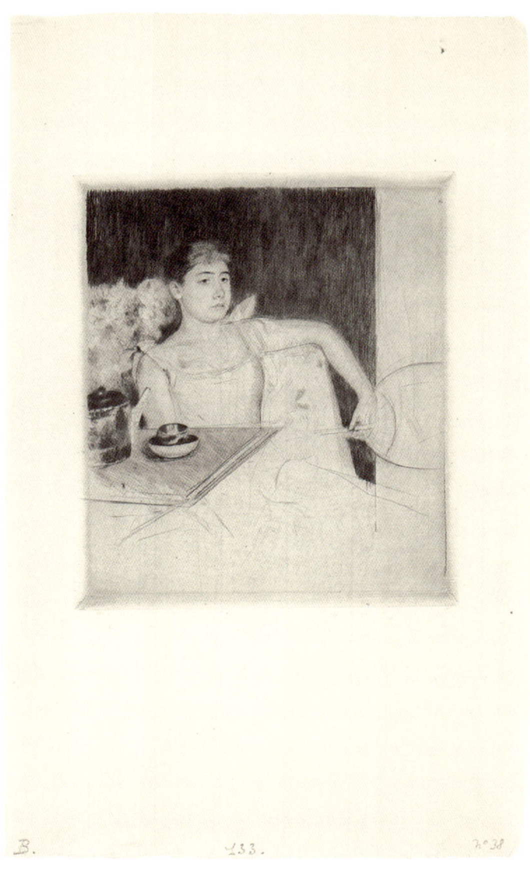

Tea, 1889–1890

Breeskin 133

Drypoint, fifth state of five, printed in brown ink, with plate tone, on laid paper with a Pro Patria watermark, the full sheet, in good condition, annotated *B.* in the lower left corner

Plate: 18.1 × 15.6 cm 7⅛ × 6⅛ in.
Sheet: 35.2 × 21.4 cm 13¾ × 8⅜ in.

One of the series of 12 drypoints exhibited by Durand-Ruel in 1890.

Tea, 1889–1890

Breeskin 133

Drypoint, fifth state of five, printed in brown ink, with plate tone, on laid paper with a Vanderley watermark, the full sheet, in good condition, annotated *H.* in the lower left corner

Plate: 18.1 × 15.7 cm 7⅛ × 6⅛ in.
Sheet: 35.5 × 21.5 cm 14 × 8⅜ in.

One of the series of 12 drypoints exhibited by Durand-Ruel in 1890.

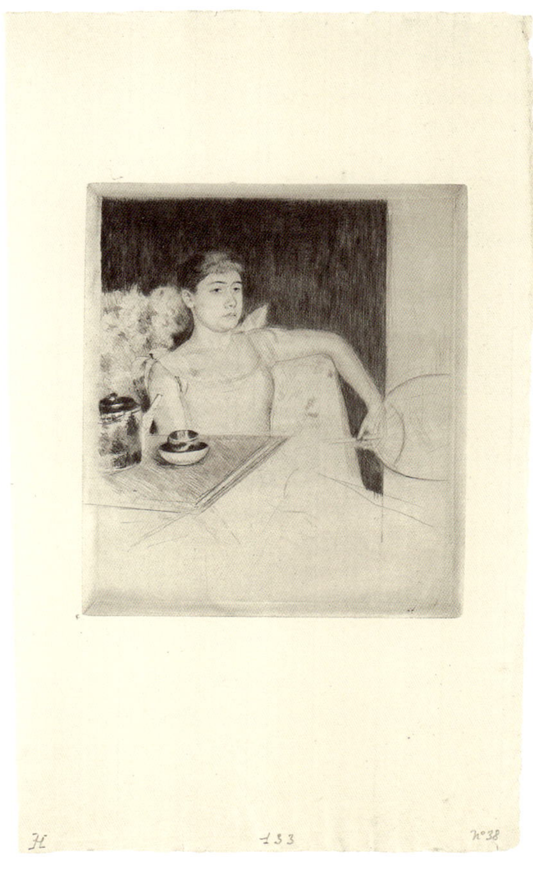

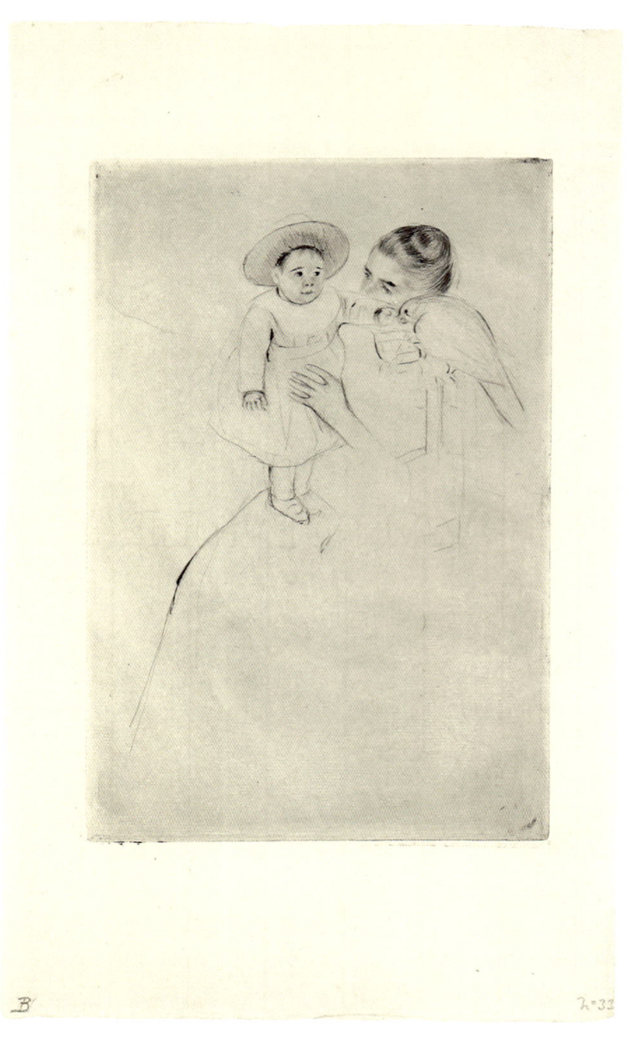

Hélène of Septeuil
[Enfant au Perroquet], 1889–1890

Breeskin 134

Drypoint, fifth state of five, printed in black ink, with rich, varied plate tone, on laid paper with a Vanderley watermark, the full sheet, in good condition apart from a few pale fox marks, annotated *B.* in the lower left corner

Plate: 23.9 × 15.7 cm 9⅜ × 6⅛ in.
Sheet: 35 × 20.9 cm 13¾ × 8¼ in.

One of the series of 12 drypoints exhibited by Durand-Ruel in 1890.

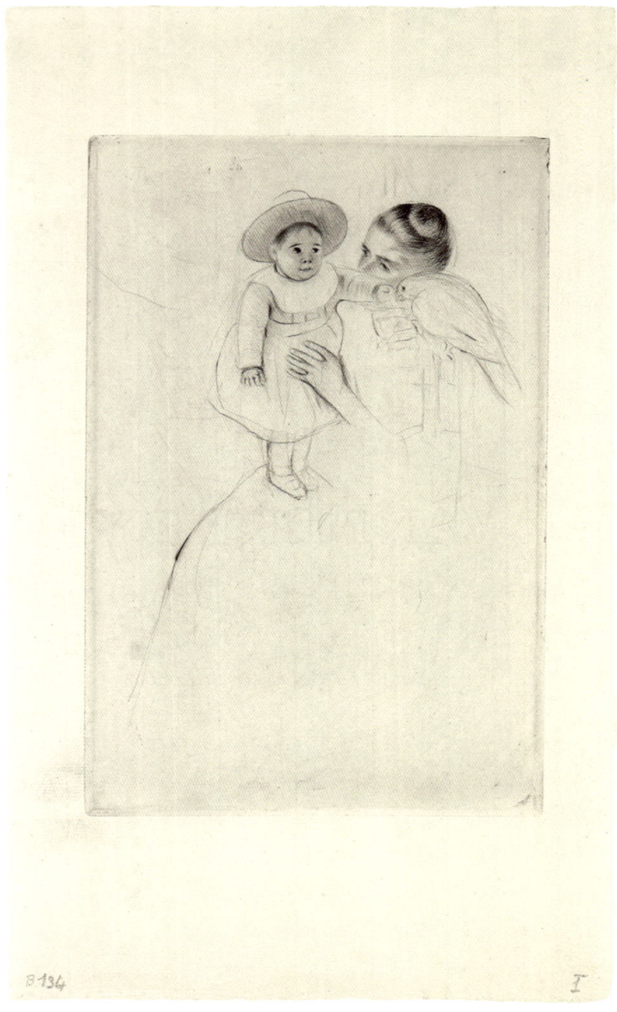

Hélène of Septeuil
[Enfant au Perroquet], 1889–1890

Breeskin 134

Drypoint, fifth state of five, printed in dark brown ink, with delicate, overall plate tone, on laid paper with a Vanderley watermark, the full sheet, in good condition apart from some foxing, annotated *I.* in the lower left corner

Plate: 23.8 × 15.7 cm 9⅜ × 6⅛ in.
Sheet: 35 × 20.9 cm 13¾ × 8¼ in.

One of the series of 12 drypoints exhibited by Durand-Ruel in 1890.

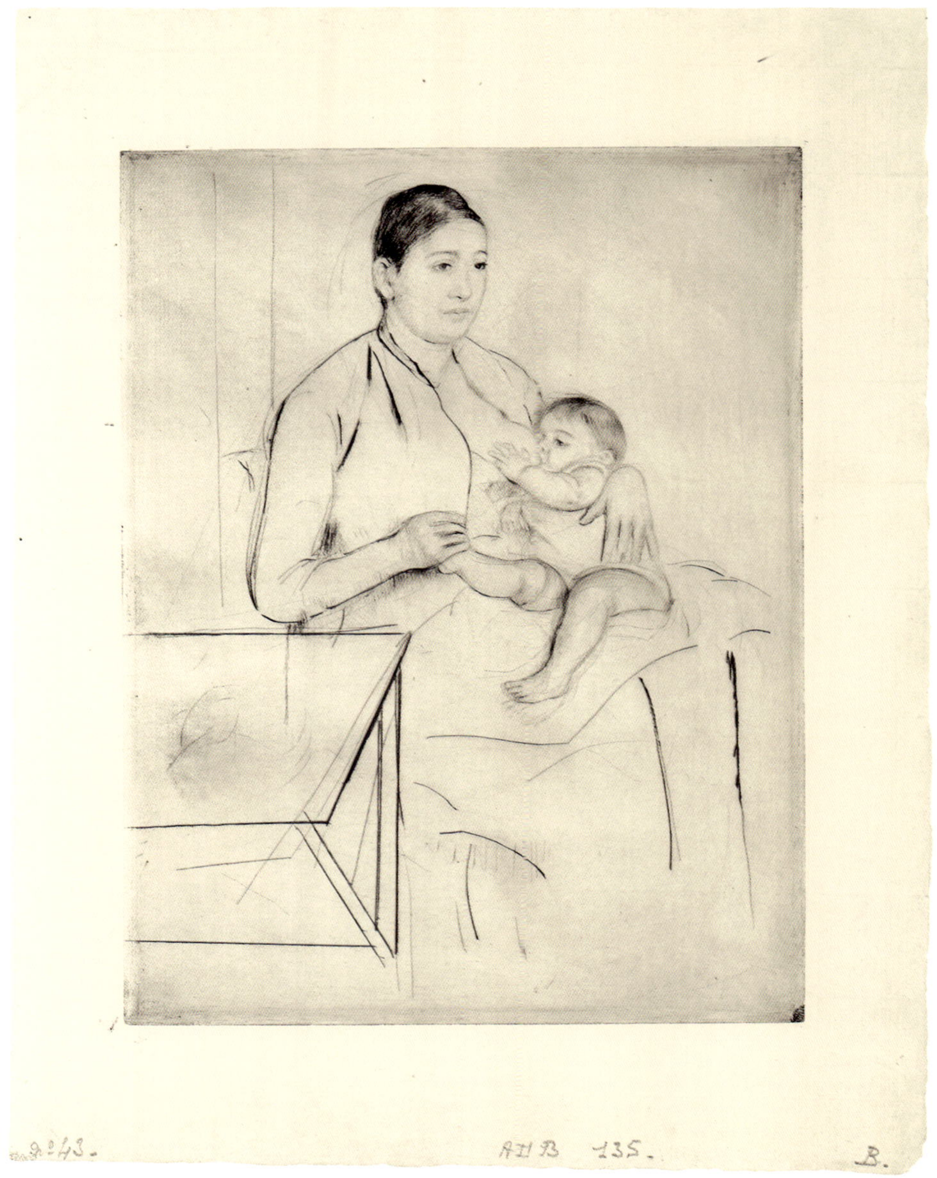

Nursing, 1889–1890 [ca. 1890]

Breeskin 135

Drypoint, third state of three, printed in brown-black ink, with strong burr and rich, varied plate tone, on laid paper with BLACONS watermark, the full sheet, in good condition

Plate: 23.6 × 17.8 cm 9¼ × 7 in.
Sheet: 31.4 × 24 cm 12⅜ × 9½ in.

One of the series of 12 drypoints exhibited by Durand-Ruel in 1890.

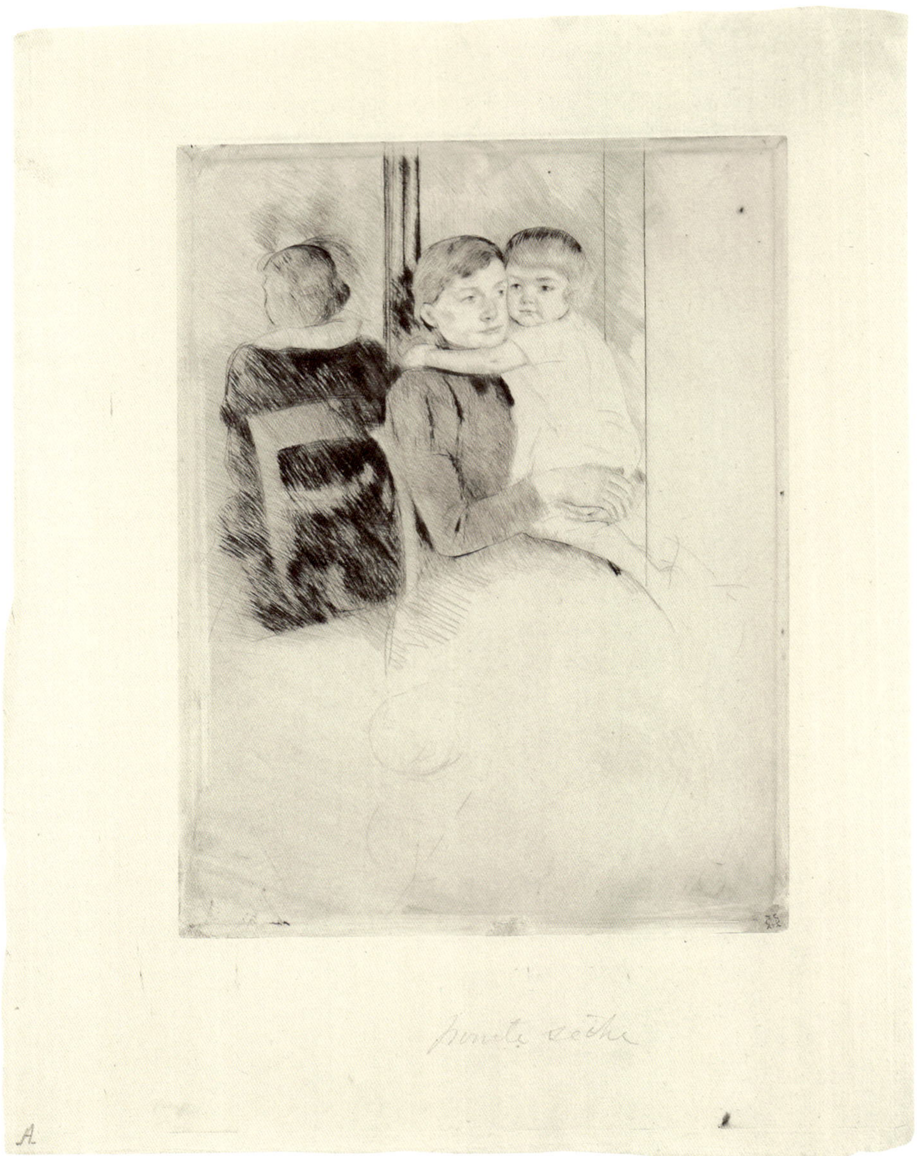

The Mirror, 1889–1890

Breeskin 136

Drypoint, a previously unrecorded and possibly unique state between Breeskin's fourth and fifth of seven, before the lower lines of the mirror frame, with the artist's blue initial stamp in the lower right plate corner (Lugt 604), printed in brown-black ink, with strong accents of burr and rich and varied plate tone, on heavy, laid paper with the crown of a Van Gelder watermark, the full sheet, in good condition (two iron flecks in the paper at upper right), annotated *A* in the lower left corner

Plate: 22.8 × 17 cm 9 × 6⅝ in.
Sheet: 33 × 25.4 cm 13 × 10 in.

One of the series of 12 drypoints exhibited by Durand-Ruel in 1890.

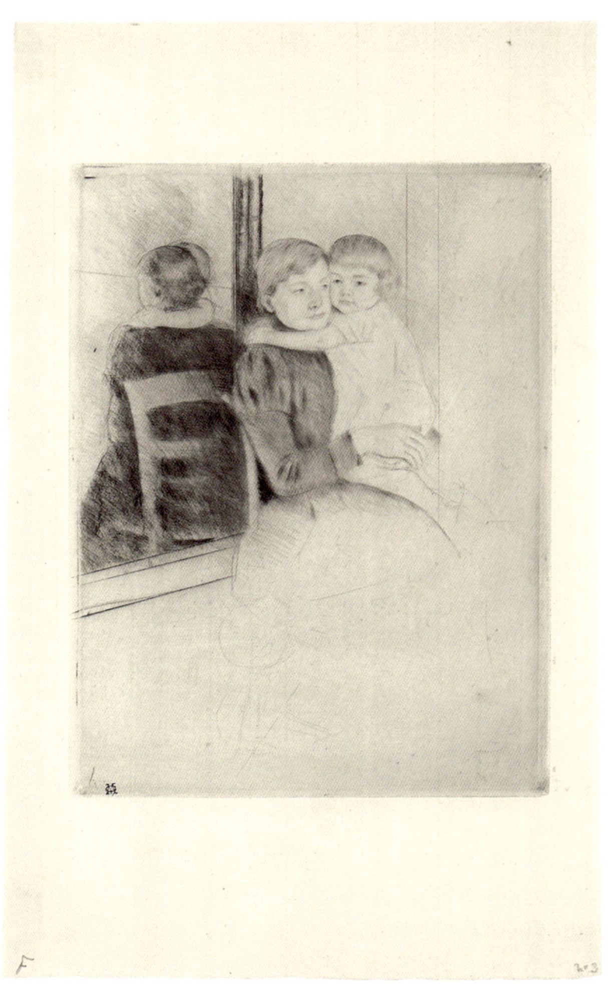

The Mirror, 1889–1890

Breeskin 136

Drypoint, Breeskin's sixth state of seven, with the artist's blue initial stamp in the lower left plate corner (Lugt 604), printed in brown ink, with even plate tone, on laid paper with a Pro Patria watermark (Vanderley), the full sheet, in good condition, annotated *F* in the lower left corner

Plate: 22.8 × 16.8 cm 9 × 6⅝ in.
Sheet: 34.5 × 20.9 cm 13⅝ × 8¼ in.

One of the series of 12 drypoints exhibited by Durand-Ruel in 1890.

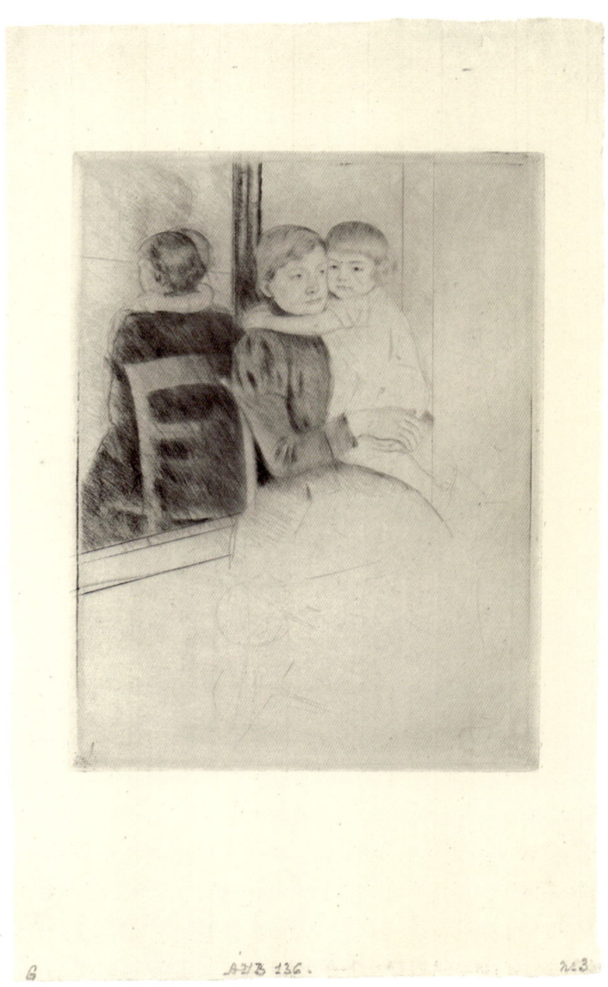

The Mirror, 1889–1890

Breeskin 136

Drypoint, Breeskin's seventh state of seven, printed in brown ink, with even plate tone, on laid paper with Vanderley watermark, the full sheet, in good condition, annotated *G* in the lower left corner

Plate: 22.8 × 16.8 cm 9 × 6⅝ in.
Sheet: 35.5 × 21.3 cm 14 × 8⅜ in.

One of the series of 12 drypoints exhibited by Durand-Ruel in 1890.

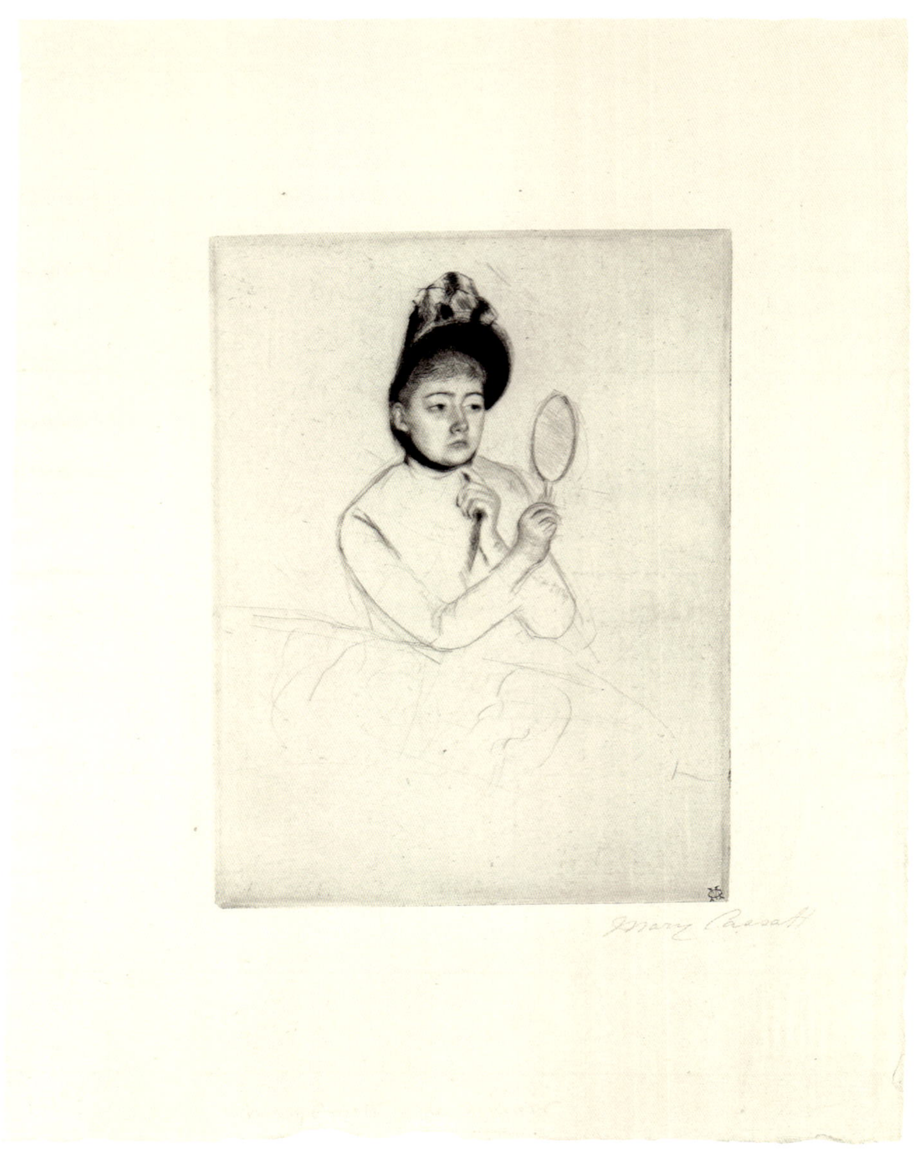

The Bonnet, 1889–1890

Breeskin 137

Drypoint, third state of three, signed in full, with the artist's blue initial stamp in the lower right plate corner (Lugt 604), from the edition of 25, on laid paper with part of a letters in shield watermark, the full sheet, in good condition

Plate: 18.5 × 13.9 cm 7¼ × 5½ in.
Sheet: 31 × 24 cm 12¼ × 9½ in.

One of the series of 12 drypoints exhibited by Durand-Ruel in 1890.

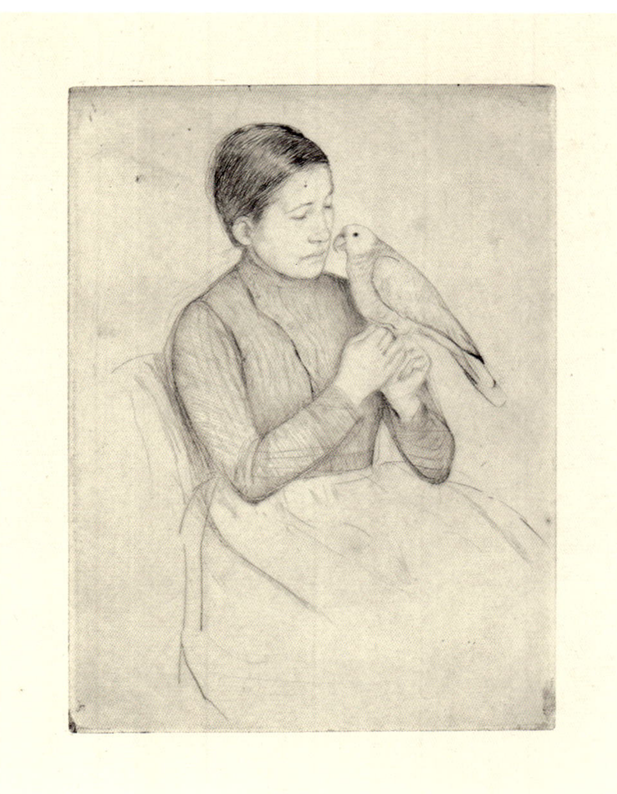

The Parrot, 1889–1890

Breeskin 138

Drypoint, fifth state of seven, printed in brown-black ink with delicate plate tone, on laid paper, the full sheet, in good condition, annotated *F.* in the lower left corner

Plate: 16.2 × 11.9 cm 6⅜ × 4¾ in.
Sheet: 34.1 × 21.3 cm 13⅜ × 8⅜ in.

One of the series of 12 drypoints exhibited by Durand-Ruel in 1890.

Breeskin illustrates the seventh (final) state, not the fifth.

The Parrot, 1889–1890

Breeskin 138

Drypoint, sixth state of seven, signed in full and inscribed *épreuve d'essai*, printed in dark brown ink with warm plate tone, on laid paper, the full sheet, in good condition (slightly darkened)

Plate: 16.2 × 12 cm 6⅜ × 4¾ in.
Sheet: 34.5 × 21.3 cm 13½ × 8⅜ in.

One of the series of 12 drypoints exhibited by Durand-Ruel in 1890.

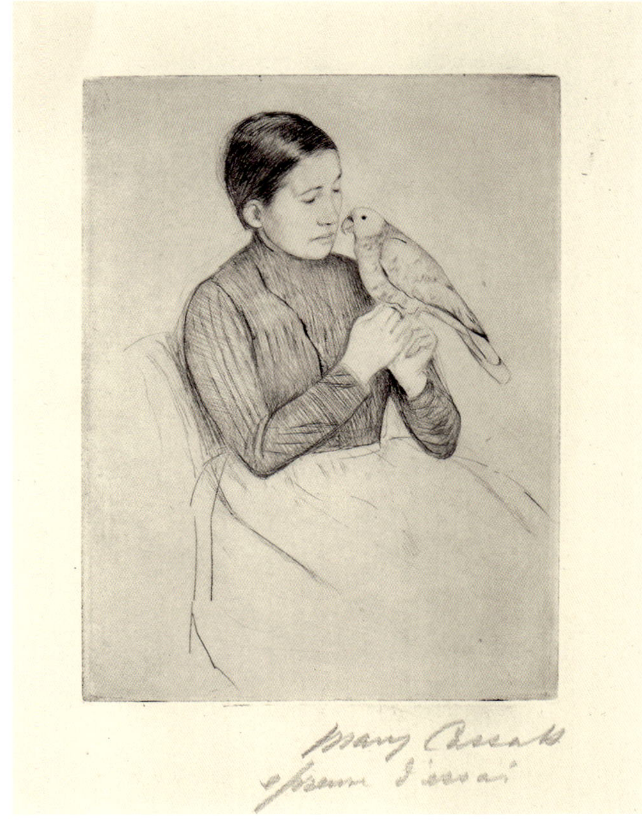

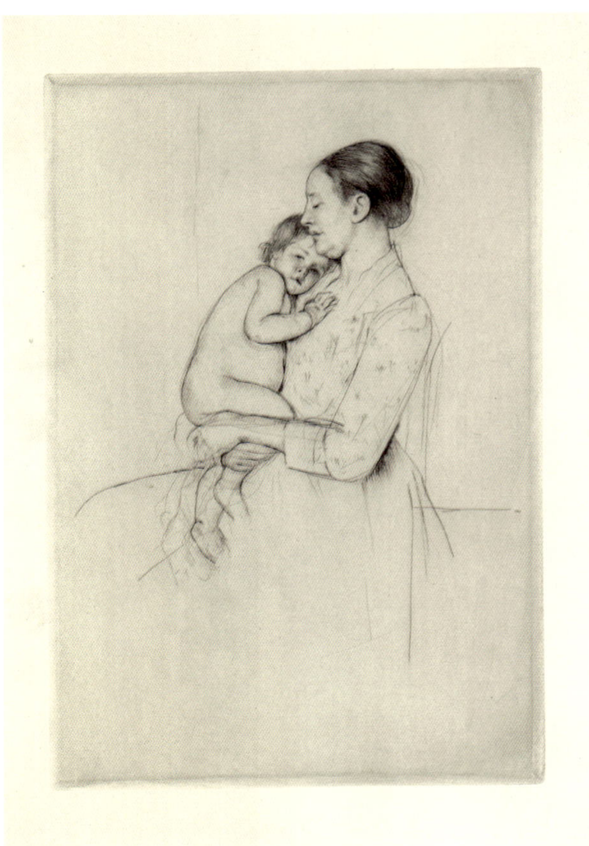

Quietude, ca. 1891

Breeskin 139

Drypoint, fourth state of five, an extremely fine impression, printed in brown-black ink, with all of the fine nuances of drypoint shading printed clearly, and with an even veil of plate tone, on laid paper with VanderLey and post horn in crowned shield watermark, the full sheet, in good condition apart from some minor handling creases in the upper margin, and slight soiling in the left edge, annotated *C* in the lower left corner

Plate: 26 × 17.6 cm 10¼ × 6⅞ in.
Sheet: 39 × 23.5 cm 15⅜ × 9¼ in.

Quietude, ca. 1891

Breeskin 139

Drypoint, fourth state of five, signed in full, printed in brown-black ink, with atmospheric plate tone, on blue laid paper with F/ANDRIA watermark, the full sheet, in good condition apart from slight handling creases, a few tiny bits of foreign matter, barely noticeable in image, annotated *A* in the lower left corner

Plate: 25.9 × 17.6 cm 10¼ × 6⅞ in.
Sheet: 39.4 × 25.5 cm 15½ × 10 in.

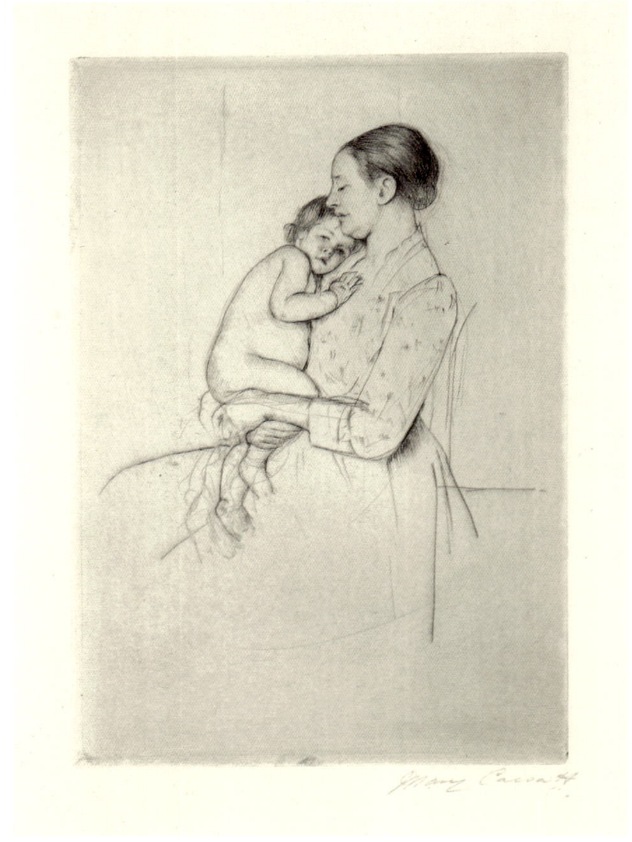

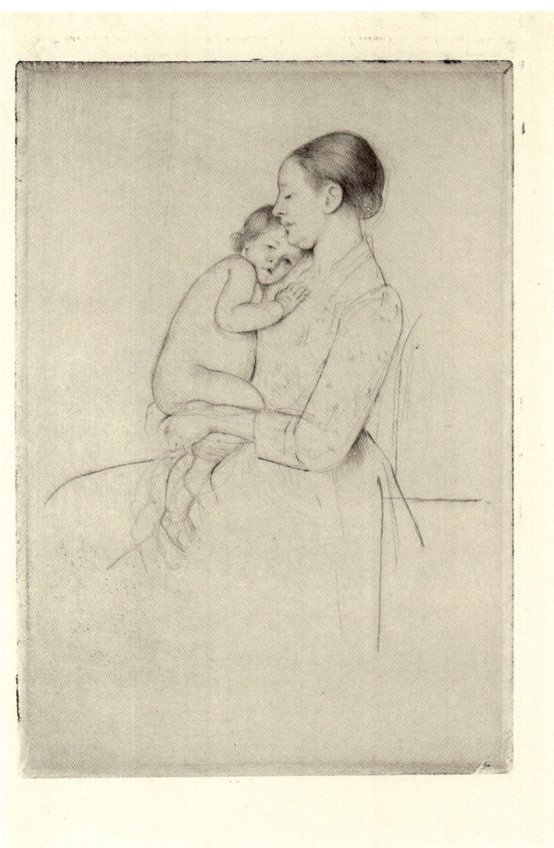

Quietude, ca. 1891

Breeskin 139

Drypoint, fourth state of five, printed in black ink, with strong and very effective plate tone, on paper with a Pro Patria (Vanderley) watermark, the full sheet (narrow margin at left), in good condition

Plate: 26 × 17.7 cm 10¼ × 7 in.
Sheet: 35 × 20.4 cm 13¾ × 8 in.

Quietude, ca. 1891

Breeskin 139

Drypoint, fifth state of five, printed in dark brown ink, with burr and even plate tone, on laid paper with Vanderley watermark, with the artist's blue initial stamp in the lower right plate corner (Lugt 604), the full sheet, in good condition (minor pale foxing), annotated *I.* in the lower left corner

Plate: 25.9 × 17.5 cm 10¼ × 6⅞ in.
Sheet: 34.7 × 20.2 cm 13⅝ × 7⅞ in.

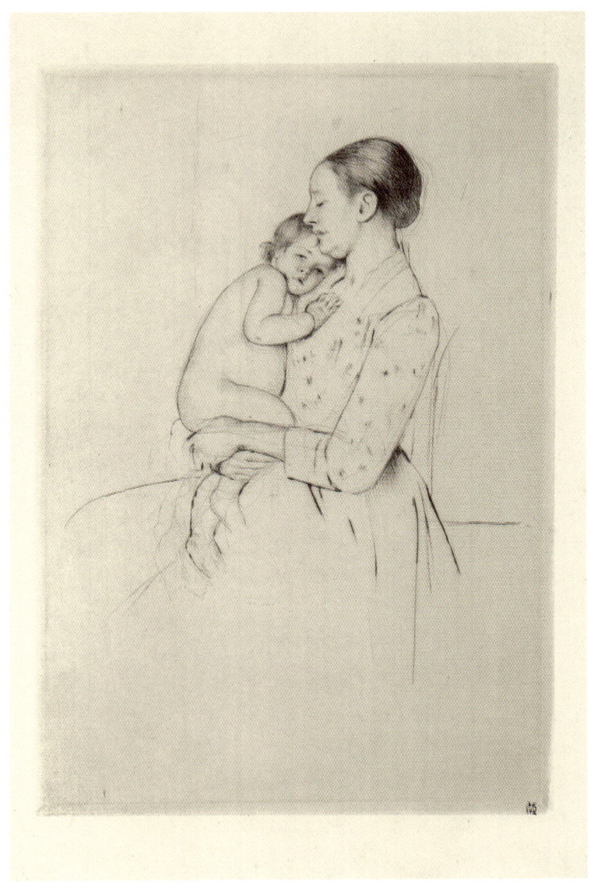

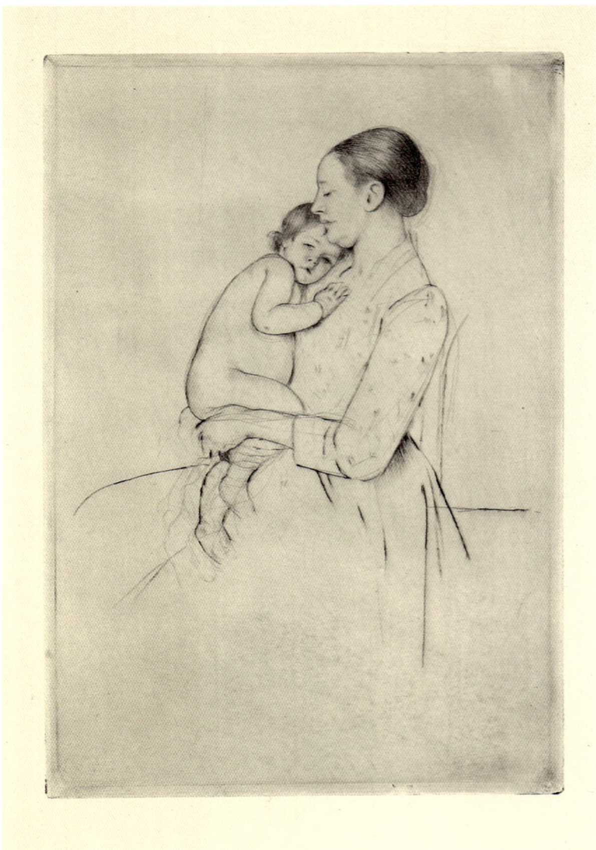

Quietude, ca. 1891

Breeskin 139

Drypoint, fifth state of five, printed in black ink, with burr and even plate tone, on laid Japan paper, the full sheet, in good condition apart from a crease across the upper corner and a few other handling creases, and an inconspicuous fingerprint or two in the image at lower right, annotated *Q* in the lower left corner

Plate: 26.1 × 17.9 cm 10¼ × 7 in.
Sheet: 37 × 27.6 cm 14½ × 10⅞ in.

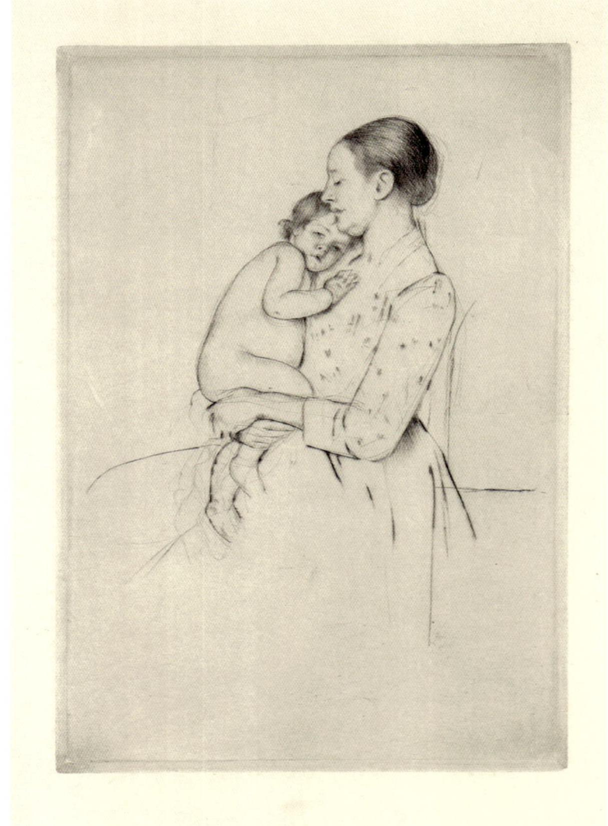

Quietude, ca. 1891

Breeskin 139

Drypoint, fifth state of five, printed in black ink, with burr and strong plate tone, on laid paper with Pro Patria (Vanderley) watermark, the full sheet, in good condition apart from a few pale fox marks in image, annotated *P.* in the lower left corner

Plate: 26 × 17.7 cm 10¼ × 7 in.
Sheet: 35.3 × 21.2 cm 13⅞ × 8⅜ in.

The Caress, ca. 1891

Breeskin 140

Drypoint, fifth state of five, a fine proof, printed in dark brown ink, with strong burr and strong plate tone, on laid paper with Pro Patria (Vanderley) watermark, the full sheet, in good condition, annotated *C. No 16* in the lower left corner

Plate: 19.7 × 14.6 cm 7¾ × 5¾ in.
Sheet: 35 × 20.3 cm 13¾ × 8 in.

An edition of 25 was intended for the final state.

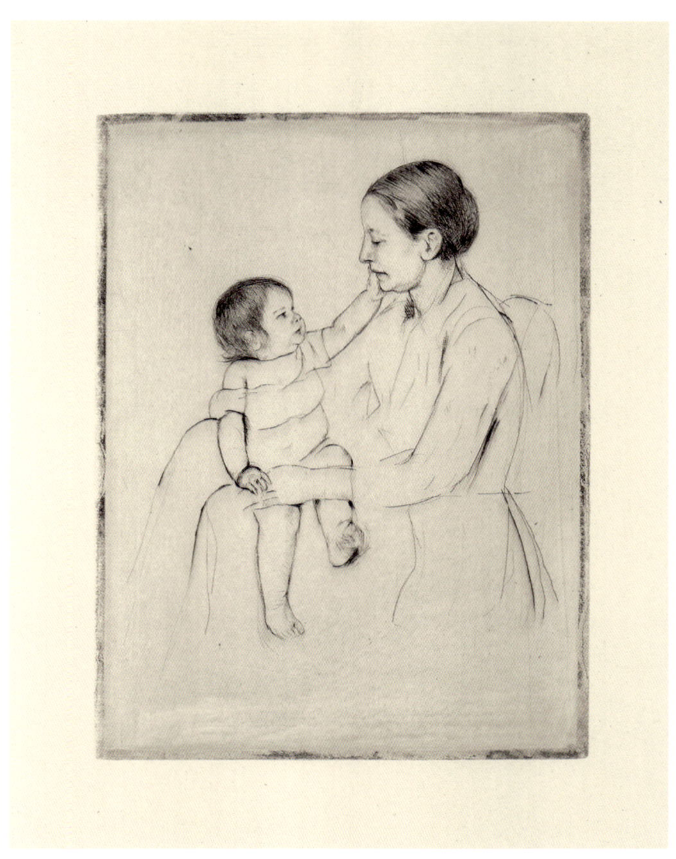

The Caress, ca. 1891

Breeskin 140

Drypoint, fifth state of five, signed in full, printed in black ink, with even plate tone, on blue laid paper with bunch of grapes watermark, the full sheet, in good condition

Plate: 19.7 × 14.8 cm 7¾ × 5¾ in.
Sheet: 39.3 × 25.8 cm 15½ × 10⅛ in.

An edition of 25 was intended for the final state.

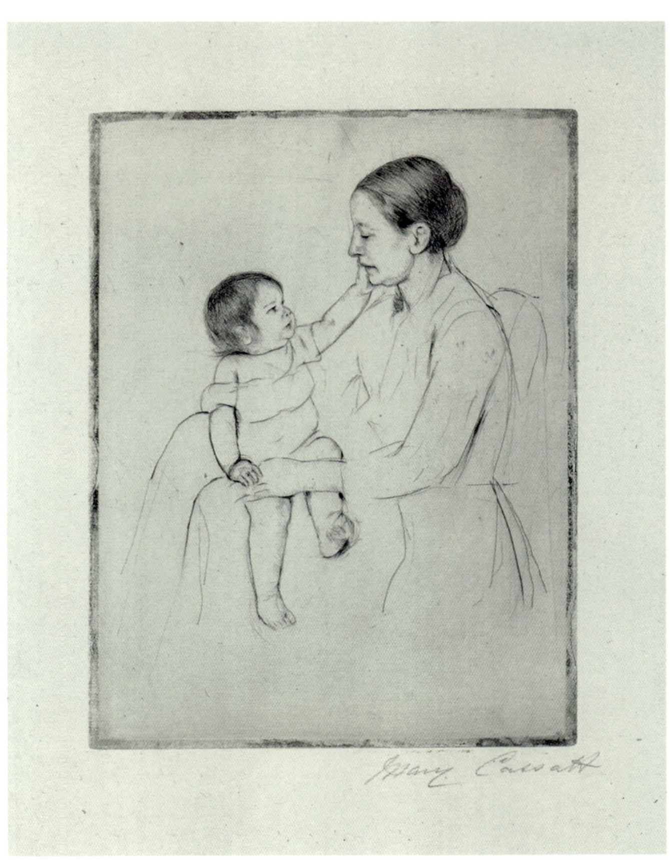

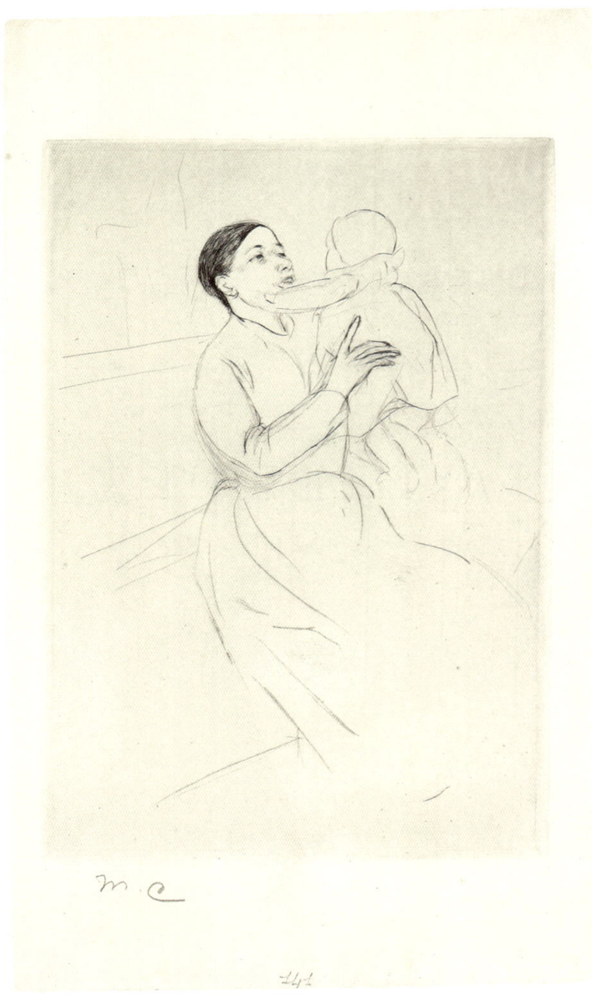

Mother Marie Holding Up Her Baby, ca. 1890

Breeskin 141

Drypoint, initialed *MC*, a trial proof, printed in sanguine, with black for the hair of the mother, and sanguine plate tone, on laid paper with Vanderley watermark, the full sheet, in good condition apart from slight foxing, mainly in the margins

Plate: 25.7 × 17.8 cm 10⅛ × 7 in.
Sheet: 35.1 × 21.4 cm 13¾ × 8⅜ in.

This perhaps unique color impression was evidently printed with a view to the series of color prints to come.

Mother Marie Dressing Her Baby after Its Bath, ca. 1890

Breeskin 142

Drypoint, second state of two, initialed *M. C*, printed in black ink, with strong burr and plate tone, on laid paper with Vanderley watermark, the full sheet, in good condition

Plate: 26 × 17.9 cm 10¼ × 7 in.
Sheet: 35.1 × 20.4 cm 13¾ × 8 in.

In this print, which is directly related to the first of the set of ten color prints, *The Bath* (Breeskin 143), Cassatt experiments with a textured tint, most notably indicating a striped pattern on the back of the mother's dress.

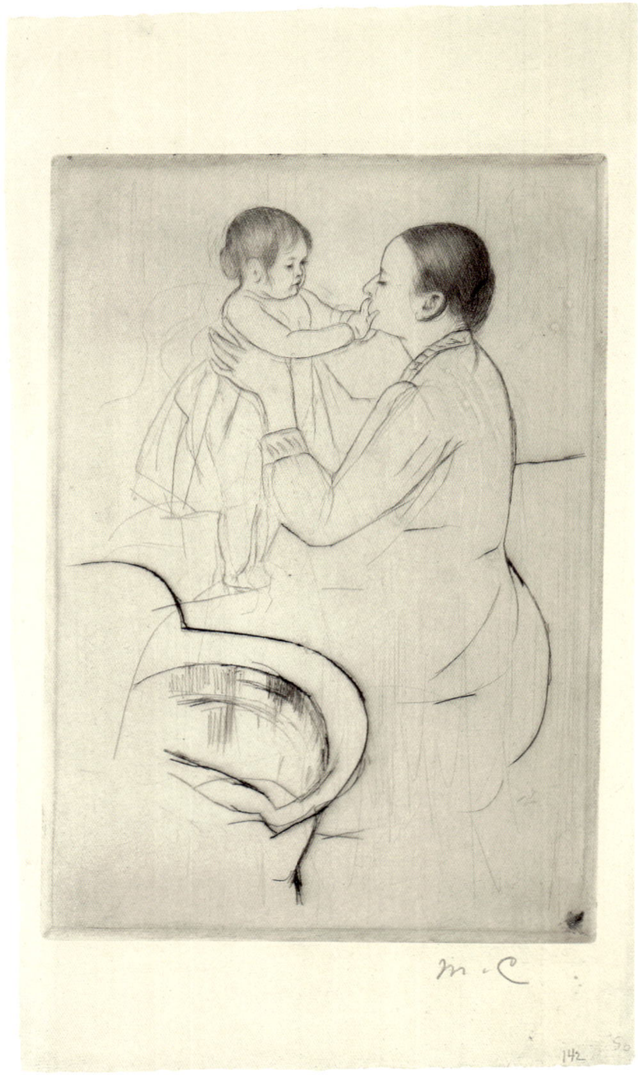

Sketch for "The Bath," ca. 1890

Breeskin 142+

Drypoint, evidently unique, initialed *M.C*, printed in gritty, black ink, with rich, atmospheric plate tone, on laid paper with VanderLey watermark, the full sheet, in good condition

Plate: 27.8 × 19.7 cm 11 × 7¾ in.
Sheet: 39 × 24 cm 15⅜ × 9⅜ in.

This work, the only impression known, is recorded and illustrated in Breeskin.

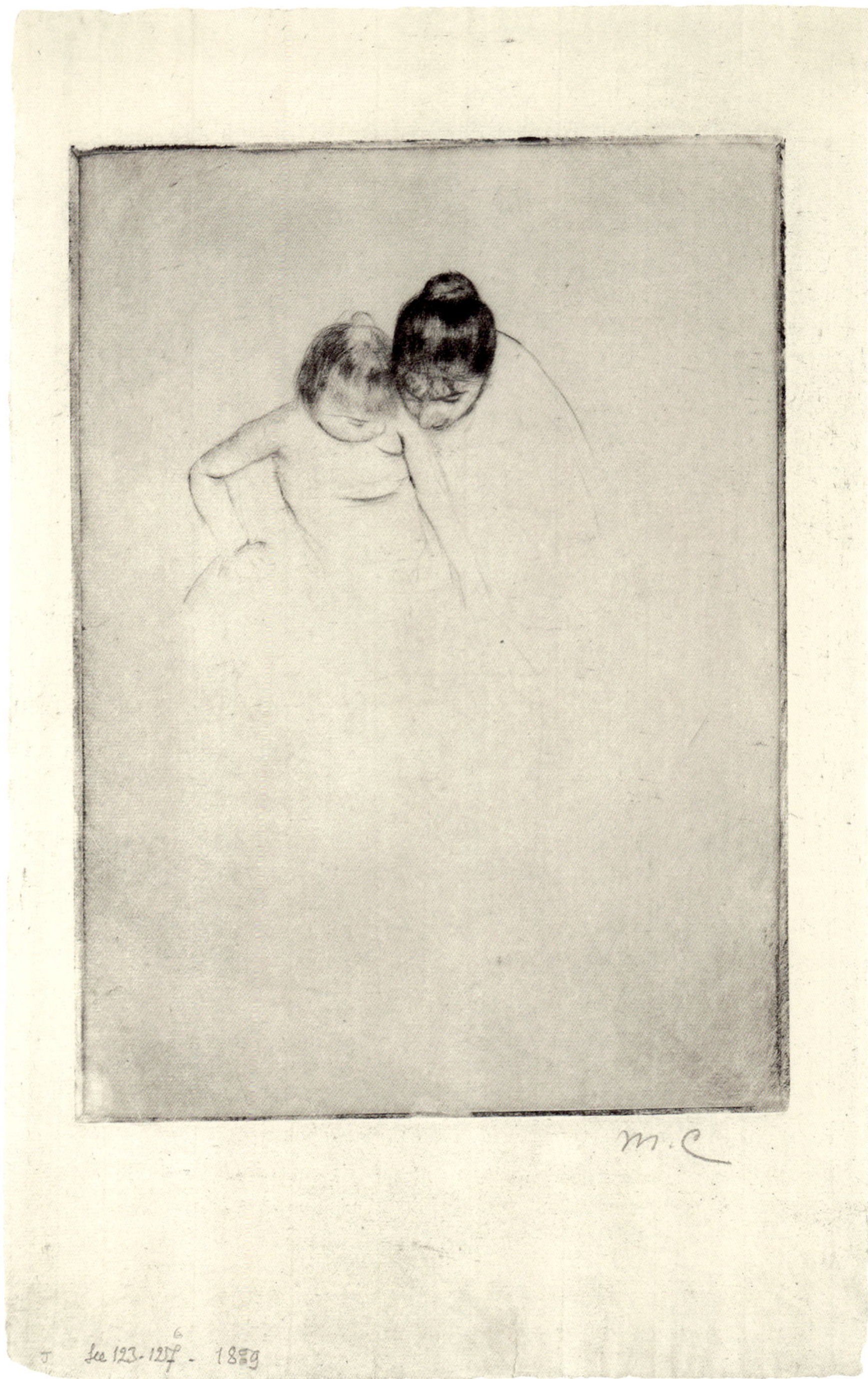

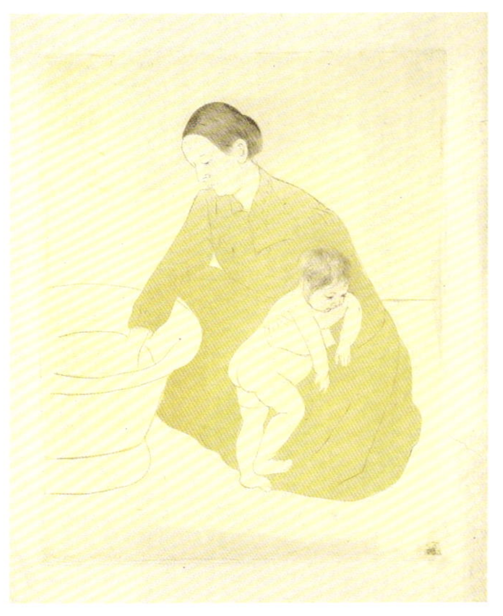

The Bath [Bain d'enfant], 1890–1891

Breeskin 143; Mathews/Shapiro 5

Drypoint, soft-ground, and aquatint, Mathews/Shapiro's fourth state of seventeen, on one plate, printed in yellow, with black for the hair and features of the figures, on heavy laid paper, the full sheet, in generally good condition apart from a tear to the platemark in the right margin, and a few lesser creases, tears, and slight soiling in the margin, annotated *B* at lower center

Plate: 32.2 × 24.4 cm 12⅝ × 9⅝ in.
Sheet: 43.6 × 30.1 cm 17⅛ × 11⅞ in.

The first of the set of ten color prints, inspired by the 1890 Paris exhibition of Japanese woodblock prints.

This is the third known impression of this state. Of the two impressions in the National Gallery of Art, Washington, DC (also previously from Vollard's collection), the one illustrated by Mathews/Shapiro is printed in black, except for the dress of the woman.

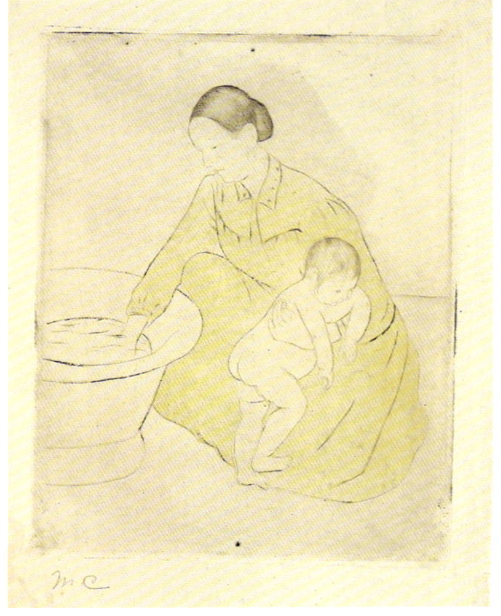

The Bath [Bain d'enfant], 1890–1891

Breeskin 143; Mathews/Shapiro 5

Drypoint, soft-ground, and aquatint, Mathews/Shapiro's seventh state of seventeen, on two plates, printed in yellow and black, with a lightly drawn pattern now showing on the dress, as well as ripples in the water, initaled *M. C,* on heavy laid paper, the full sheet, in generally good condition apart from a horizontal fold at center, some soiling, nicks, and small losses from the lower margin corners, annotated *F.* at lower center

Plate: 32.2 × 24.8 cm 12⅝ × 9¾ in.
Sheet: 43.2 × 29.9 cm 17 × 11¾ in.

The first of the set of ten color prints inspired by the 1890 Paris exhibition of Japanese woodblock prints.

This is the second known impression of this state. The other, also from the Vollard collection, is in the National Gallery of Art, Washington, DC.

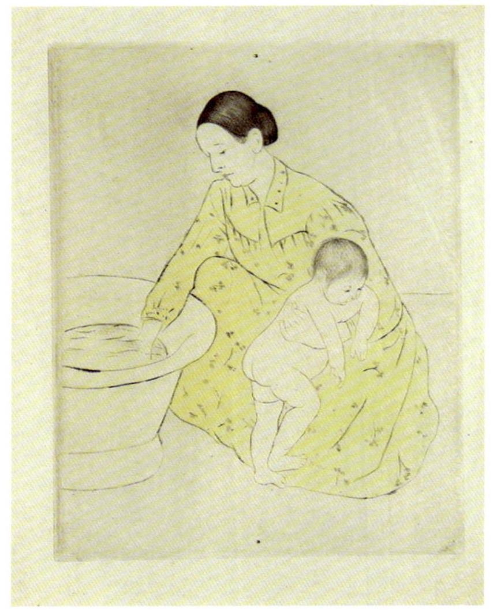

The Bath [Bain d'enfant], 1890–1891

Breeskin 143; Mathews/Shapiro 5

Drypoint, soft-ground, and aquatint, Mathews/Shapiro's ninth state of seventeen, on two plates, printed in black, yellow, and sanguine, on pale, blue-green laid paper with elaborate, interlaced initials, the full sheet, in good condition apart from some old creases, including a few within the plate area, annotated *P.* at lower center

Plate: 31.9 × 24.6 cm 12½ × 9¾ in.
Sheet: 47 × 30.6 cm 18½ × 12 in.

The first of the set of ten color prints inspired by the 1890 Paris exhibition of Japanese woodblock prints.

This is the only known impression of this state (described and illustrated in Mathews/Shapiro, pp. 106, 108, and 110).

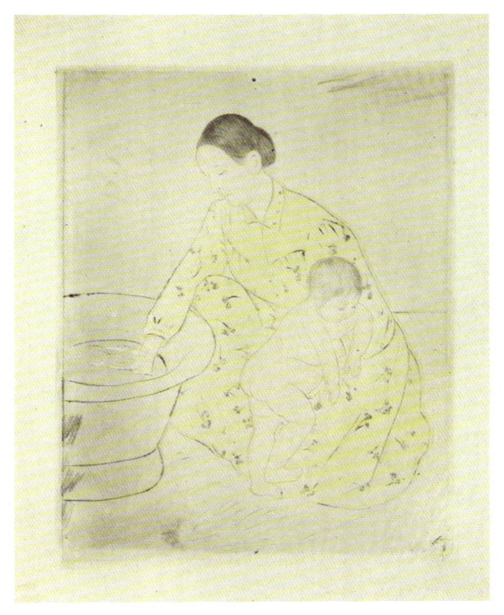

The Bath [Bain d'enfant], 1890–1891

Breeskin 143; Mathews/Shapiro 5

Drypoint, soft-ground, and aquatint, Mathews/Shapiro's tenth state of seventeen, on two plates, printed in yellow, black and sanguine, on pale green, laid paper with a watermark of interlaced letters, the full sheet, in good condition (minor discoloration at edges, and small crease across top left corner), annotated *K.* at lower center

Plate: 32.2 × 24.6 cm 12⅝ × 9¾ in.
Sheet: 46.9 × 30.7 cm 18½ × 12 in.

The first of the set of ten color prints inspired by the 1890 Paris exhibition of Japanese woodblock prints.

Mathews/Shapiro note that, "The tenth state marks the point in the development of this print in which the work is finally separated onto the two plates as they will be carried out to the final, editioned state."

This is the second known impression of this state. The other, also from the Vollard collection, is in the National Gallery of Art, Washington, DC.

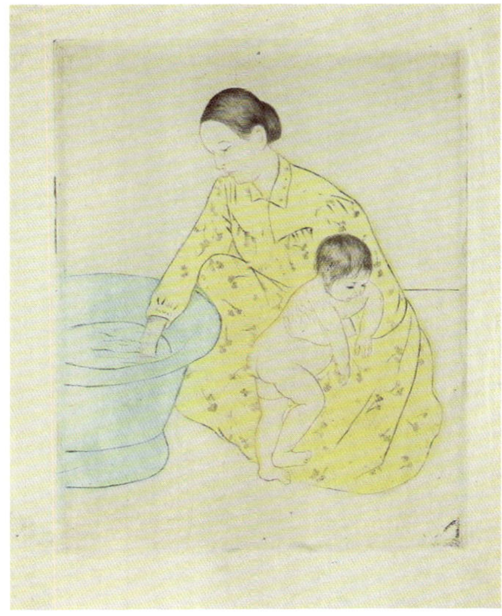

The Bath [Bain d'enfant], 1890–1891

Breeskin 143; Mathews/Shapiro 5

Drypoint, soft-ground and aquatint, Mathews/Shapiro's eleventh state of seventeen, on two plates, printed in black, yellow, sanguine, and blue, on pale green, laid paper with a watermark Buges in script, the full sheet, in good condition apart from a few creases, and a tiny hole in the manufacture of the sheet at lower right, annotated *V* at lower center

Plate: 31.8 × 24.7 cm 12½ × 9¾ in.
Sheet: 46.6 × 30.7 cm 18⅜ × 12 in.

The first of the set of ten color prints inspired by the 1890 Paris exhibition of Japanese woodblock prints.

This is the third known impression of this state. Of the two others, the one in the National Gallery of Art is also from the Vollard collection.

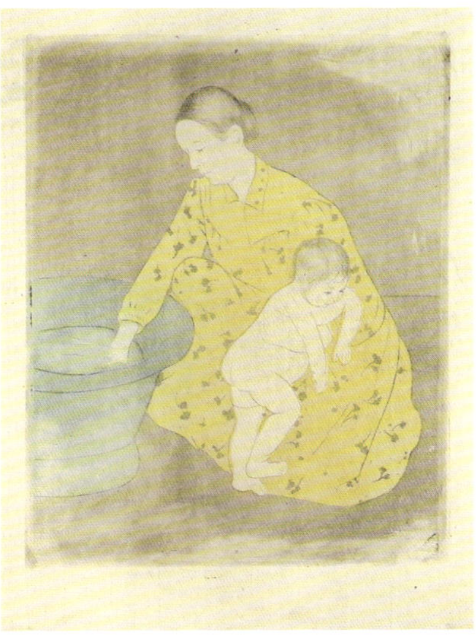

The Bath [Bain d'enfant], 1890–1891

Breeskin 143; Mathews/Shapiro 5

Drypoint, soft-ground, and aquatint, Mathews/Shapiro's twelfth state of seventeen, on two plates, printed in black, yellow, sanguine, and blue, on laid paper with an Adriaan Rogge watermark, the full sheet, in good condition (minor crinkling), annotated *O.* at lower center

Plate: 32 × 24.6 cm 12⅝ × 9¾ in.
Sheet: 44.2 × 28.1 cm 17⅜ × 11⅛ in.

The first of the set of ten color prints inspired by the 1890 Paris exhibition of Japanese woodblock prints.

This is the second known impression of this state. The other, also from the Vollard collection, is in the National Gallery of Art, Washington, DC. That impression is illustrated in Mathews/Shapiro and is printed in only black, yellow and sanguine, without the blue for the tub.

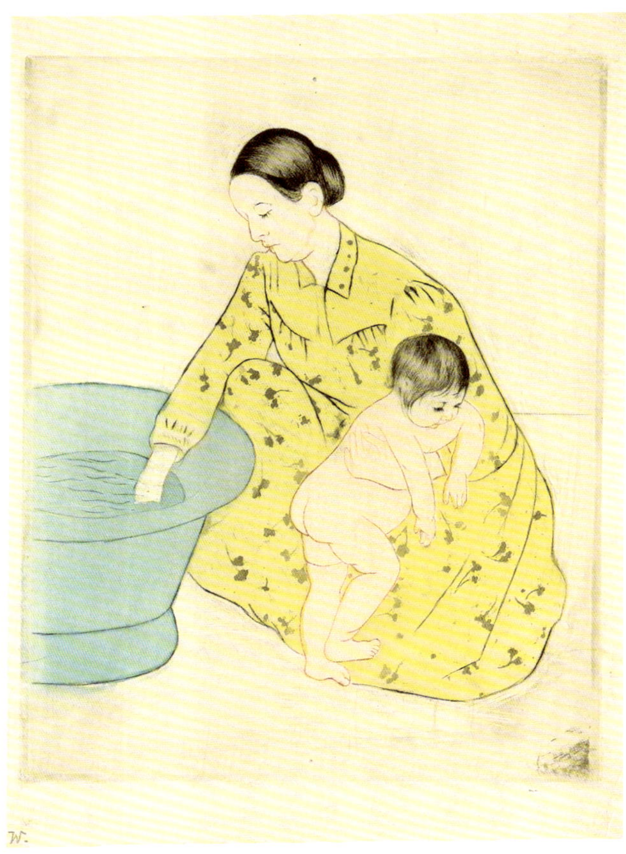

The Bath [Bain d'enfant], 1890–1891

Breeskin 143; Mathews/Shapiro 5

Drypoint, soft-ground, and aquatint, a proof of Mathews/Shapiro's seventeenth (final) state, on two plates, a fine, lustrous impression, printed in black, clear, bright, yellow, sanguine, and blue, initialed *M. C* within the lower left plate corner, with the artist's blue initial stamp (Lugt 604) at center of the lower platemark, on laid Japan paper, the full sheet, in good condition apart from slight creasing in the paper, most probably present at time of printing

Plate: 32.2 × 25 cm   12⅝ × 9⅞ in.
Sheet: 37.1 × 27.6 cm   14⅝ × 10⅞ in.

The first of the set of ten color prints inspired by the 1890 Paris exhibition of Japanese woodblock prints.

The Bath [Bain d'enfant], 1890–1891

Breeskin 143; Mathews/Shapiro 5

Drypoint, soft-ground, and aquatint, Mathews/Shapiro's fourteenth state of seventeen, on two plates, a fine, lustrous impression, printed in black, yellow, sanguine, and blue, on laid Japan paper, the full sheet, in good condition (minor handling creases), annotated *W.* at lower center

Plate: 32.1 × 25 cm   12⅝ × 9⅞ in.
Sheet: 36.6 × 26.6 cm   14⅜ × 10½ in.

The first of the set of ten color prints inspired by the 1890 Paris exhibition of Japanese woodblock prints.

Only two other impressions are known of this state, one of which is in the Bibliothèque Nationale, Paris.

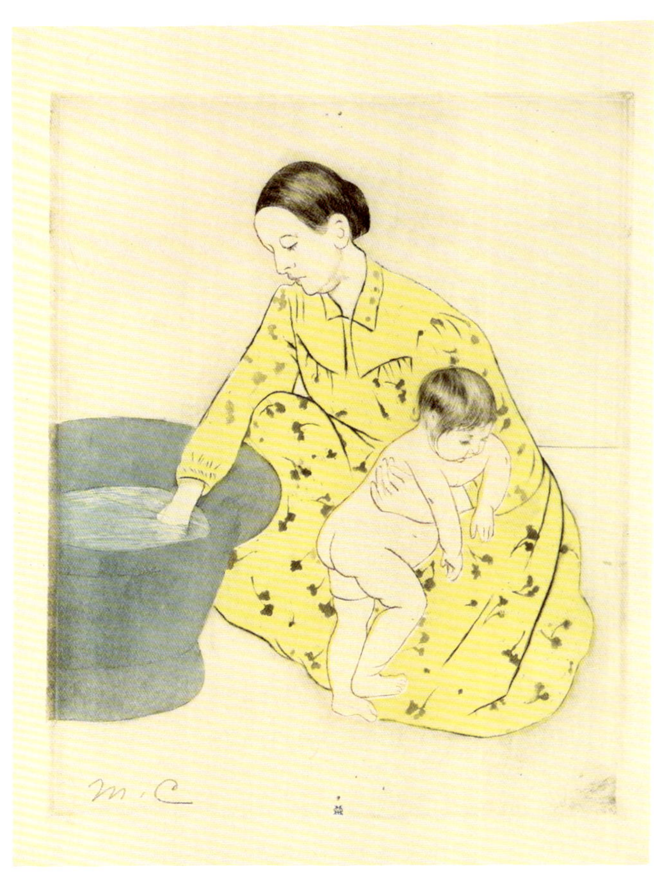

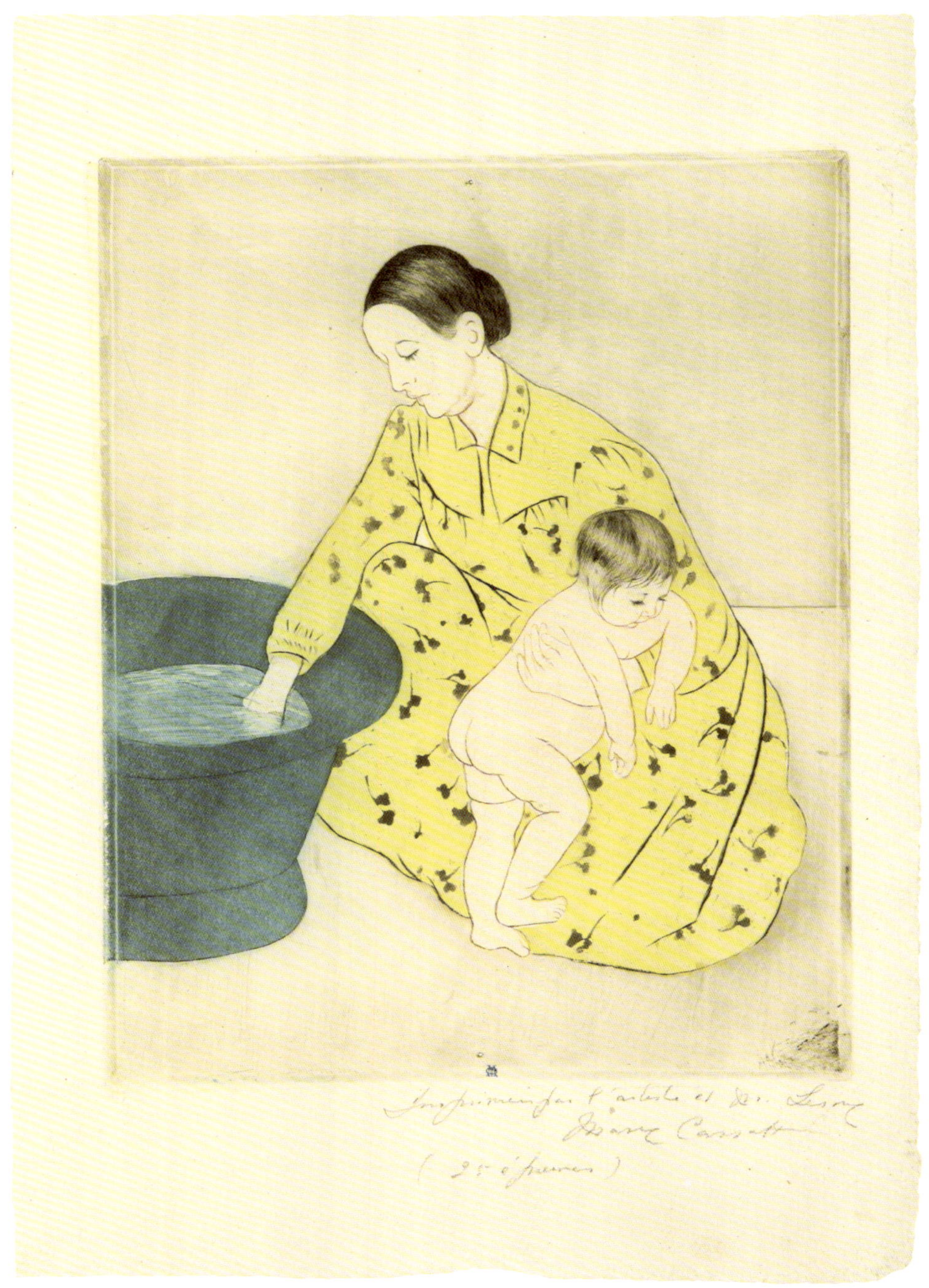

The Bath [Bain d'enfant], 1890–1891

Breeskin 143; Mathews/Shapiro 5

Drypoint, soft-ground, and aquatint, an exceptionally fine impression, printed in black, clear yellow, sanguine, and deep blue, with background plate tone, with the full signature and inscription, *Imprimé par l'artiste et M. Leroy/(25 épreuves)*, with the artist's blue initial stamp (Lugt 604) at center of the lower platemark, on laid paper with Arches watermark, the full sheet, in good condition

Plate: 31.9 × 24.9 cm   12½ × 9⅞ in.
Sheet: 43.5 × 30.4 cm   17⅛ × 11⅞ in.

The first of the set of ten color prints inspired by the 1890 Paris exhibition of Japanese woodblock prints.

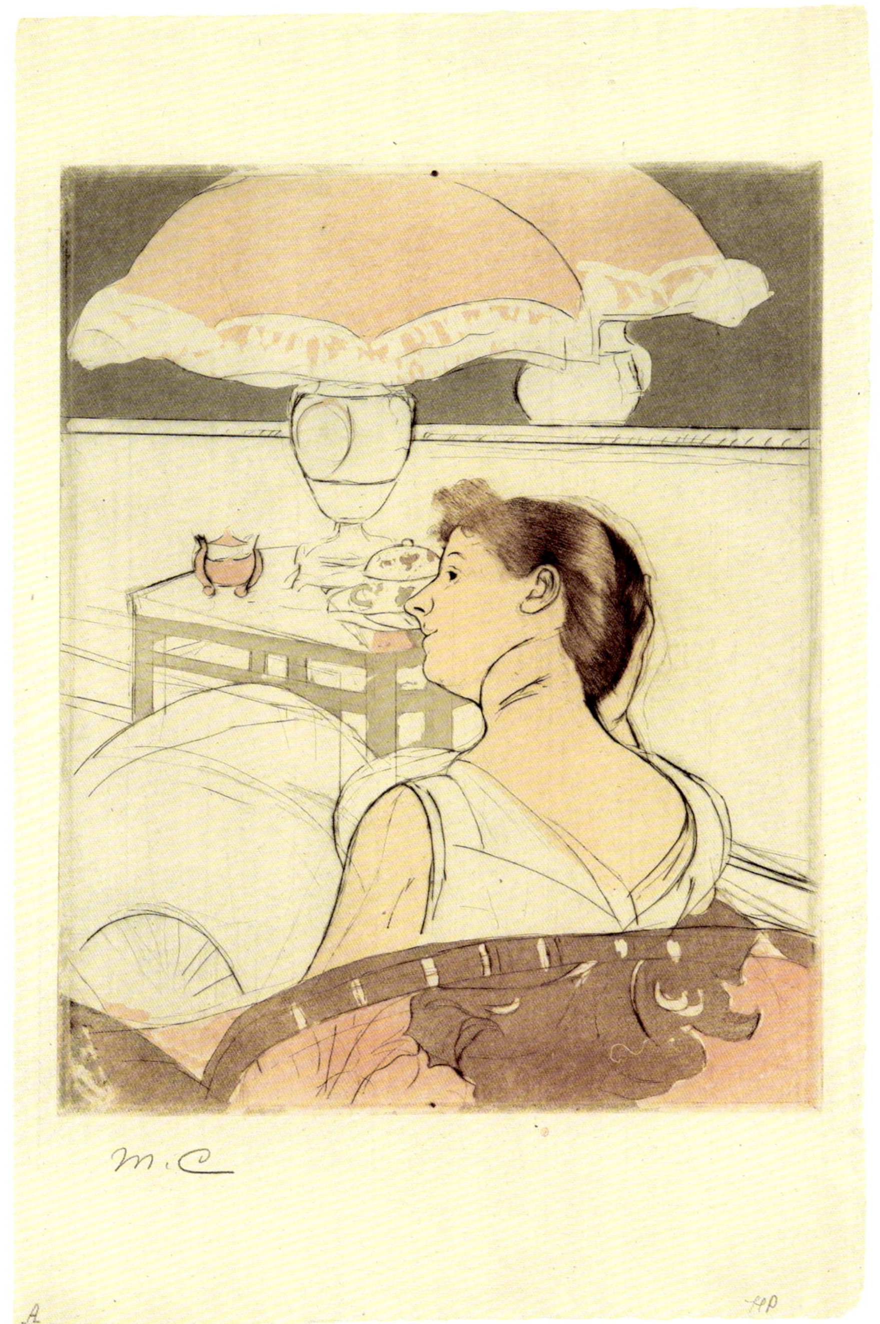

The Lamp [La Lampe], 1890–1891

Breeskin 144; Mathews/Shapiro 6

Drypoint, soft-ground, and aquatint, a previously unknown state, between Mathews/Shapiro's first and second states of four, on two plates, printed in black, russet-brown, violet-brown, and pink (all of these colors except the pink, which in various places overlaps them, appear to be printed from the first plate, except that the artist appears to have dabbed some of the same pink onto the first plate for the pattern on the lid on the dish), initialed *M. C* at lower left, on laid paper with Adriaan Rogge watermark, the full sheet, in good condition, annotated *A* in the lower left corner, initialed *HP* in the lower right corner

Plate: 32.2 × 25 cm 12⅝ × 9⅞ in.
Sheet: 44.5 × 28.3 cm 17½ × 11⅛ in.

One of the set of ten color prints inspired by the 1890 Paris exhibition of Japanese woodblock prints.

In this state, the lamp and its reflection (which will subsequently be printed with an aquatint grain in blue) have not yet received their aquatint grain. The work on the second plate includes some aquatint printed in pink near the base of the fan and in the area below, representing the arm, which is subsequently altered.

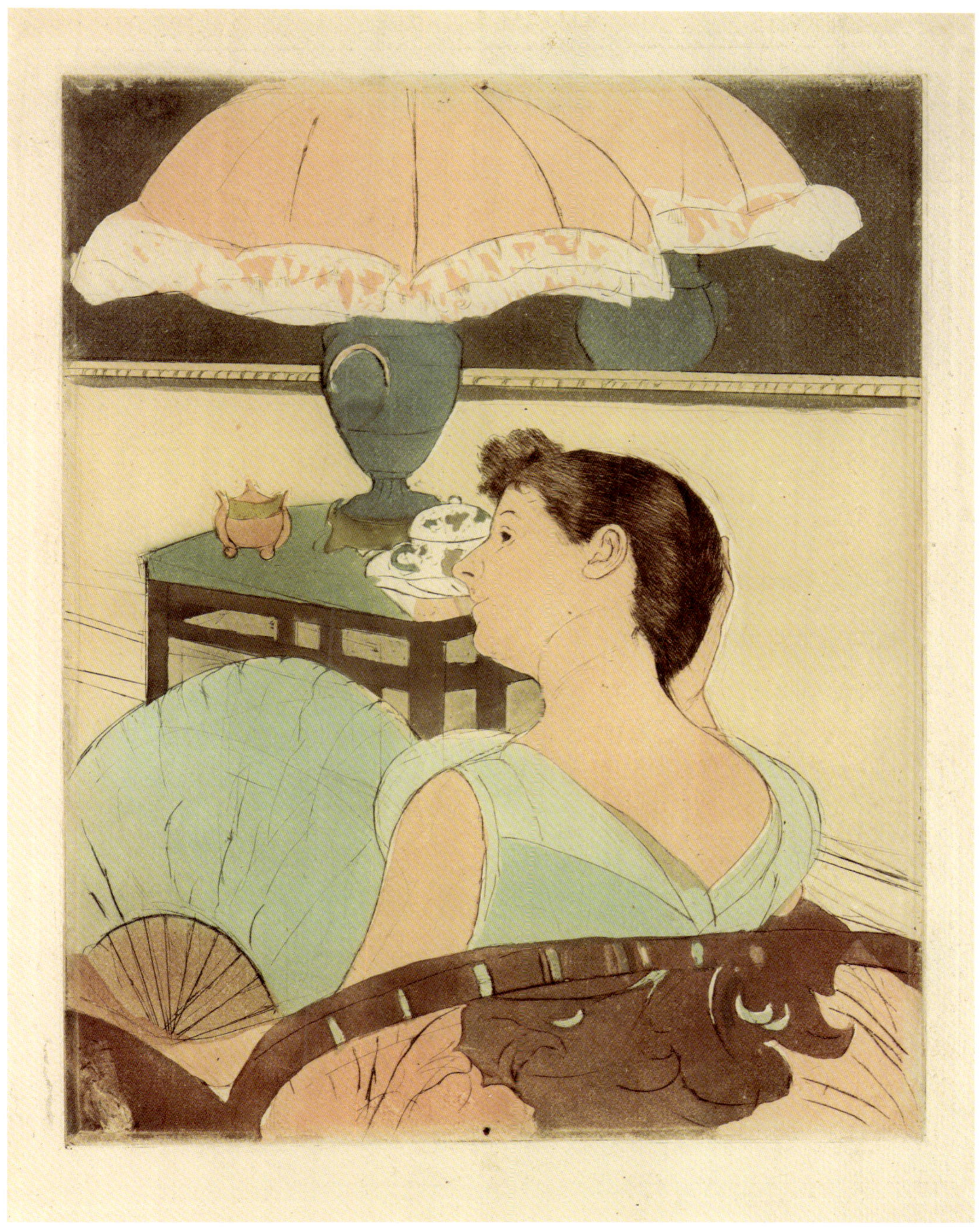

The Lamp [La Lampe], 1890–1891

Breeskin 144; Mathews/Shapiro 6

Drypoint, soft-ground, and aquatint, Mathews/Shapiro's fourth state of four, on three plates, a proof printed in vivid colors, aside from the edition of 25, on sturdy laid paper, the full sheet, in good condition apart from some glue and discoloration where previously mounted at edges, mainly on *verso*

Plate: 32.4 × 25.5 cm 12¾ × 10 in.
Sheet: 43.1 × 30 cm 17 × 11¾ in.

One of the set of ten color prints inspired by the 1890 Paris exhibition of Japanese woodblock prints.

In the Omnibus [Intérior d'un tramway passant un pont], 1890–1891

Breeskin 145; Mathews/Shapiro 7

Drypoint and aquatint, Mathews/Shapiro's sixth state of seven, on three plates, initialed *M C* at lower left, a superb impression, printed with strong burr and exceptionally vivid colors, on laid paper with an Arches watermark, the full sheet, in good condition (a small tear and crease in the lower right corner of the margin and just to the plate), annotated *B* and initialed *HP* in lower edge at left

Plate: 36.7 × 26.9 cm   14½ × 10⅝ in.
Sheet: 43.8 × 30.3 cm   17¼ × 11⅞ in.

One of the set of ten color prints inspired by the 1890 Paris exhibition of Japanese woodblock prints.

The only other recorded impression of this state, in the Museum of Fine Arts, Boston, and illustrated by Mathews/Shapiro, shows the barge at left uninked, whereas here, fine aquatint grain has been added to the barge and is printed in light grey.

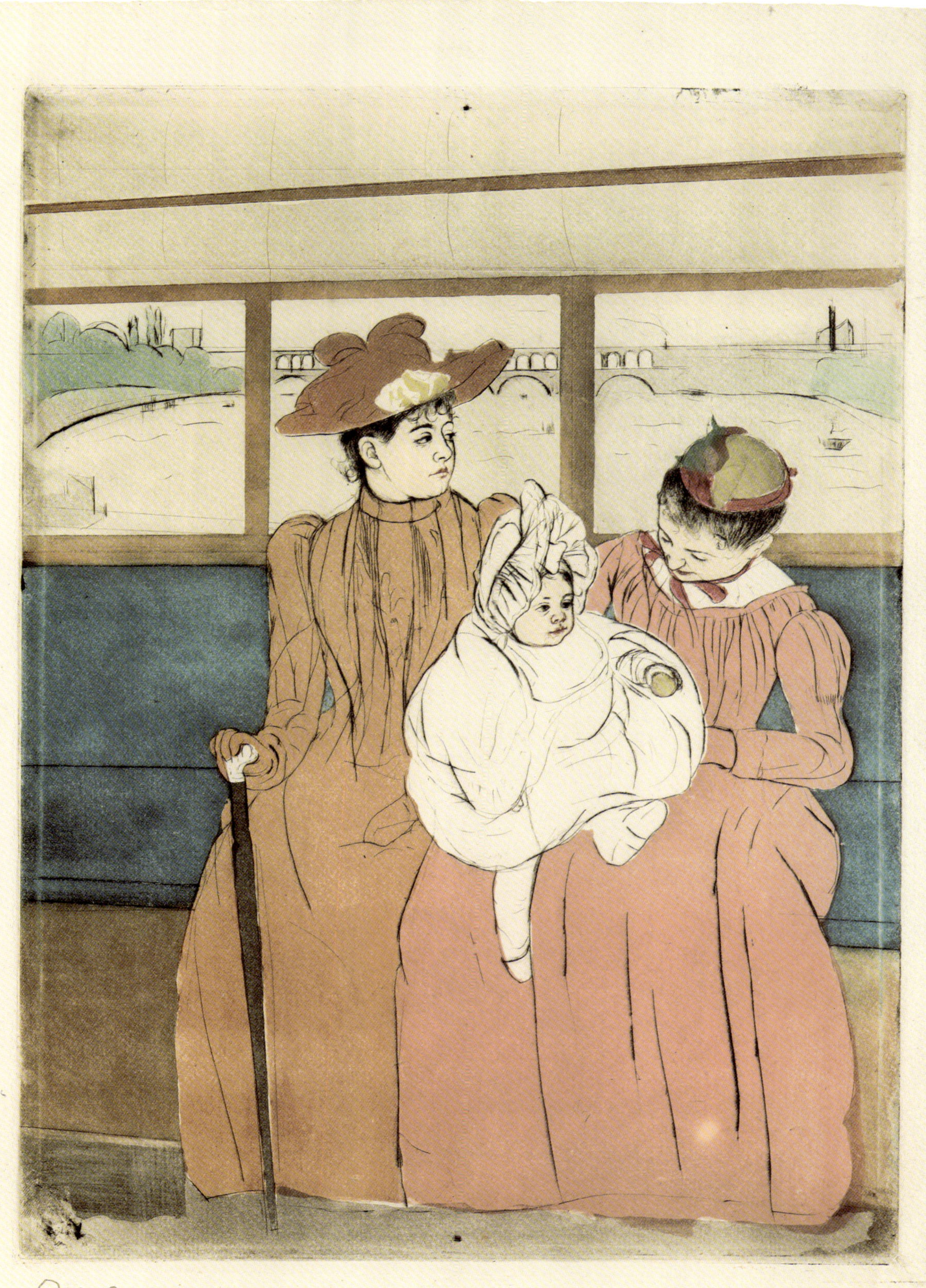

The Letter [La Lettre], 1890–1891

Breeskin 146; Mathews/Shapiro 8

Drypoint and aquatint, Mathews/Shapiro's fourth state of four, on three plates, a trial proof aside from the edition of 25, printed in colors with indications of a pattern on the chair suggested by monotype inking in green and purple, while the desk is printed in a lighter than usual brown, and the dress in a more transparent blue, on sturdy laid paper (Arches), the full sheet, in good condition apart from a few barely perceptible streaks of extraneous color on the face, a slight fox mark on the envelope, annotated *A* in the lower left corner

Plate: 34.8 × 23 cm 13⅝ × 9 in.
Sheet: 43.4 × 30.4 cm 17⅛ × 12 in.

One of the set of ten color prints inspired by the 1890 Paris exhibition of Japanese woodblock prints.

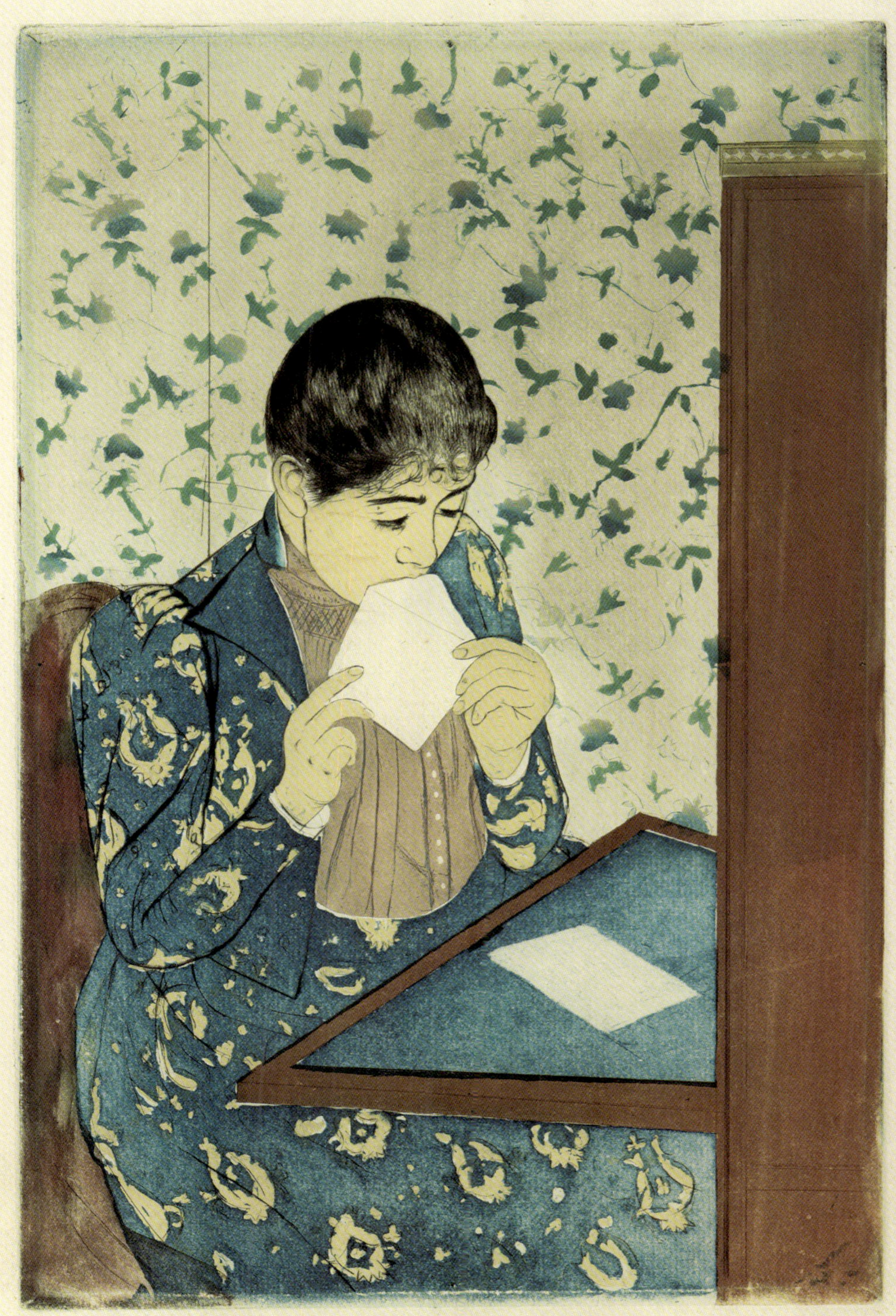

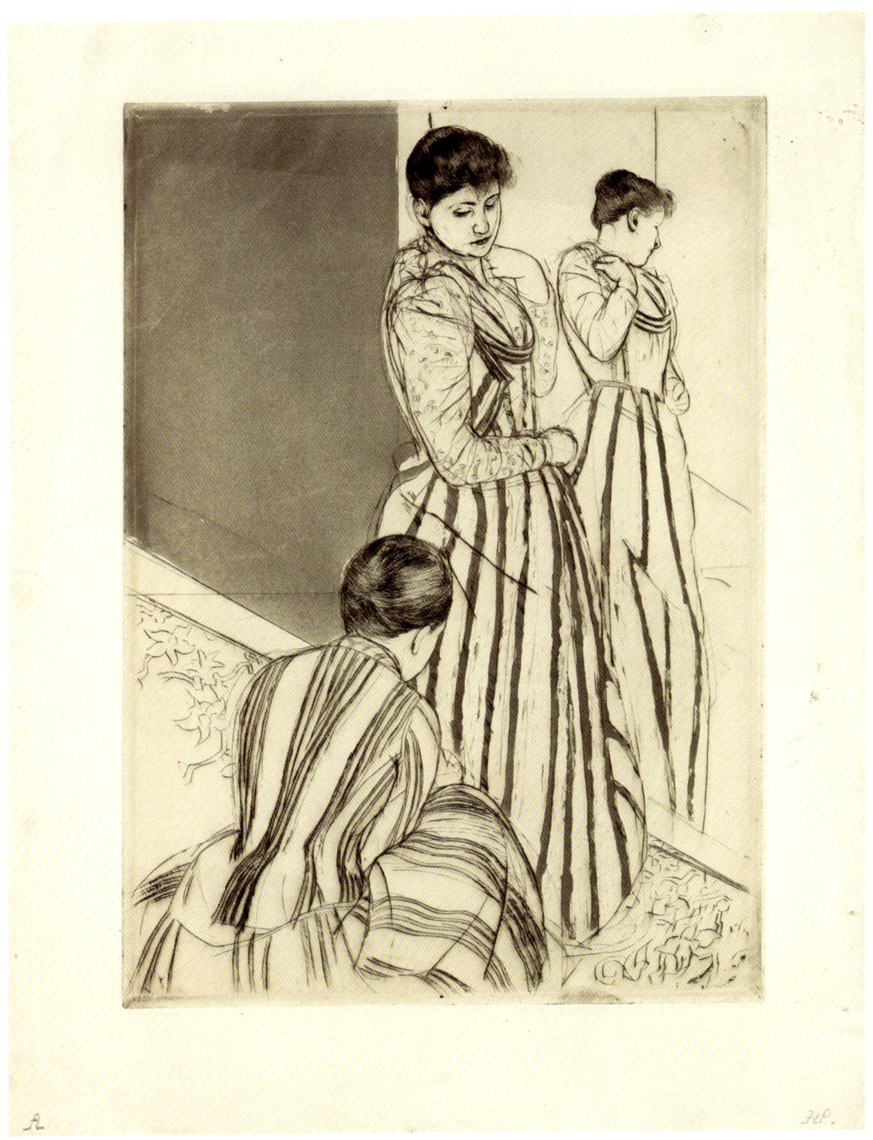

The Fitting [Jeune Femme essayant une robe], 1890–1891

Breeskin 147; Mathews/Shapiro 9

Drypoint and aquatint, a very fine trial proof, a variant of Mathews/Shapiro's fifth state of seven, apparently printed from only the first plate and without the tint for flesh tones, dress and reflection, printed in rich, dark brown ink, on wove paper, the full sheet, in good condition except for some crinkling and creases, and two short tears in the left margin, annotated *A* in the lower left corner and *HP* at lower right

Plate: 37.3 × 25.7 cm 14¾ × 10⅛ in.
Sheet: 46 × 34.3 cm 18⅛ × 13½ in.

One of the set of ten color prints inspired by the 1890 Paris exhibition of Japanese woodblock prints.

This is a unique example of this state printed from the first plate alone, though registration marks are present. The only previously known example of the state, printed monochromatically from two plates, shows less burr (Art Institute of Chicago).

The Fitting [Jeune Femme essayant une robe], 1890–1891

Breeskin 147; Mathews/Shapiro 9

Drypoint and aquatint, a fine, trial proof of a previously unknown state between Mathews/Shapiro's fifth and sixth states of seven, printed in colors, from two plates, on laid paper with watermark Adriaan Rogge, the full sheet, in good condition, annotated *C.* in the lower left corner and *HP.* at lower right

Plate: 37.6 × 25.5 cm 14¾ × 10⅛ in.
Sheet: 44.4 × 28.4 cm 17½ × 18⅛ in.

One of the set of ten color prints inspired by the 1890 Paris exhibition of Japanese woodblock prints.

In this intermediate state, on the first plate, the aquatint stripes on the standing woman's dress have been redefined, the aquatint baseboard added, and the stripes on the seamstress's dress changed to aquatint, but there is not yet a pattern on the wall. In the second plate, the aquatint floral pattern on the carpet has been introduced (with some drypoint lines), but not yet extended to the reflection in the mirror; and aquatint has not yet been added to the pattern on the sleeves of the standing woman's dress.

[See illustration on facing page]

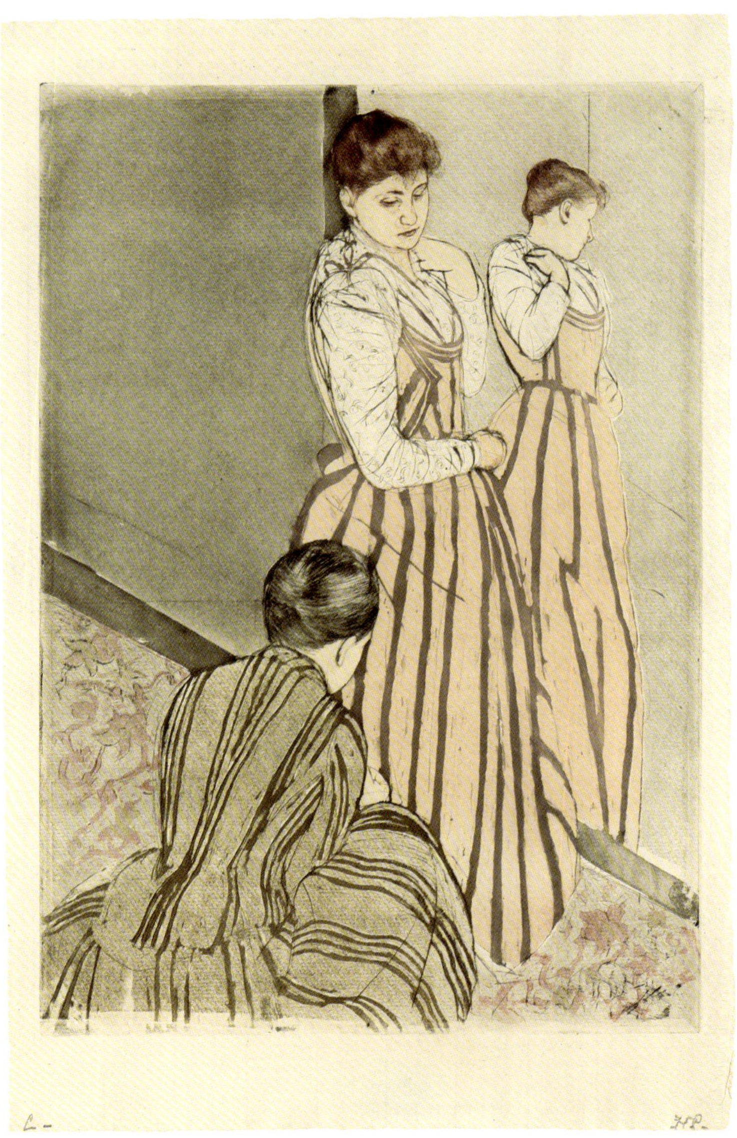

The Fitting [Jeune Femme essayant une robe], 1890–1891

Breeskin 147; Mathews/Shapiro 9

Drypoint and aquatint, a superb proof of a previously unknown state, before Mathews/Shapiro's sixth state of seven, printed in colors, from three plates, with the patterned wall and baseboard printed in vivid russet-brown, and the pink and purple-grey stripes of the dress, as well as the stopped-out aquatint pattern on the sleeves, also unusually strong, and the hair of the seamstress unusually dark and rich, on sturdy, laid paper, the full sheet, in good condition, annotated *G* at lower right, and *HP.* in the lower left corner

Plate: 37.4 × 25.7 cm 14¾ × 10⅛ in.
Sheet: 43.1 × 30 cm 17 × 11¾ in.

One of the set of ten color prints inspired by the 1890 Paris exhibition of Japanese woodblock prints.

In this intermediate state, there is an aquatint grain on the sleeve of the dress reflected in the mirror, consistent with the tone of the bodice. In Mathews/Shapiro's sixth state of seven this has been removed and replaced with diagonal scratched lines.

[See illustration on page 88]

The Fitting [Jeune Femme essayant une robe], 1890–1891

Breeskin 147; Mathews/Shapiro 9

Drypoint and aquatint, Mathews/Shapiro's seventh state of seven, an astonishing trial proof, printed in colors from three plates: the patterned wall printed in blue, with the mirror in a more subdued tint, in which the burnishing produces effects of reflected light, and with the stripes of the seamstress's dress printed in an unusually light brown to give her form a more muted presence, initialed *M. C,* on sturdy, laid paper, the full sheet, in good condition (slight paper loss in upper deckle, probably present since time of printing), annotated *H.* in the lower left corner, and *HP* at lower right

Plate: 37.6 × 25.7 cm 14¾ × 10⅛ in.
Sheet: 42.3 × 31.3 cm 16⅝ × 12¼ in.

One of the set of ten color prints.

In this fine and vivid impression, the change in the work on the reflected sleeve from aquatint grain to diagonal scratch work is readily apparent.

[See illustration on page 89]

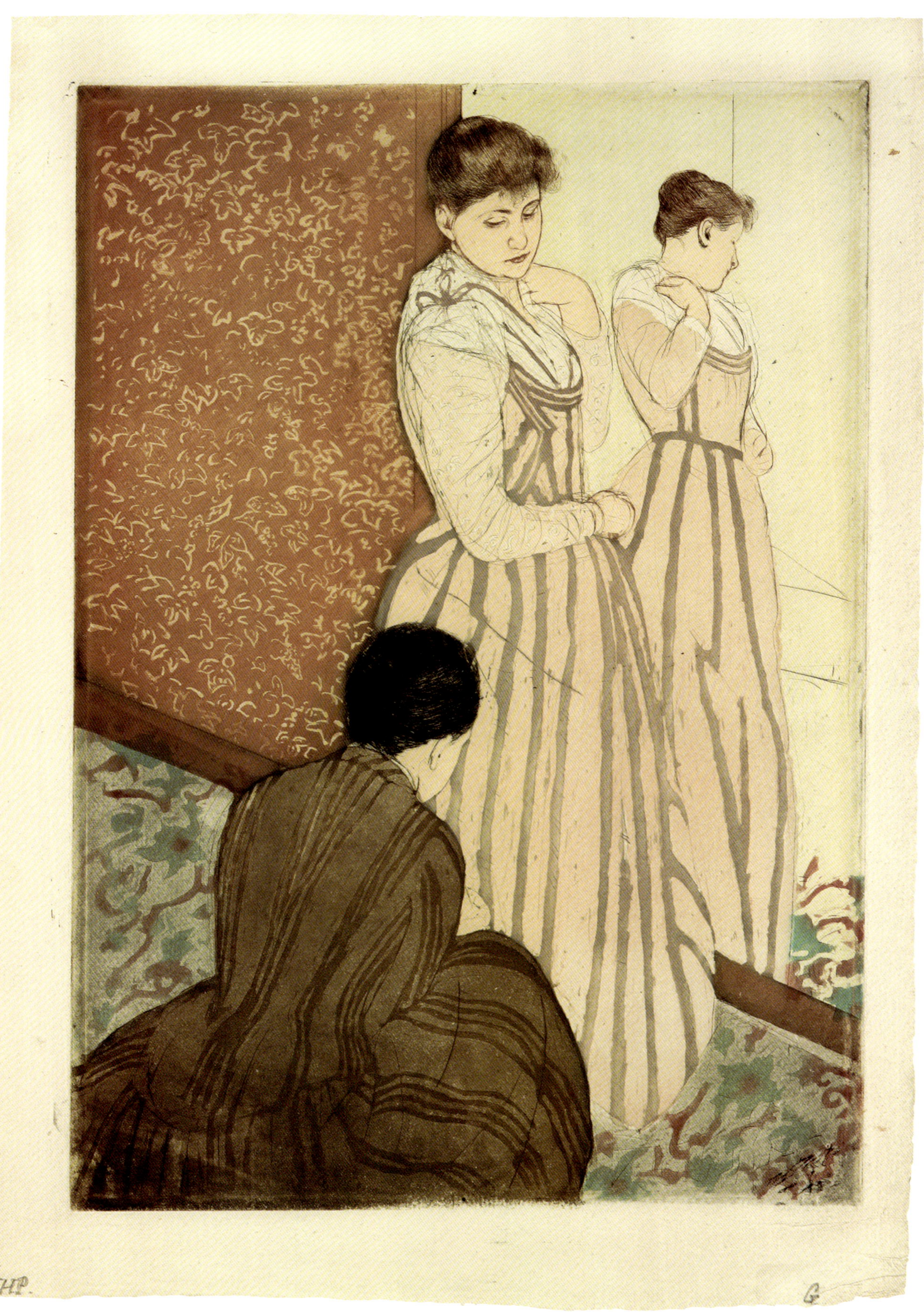

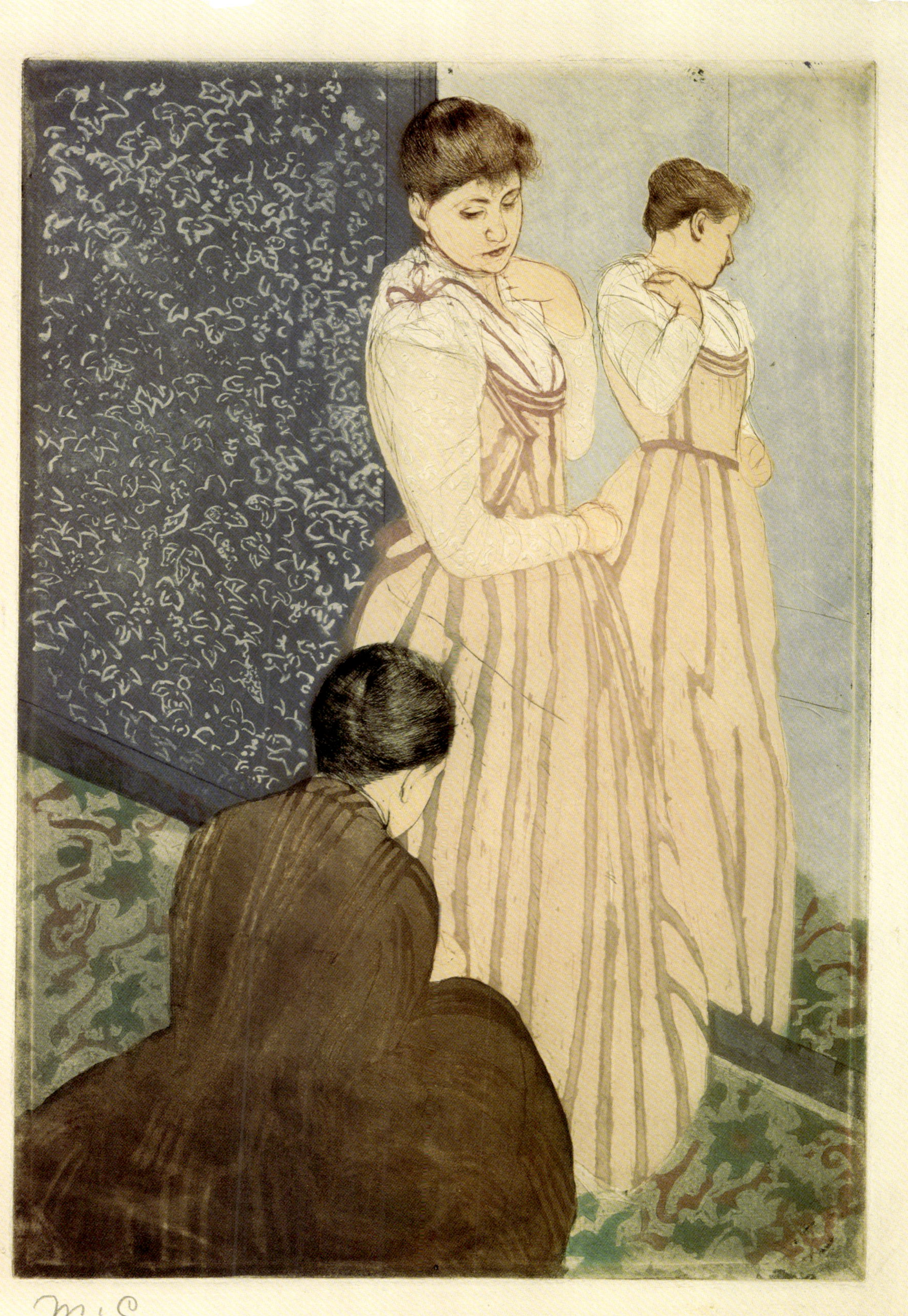

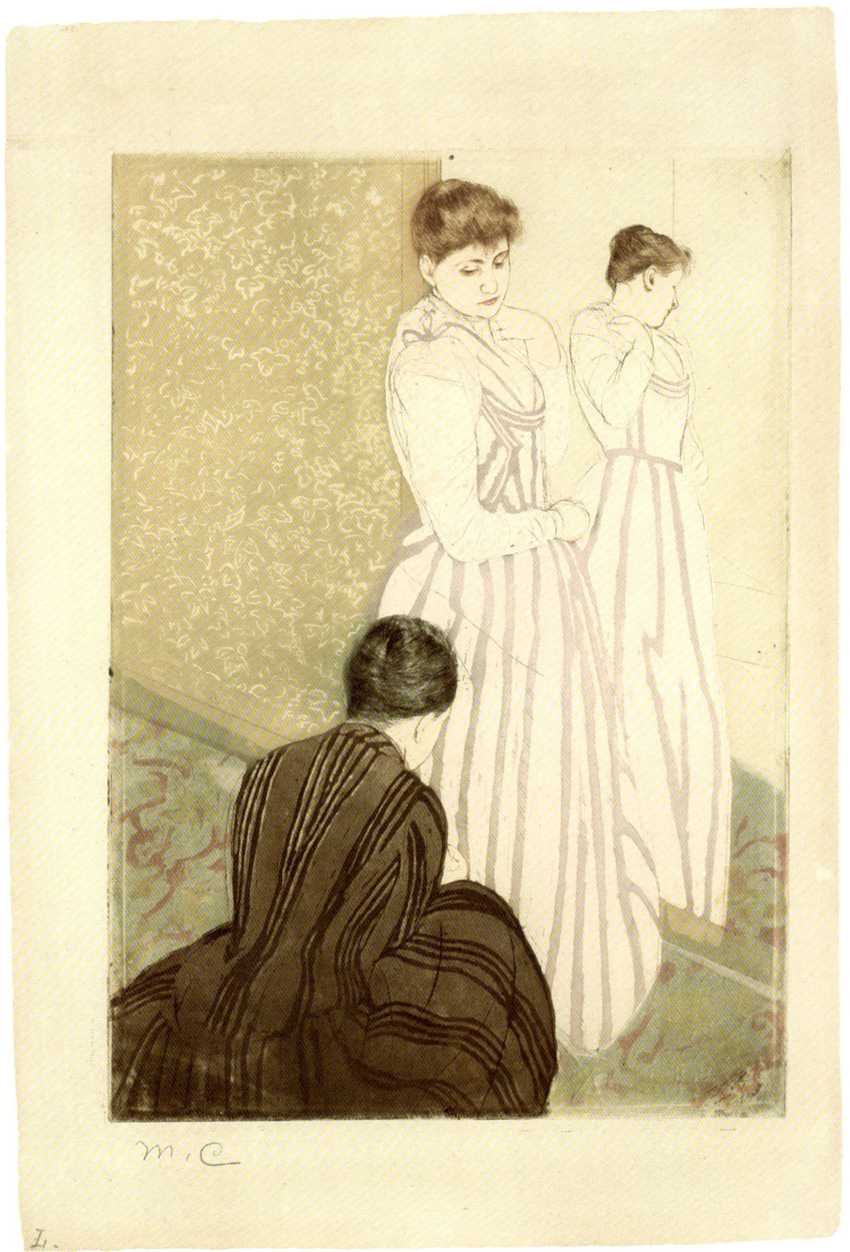

The Fitting [Jeune Femme essayant une robe], 1890–1891

Breeskin 147; Mathews/Shapiro 9

Drypoint and aquatint, Mathews/Shapiro's seventh state of seven, a proof aside from the edition of 25, printed in colors, from three plates, initialed *M. C*, with the artist's blue initial stamp (Lugt 604) at center of the lower platemark, on sturdy, laid paper with watermark PL Bas, the full sheet, in good condition apart from overall discoloration, annotated *L.* in the lower left corner

Plate: 37.6 × 25.6 cm 14¾ × 10⅛ in.
Sheet: 47.9 × 31.5 cm 18⅞ × 12⅜ in.

One of the set of ten color prints inspired by the 1890 Paris exhibition of Japanese woodblock prints.

Woman Bathing [La Toilette], 1890–1891

Breeskin 148; Mathews/Shapiro 10

Drypoint and aquatint, Mathews/Shapiro's fourth state of four, printed in colors, from three plates, initialed *M. C* at lower left, a very fine, strong, fresh proof, aside from the edition of 25, with the wall and mirror in an unusually deep, dark blue that serves all the more to set off the subject, and with the aquatint grain on the top of the commode very lightly inked in a delicate blue, on sturdy, laid paper, the full sheet, in good condition (stray color smudges in margins), annotated *D* in the lower left corner and *HMP.* in the lower right corner

Plate: 36.5 × 27 cm 14⅜ × 10⅝ in.
Sheet: 43.3 × 30.5 cm 17 × 12 in.

One of the set of ten color prints inspired by the 1890 Paris exhibition of Japanese woodblock prints.

[See illustration on facing page]

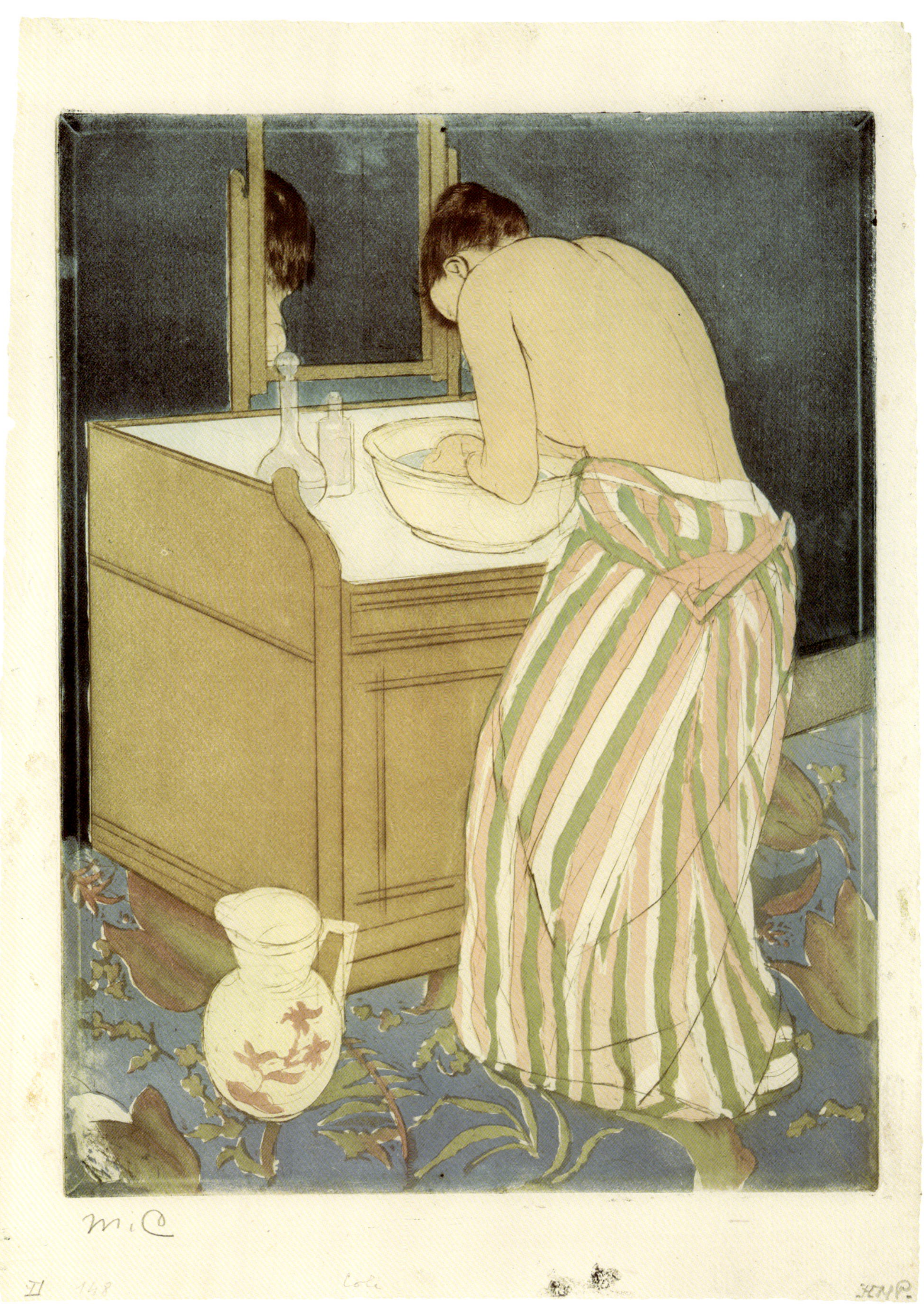

Mother's Kiss [Le Baiser], 1890–1891

Breeskin 149; Mathews/Shapiro 11

Drypoint, Mathews/Shapiro's first state of five, on one plate, printed in black, on laid Japan paper, the full sheet (narrow margin at top), in good condition apart from a smudge at the top of the plate, an unobtrusive, nearly horizontal printer's crease at level of child's elbow, annotated *B* in the lower left corner

Plate: 34.8 × 22.9 cm   13¾ × 9 in.
Sheet: 37.1 × 27.8 cm   14⅛ × 10⅞ in.

One of the set of ten color prints inspired by the 1890 Paris exhibition of Japanese woodblock prints.

This is the second known impression of this state. The other, also from the Vollard collection, is in the National Gallery of Art, Washington, DC.

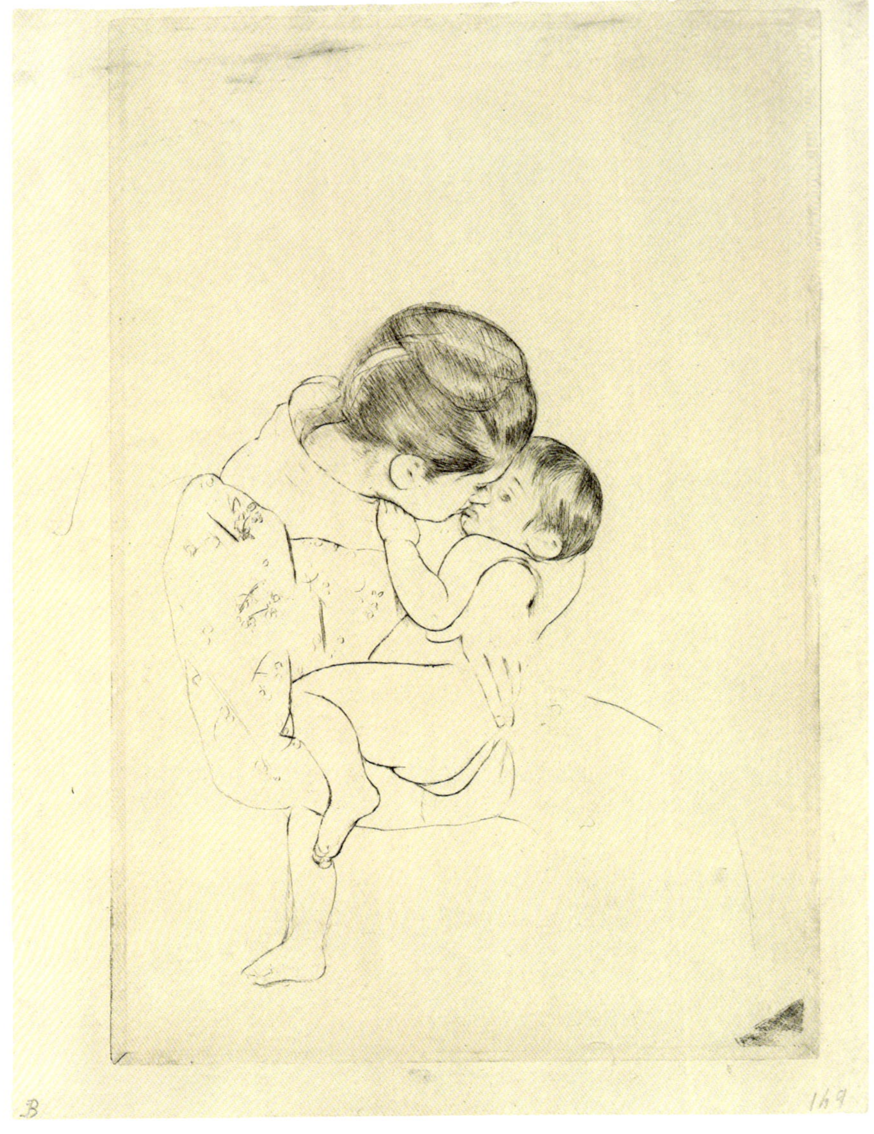

Mother's Kiss [Le Baiser], 1890–1891

Breeskin 149; Mathews/Shapiro 11

Drypoint and aquatint, Mathews/Shapiro's fifth state of five, on two plates, a brilliant proof, aside from the edition of 25, printed with an intense blue background, and a fresh, aqua-blue tint for the dress, initialed *M. C*, on wove paper with watermark J Whatman 1862, the full sheet, in good condition apart from three short tears in the margins, and one in the right margin, extending a little into the plate (casually mended), annotated *G.* at lower left

Plate: 34.8 × 22.9 cm   13¾ × 9 in.
Sheet: 37.1 × 27.8 cm   14⅛ × 10⅞ in.

One of the set of ten color prints inspired by the 1890 Paris exhibition of Japanese woodblock prints.

[See illustration on facing page]

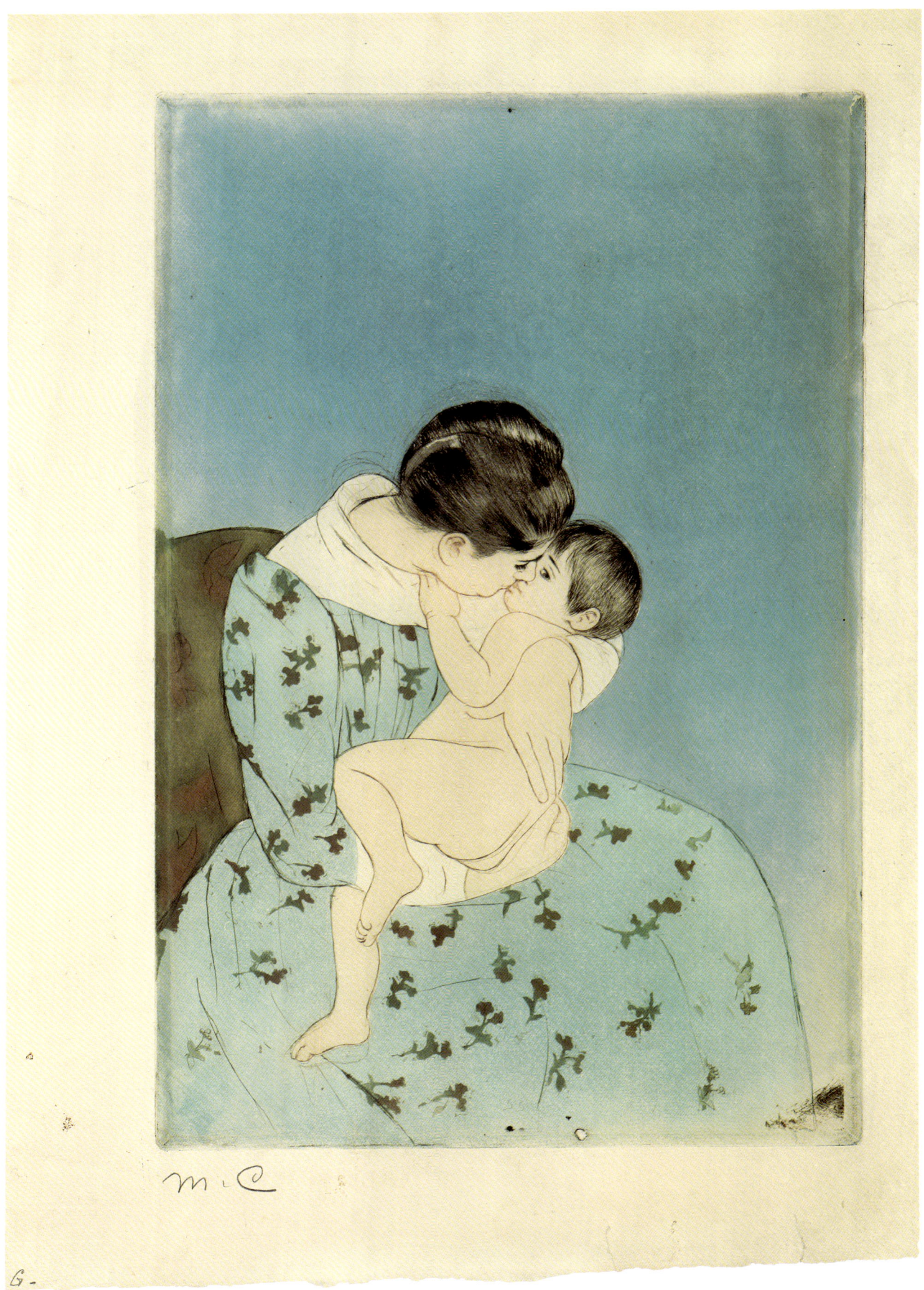

Afternoon Tea Party [La Visite], 1890–1891

Breeskin 151; Mathews/Shapiro 13

Drypoint and aquatint, Mathews/Shapiro's fifth state of five, printed in colors, from three plates, a very fine proof, aside from the edition of 25, printed with strong burr, fresh bright colors, and with the added gold paint accents on the tea service, on sturdy, laid paper, the full sheet, in good condition apart from a tear and small crease in the lower margin at left, bits of stamp hinging at edge of upper margin, annotated *H* in the lower left corner and *HP* in the lower right corner

Plate: 34.8 × 27 cm 13¾ × 10⅝ in.
Sheet: 43.6 × 30.5 cm 17⅛ × 12 in.

One of the set of ten color prints inspired by the 1890 Paris exhibition of Japanese woodblock prints.

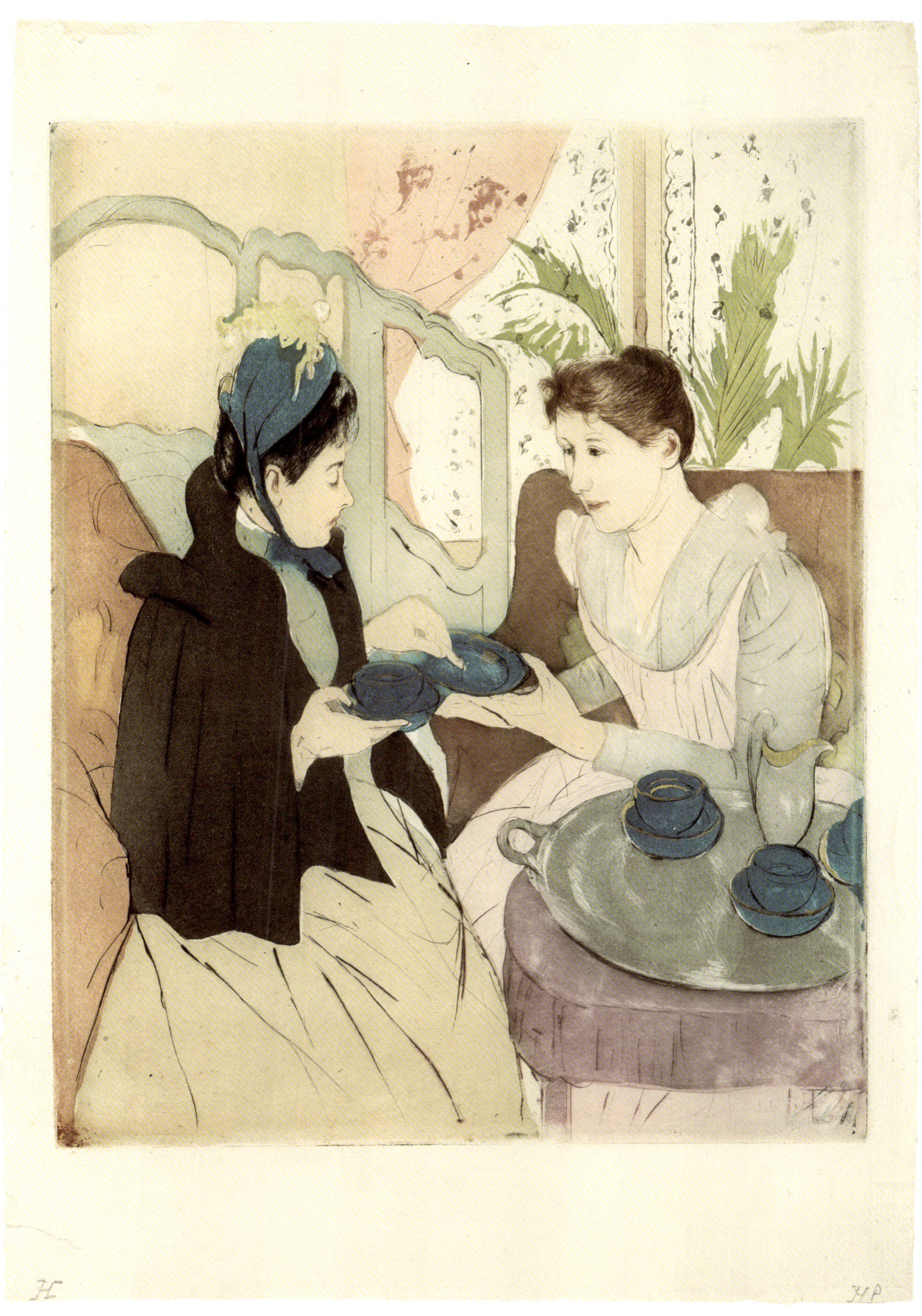

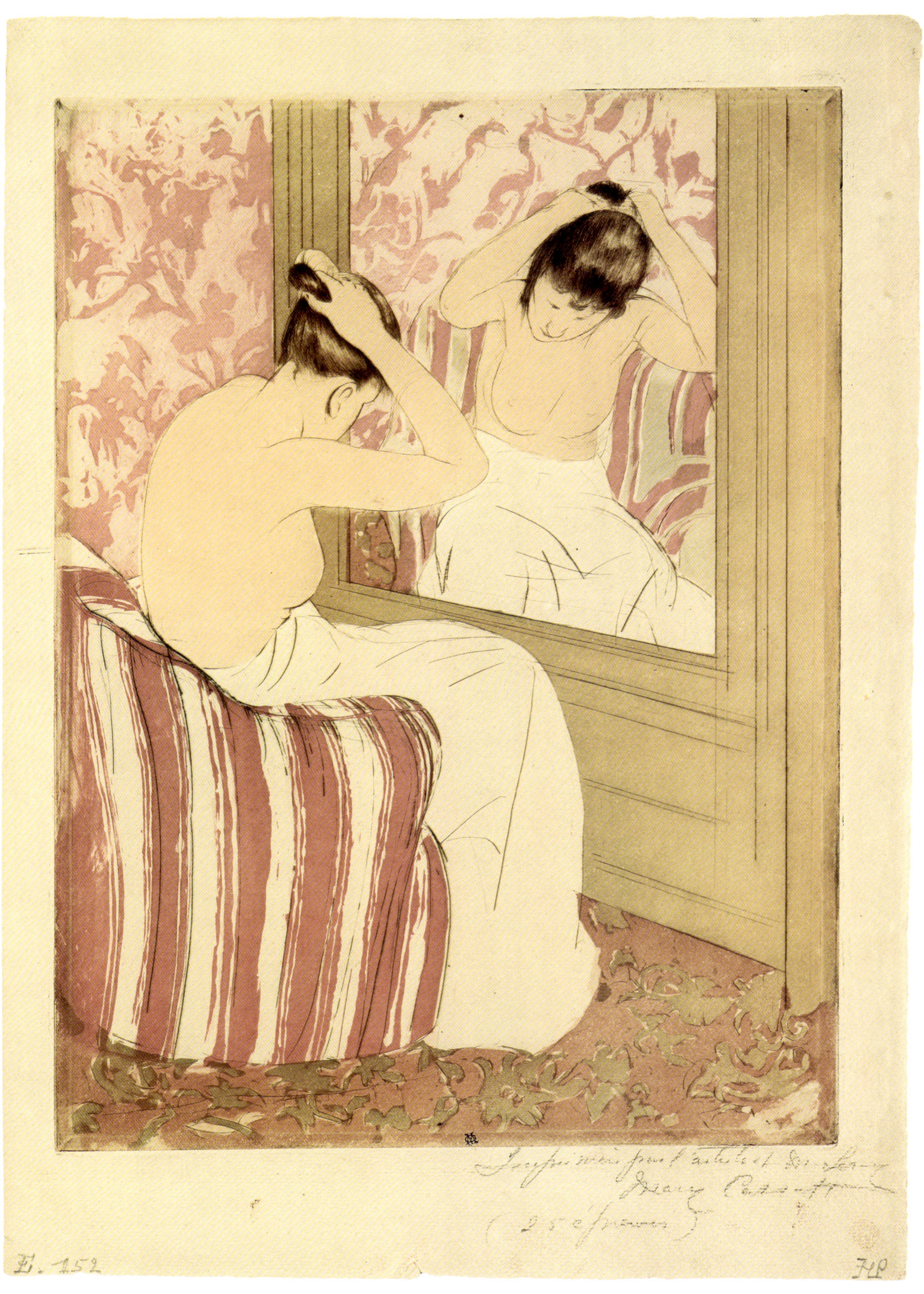

The Coiffure [Etude], 1890–1891

Breeskin 152; Mathews/Shapiro 14

Drypoint and aquatint, Mathews/Shapiro's fifth state of five, a fine impression, printed in exceptionally strong colors, from three plates, with the full signature and inscription, *Imprimé par la artiste et M. Leroy/ (25 épreuves)*, with the artist's blue initial stamp (Lugt 604) at center of the lower platemark, on laid paper with watermark PL Bas, the full sheet, in good condition except for darkening of paper tone, annotated *E.* in the lower left corner and *HP* in the lower right corner

Plate: 31.9 × 24.9 cm 12½ × 9⅞ in.
Sheet: 43.5 × 30.4 cm 17⅛ × 11⅞ in.

One of the set of ten color prints inspired by the 1890 Paris exhibition of Japanese woodblock prints.

[See illustration on facing page]

Blanche without Her Hat, ca. 1895

Breeskin 154

Drypoint, initialed *M. C*, a previously unknown and possibly unique impression of a state between Breeskin's first and second of three, with the legs of the chair indicated, but with the right arm still bent at the elbow, rather than hanging straight down alongside the chair, printed in dark brown ink with strong burr and plate tone, on laid paper with a Pro Patria watermark, the full sheet (lacking lower corner of lower right margin), severely crinkled from pressure of printing and rubbed, with a tiny hole in the hair

Plate: 25.2 × 17.8 cm 9⅞ × 7 in.
Sheet: 35.1 × 20.8 cm 13⅞ × 8⅛ in.

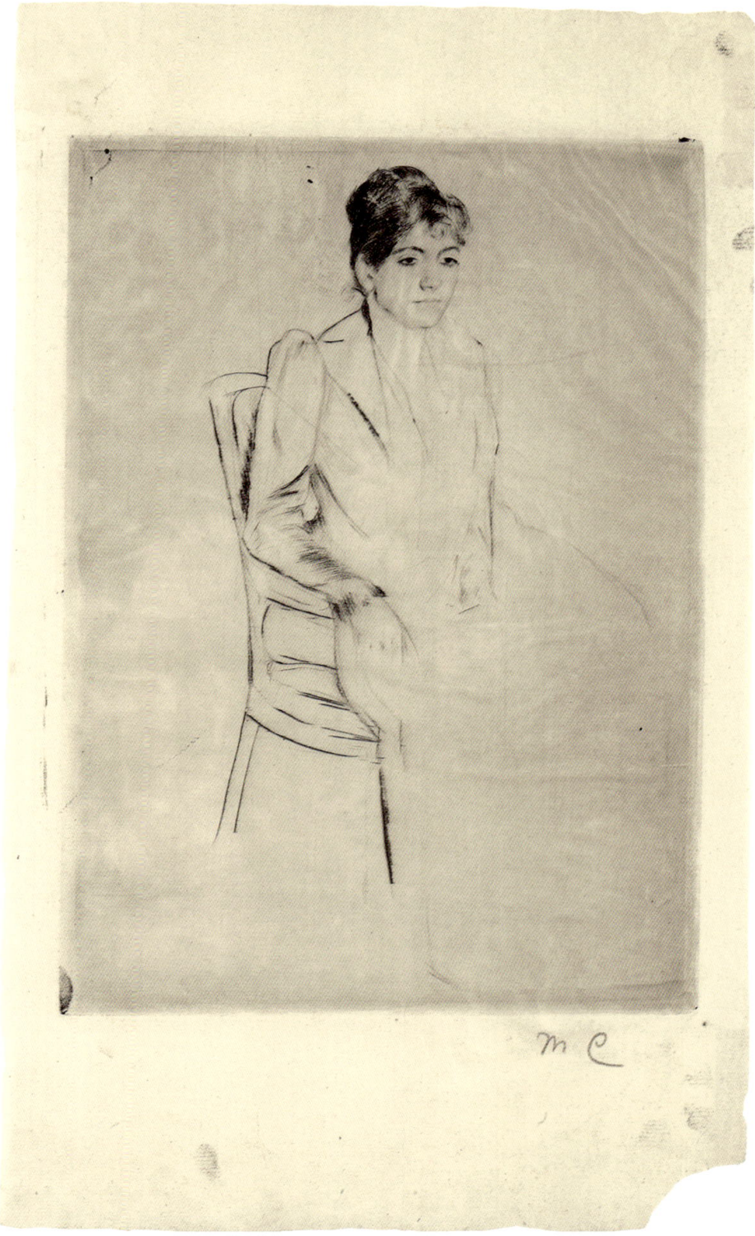

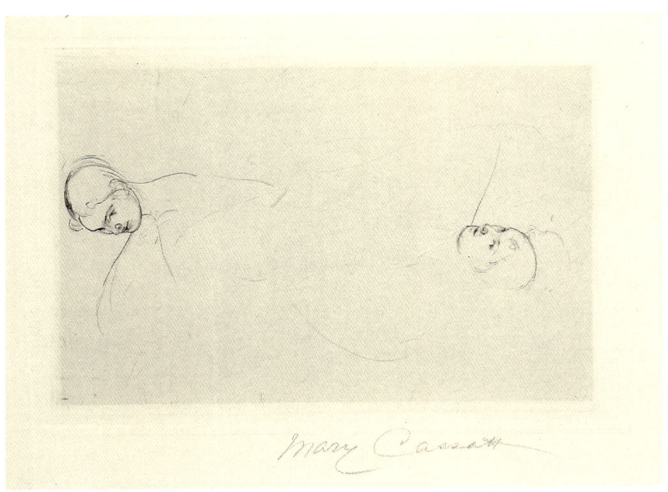

Two Heads: One Upside Down, ca. 1893

Breeskin 154+

Drypoint, signed in full, printed in black ink with delicate plate tone, wiped clean at the edges, on wove paper, the full sheet, in good condition (minor soiling and some very faint foxing in margins)

Plate: 15.8 × 23.6 cm   6¼ × 9¼ in.
Sheet: 27 × 38.2 cm   10¾ × 15 in.

This impression, described and illustrated by Breeskin, is the only known example of the work. It is a sketch plate conceivably related to *The Banjo Lesson*, in which the head is sketched on the copper in a surprisingly Leonardoesque manner.

PROVENANCE
Annotated *Collection Ardail*, possibly A. Ardail (see Lugt 1728)

With initials *P. E* stamped in violet in the margin on *verso* (unidentified)

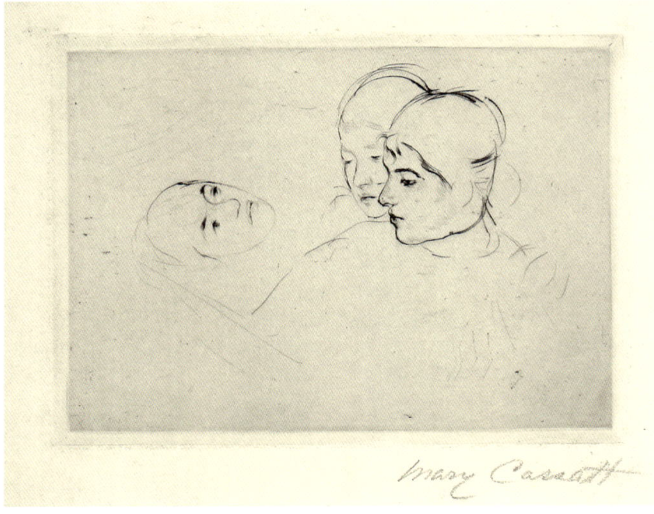

Blanche and Her Sister (Croquis), ca. 1893

Breeskin 155

Drypoint, signed in full, printed in black ink, with burr and even plate tone, wiped clean at the edges, on wove paper, the full sheet, in good condition apart from a handling crease at lower center, and pale, mottled discoloration

Plate: 13 × 17.8 cm   5⅛ × 7 in.
Sheet: 18.6 × 24.6 cm   7⅜ × 9⅝ in.

A study plate for the figures in *The Banjo Lesson*.

The Banjo Lesson, ca. 1893

Breeskin 156; Mathews/Shapiro 16

Drypoint, a previously unknown and apparently unique state between Mathews/Shapiro's first and second states of four, before much additional work on the skirt and banjo, etc., a richly inked impression, printed in dark brown with enveloping plate tone, initialed *M. C* within the plate area at lower right, on grey-green laid paper, the full sheet, in good condition apart from a pinhole inherent in the paper at upper left, a small tear in the lower left margin, and slight crinkling, annotated *HP* at lower left

Plate: 29.8 × 23.7 cm   11¾ × 9¼ in.
Sheet: 35.8 × 31.1 cm   14⅛ × 12¼ in.

[See illustration on facing page, top]

The Banjo Lesson, ca. 1893

Breeskin 156; Mathews/Shapiro 16

Drypoint and aquatint, with additions in monotype, Mathews/Shapiro's fourth state of four, printed from two plates, a fine trial proof (aside from the planned edition of 40, of which many fewer may have been printed), with the first plate printed in black with strong burr, and the second plate delicately tinted *à la poupée* for flesh tone, the ribs of the banjo, and the pale turquoise and pale rose dresses, with accents of pink on the lips, bodice and sleeves, and polka dots on the skirt added in brushed monotype, as well as the golden ochre collar of the woman, initialed *M. C* within the plate area at lower right, on laid paper with watermark VanderLey, the full sheet (irregularly cut along the right edge), in good condition (minor ripples in the right corners from printing), annotated *HP* in the lower left corner

Plate: 29.8 × 23.7 cm   11¾ × 9¼ in.
Sheet: 38.9 × 25.4 cm   15¼ × 10 in.

[See illustration on facing page, lower left]

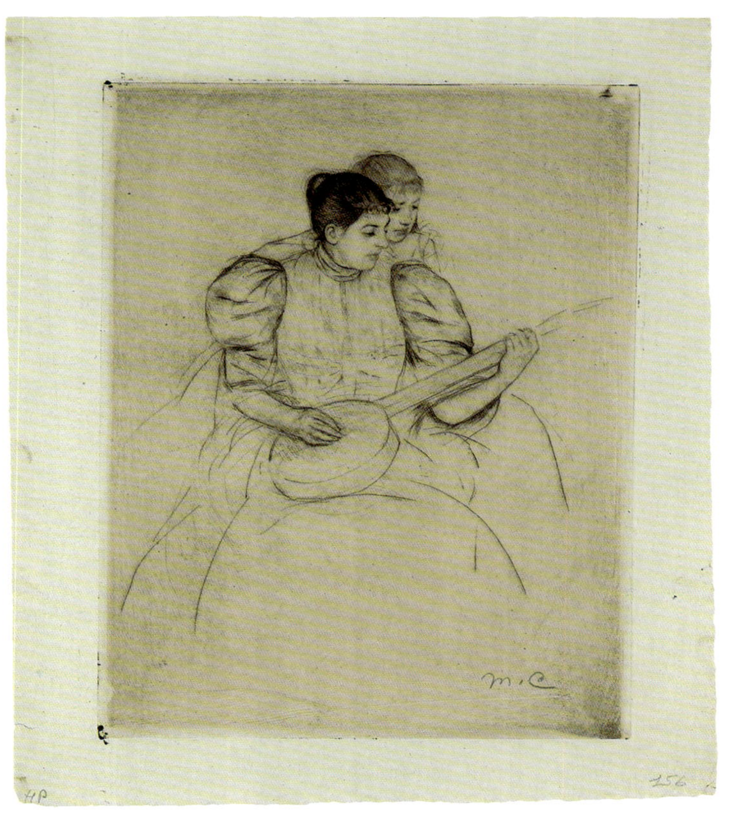

The Banjo Lesson, ca. 1893

Breeskin 156; Mathews/Shapiro 16

Drypoint and aquatint, with additions in monotype, Mathews/Shapiro's fourth state of four, printed from two plates, a proof with the monotype coloring of the sleeves applied with a thin slate blue ink, which bleeds into the paper (aside from the planned edition of 40, of which many fewer may have been printed), initialed *M. C* in the lower margin at right, with the artist's blue initial stamp (Lugt 604) at center of the lower platemark, on pale, blue-green laid paper with watermark F/ANDRIA, the full sheet, in good condition (minor crinkling from printing pressure at corners) annotated *HP.* in the lower left corner

Plate: 29.8 × 23.7 cm 11¾ × 9¼ in.
Sheet: 40.4 × 26.2 cm 15⅞ × 10¼ in.

[See illustration below, right]

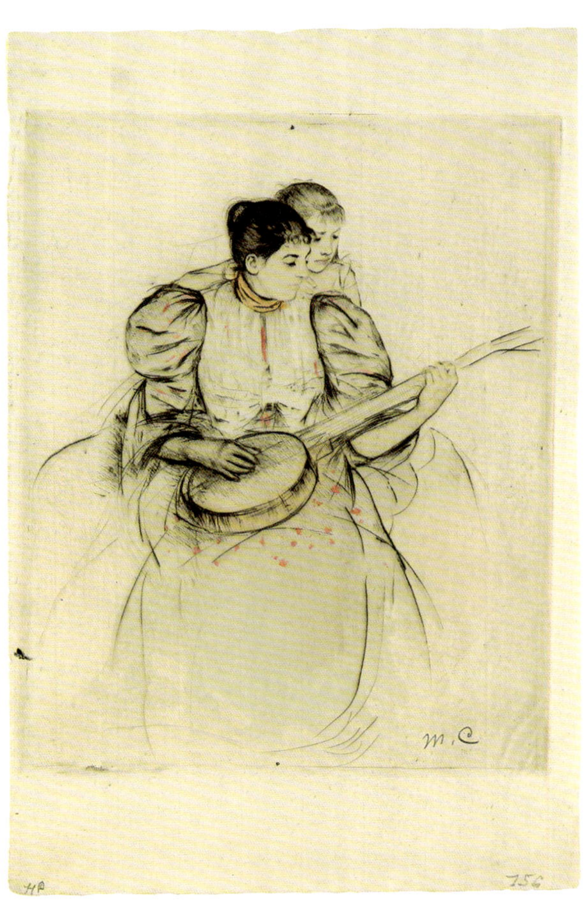

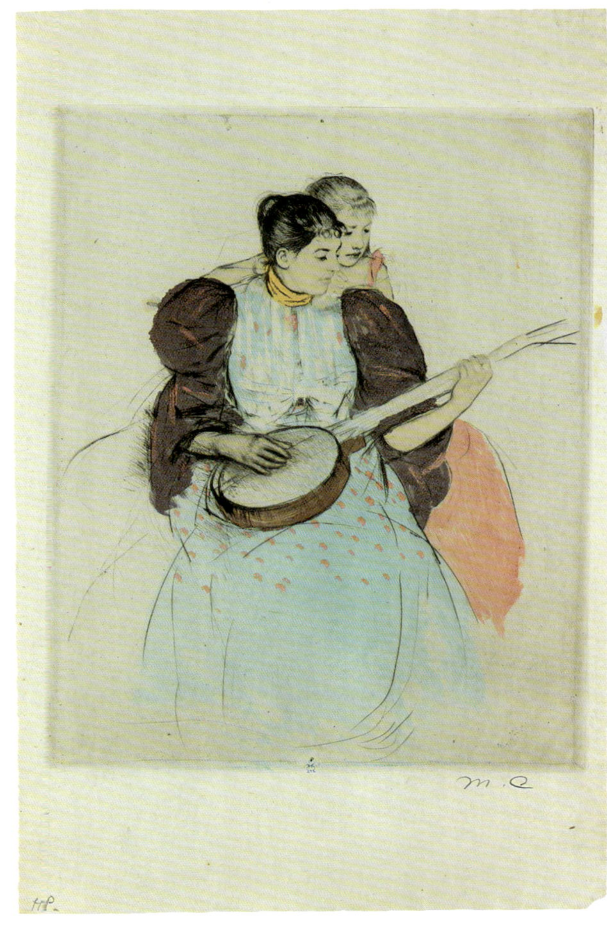

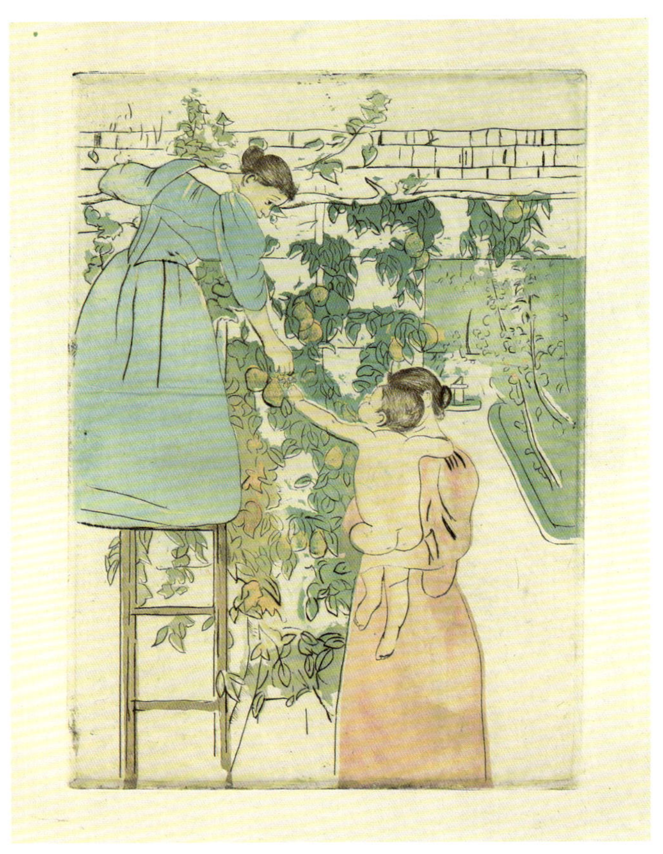

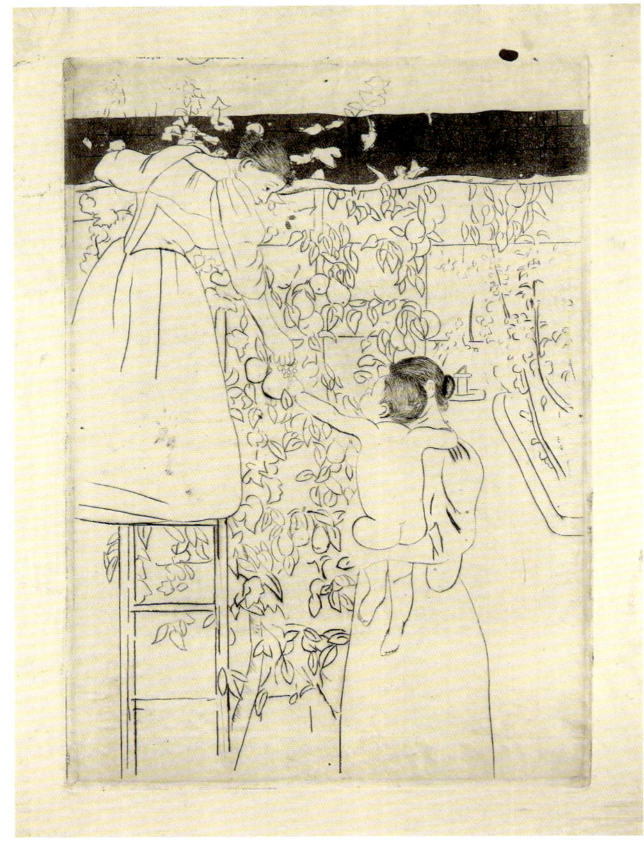

Gathering Fruit [Le Potager], 1893

Breeskin 157; Mathews/Shapiro 15

Drypoint, soft-ground, and aquatint, Mathews/Shapiro's third state of eleven, printed in colors from three plates, a fine impression of this state, with strong burr and experimental coloring, on fine laid paper with watermarks Adriaan Rogge, fleur-de-lys in crowned shield, and interlaced letters, the full sheet, in generally good condition except crinkled across the center from the pressure of printing, and with some soiling and handling creases, particularly at the edges of the large margins, and a few stray spots of color, a few nicks in the lower edge, annotated *D* in the lower margin at center

Plate: 42.5 × 29.7 cm   16¾ × 11⅝ in.
Sheet: 56.1 × 44.1 cm   22⅛ × 17⅜ in.

The flesh tones in this impression are in a paler tone than in the National Gallery of Art impression, while the dress at left is a more intense blue, and printed with light monotype strokes to the gathers at the neckline, sleeve and skirt, and with freer monotype coloring of the pink dress.

Gathering Fruit [Le Potager], 1893

Breeskin 157; Mathews/Shapiro 15

Drypoint, soft-ground, and aquatint, Mathews/Shapiro's fourth state of eleven, a previously unknown proof, printed in black only from the first plate, a fine impression, with strong burr, on laid paper with watermarks VanderLey and Fortuna, the full sheet, in good condition apart from some crinkling from printing pressure, several creases in the margins, and a few soft horizontal creases in the image, a few pale ink stains in the skirt of the dress at left, a small ink spot in the upper platemark at right, annotated *C* in lower left corner

Plate: 42.1 × 29.8 cm   16½ × 11¾ in.
Sheet: 50.1 × 38.8 cm   19¾ × 15¼ in.

One other impression of this state is recorded, but printed from plates I and III (location unknown).

It appears that the artist may have used this impression to transfer the image to a new plate, since there appear to be two platemarks and two, not quite coinciding, registration marks at the top.

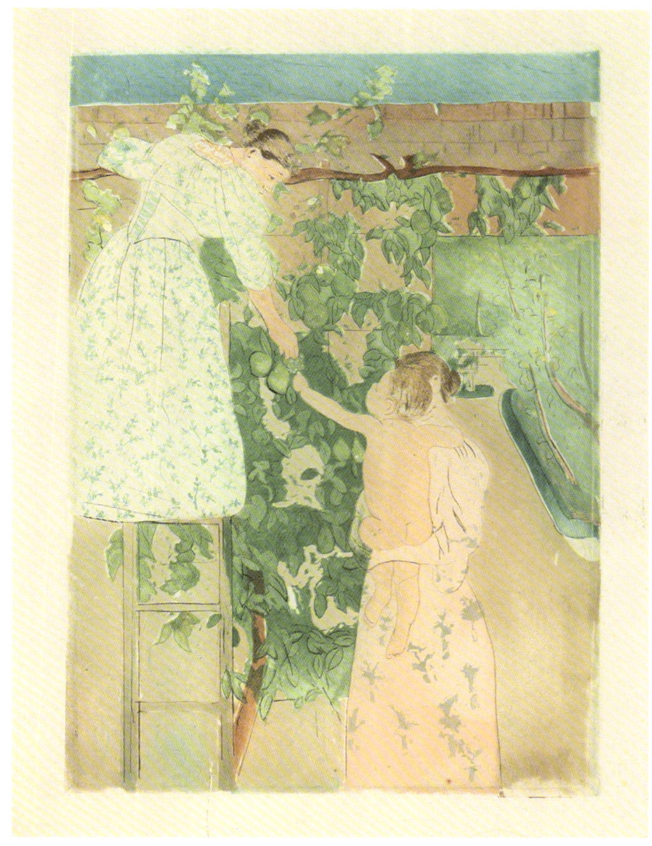

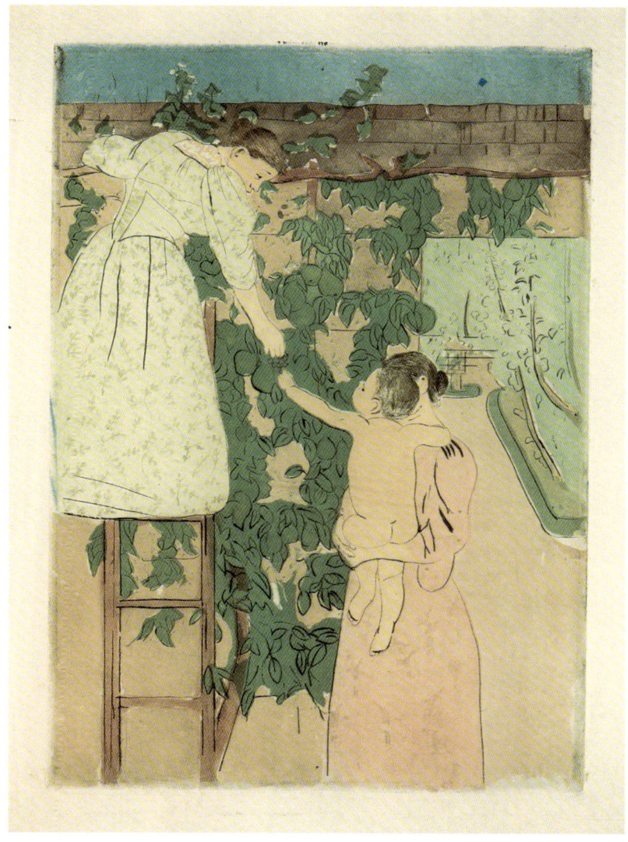

Gathering Fruit [Le Potager], 1893

Breeskin 157; Mathews/Shapiro 15

Drypoint, soft-ground, and aquatint, a previously unknown and apparently unique state between Mathews/Shapiro's eighth and ninth states of eleven, printed in colors from three plates, a fine impression, with elegantly balanced, airy colors, on sturdy, laid paper, the full sheet, in good condition except for a mended tear running from the lower edge at left a little into the plate area, some foxing, noticeable mainly in the margins, and a waterstain in the outer half of the lower margin, annotated *H* at lower left

Plate: 42.8 × 29.8 cm   16⅞ × 11¾ in.
Sheet: 51.3 × 38.2 cm   20⅛ × 15 in.

In this state, the second plate shows some of the new aquatint grain on the garden border at right and around the base of the sundial, but the aquatint of the foliage has not yet been filled in to a uniform green. (Notice that the leaves between the figures stand out in a lighter tone.)

Gathering Fruit [Le Potager], 1893

Breeskin 157; Mathews/Shapiro 15

Drypoint, soft-ground, and aquatint, a variant proof of Mathews/Shapiro's ninth state of eleven, printed in colors from three plates, on laid paper with watermarks VanderLey and Fortuna, the full sheet (deckle trimmed at top and right), in good condition apart from slight soiling in margins, some nearly vertical handling creases in the left margin, annotated *J* at lower left

Plate: 42.5 × 29.8 cm   16¾ × 11¾ in.
Sheet: 49.8 × 38.6 cm   19⅝ × 15⅛ in.

In this impression, the work on the path at right, printed from the third plate, has some new aquatint grain, but is not yet brought up to meet the dark green border of the garden. The dress of the woman on the ladder is printed in light green rather than turquoise.

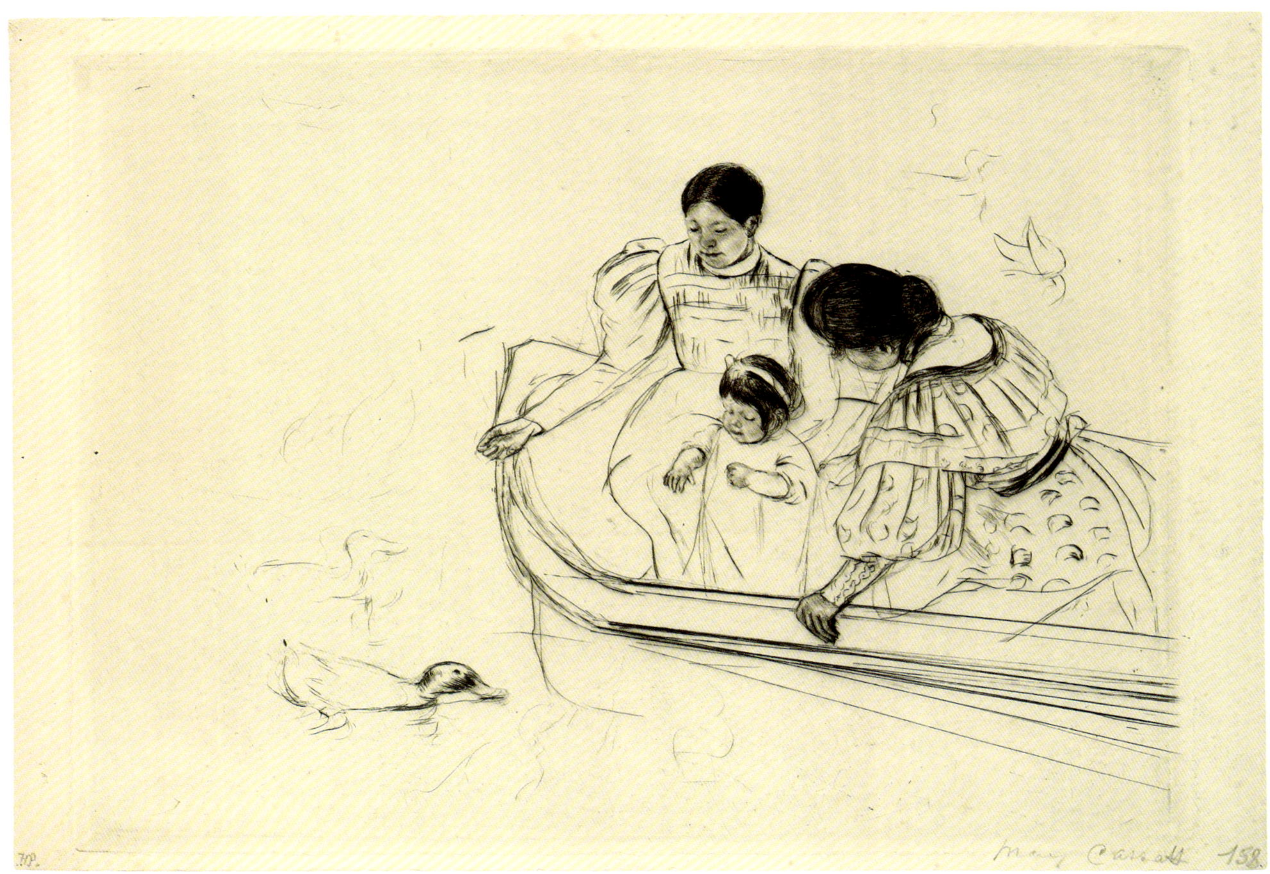

Feeding the Ducks, ca. 1895

Breeskin 158; Mathews/Shapiro 18

Drypoint, Mathews/Shapiro's first state of four, printed in black, from one plate, a fine impression, printed with strong burr and very delicate plate tone, signed in full across the platemark at lower right, on sturdy, white wove paper, the full sheet (with small margins at top and bottom as when printed), in good condition apart from foxing and some handling creases, annotated *HP.* in lower left corner

Plate: 29.7 × 40 cm 11¾ × 15¾ in.
Sheet: 31.8 × 44.9 cm 12½ × 17⅝ in.

The only other known impression of this state, in the Metropolitan Museum of Art, was previously thought to be unique.

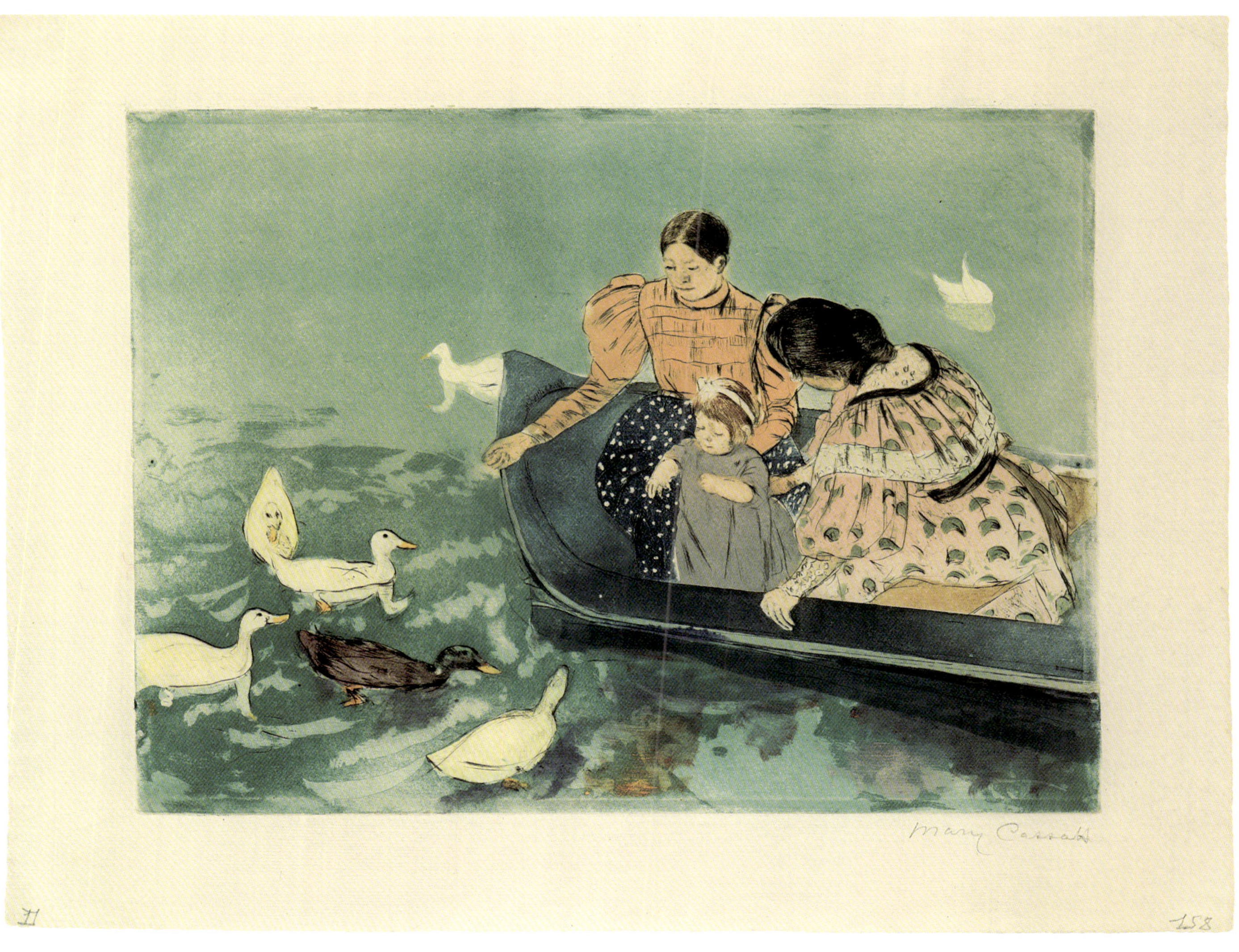

Feeding the Ducks, ca. 1895

Breeskin 158; Mathews/Shapiro 18

Drypoint, soft ground and aquatint, Mathews/Shapiro's fourth state of four, printed in colors, from three plates, a fine impression, printed with monotype inking for the reflections in the water, and the beaks and feet of the ducks, signed in full, on laid paper with VanderLey and Fortuna watermarks, the full sheet, in good condition (usual soft vertical fold present from time of printing), annotated *D* in the lower left corner

Plate: 29.8 × 39.5 cm 11¾ × 15½ in.
Sheet: 38.5 × 50.5 cm 15⅛ × 19⅞ in.

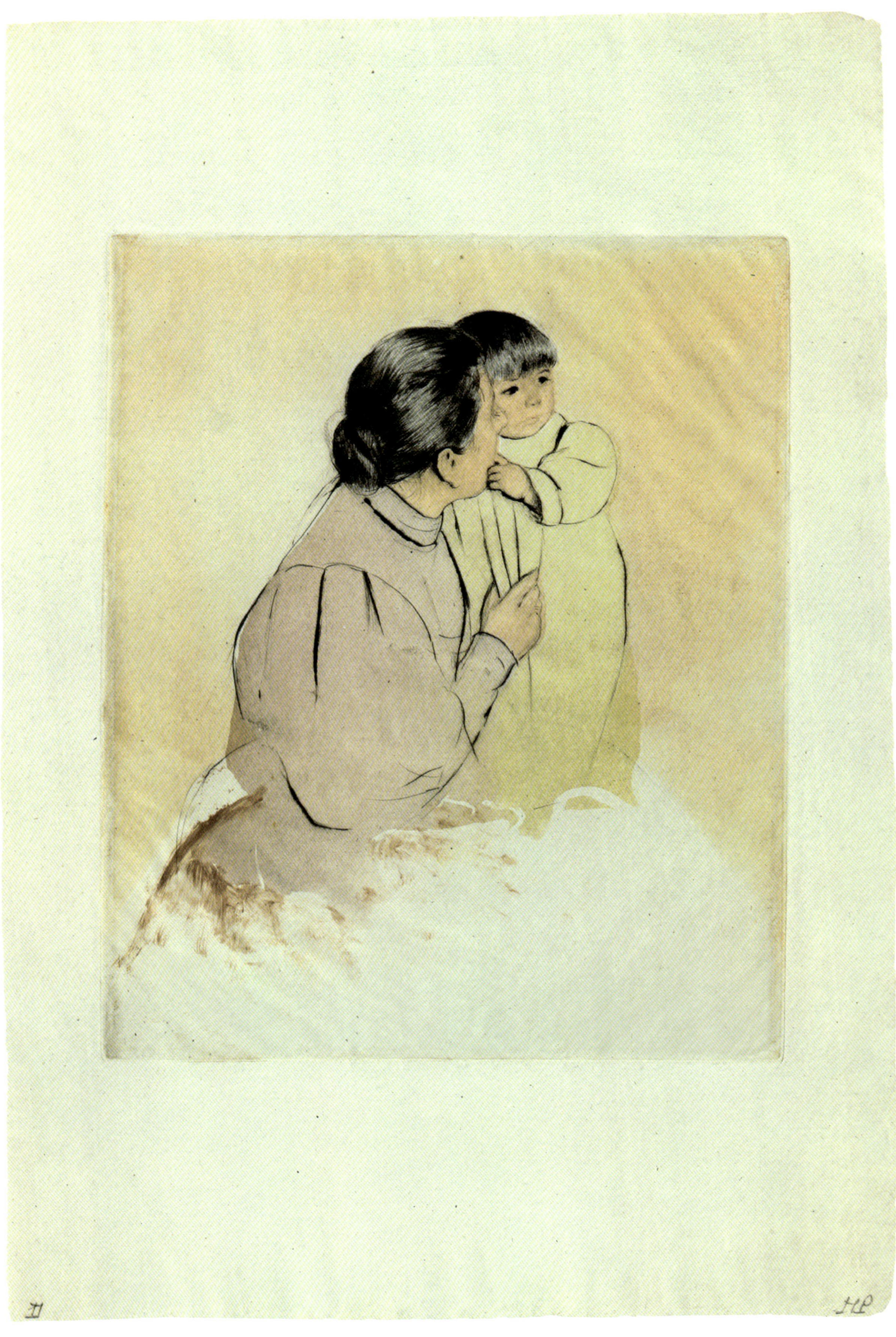

Peasant Mother and Child, ca. 1894

Breeskin 159; Mathews/Shapiro 17

Drypoint and aquatint, Mathews/Shapiro's eighth state of ten, printed in black, green, purple, apricot and rose-apricot, from three plates, a superb impression of this state, with strong burr, in a previously unknown color combination, and with experimental extension of the skirt of the woman's dress by monotype inking, on blue-green laid paper, the full sheet, in good condition (crinkling at plate corners from printing pressure), annotated *D* in the lower left corner, and *HP* at lower right

Plate: 29.6 × 24.1 cm 11⅝ × 9½ in.
Sheet: 46.8 × 31.6 cm 18½ × 12⅜ in.

The only other impression of this state, a duplicate from the Vollard collection, now in the National Gallery of Art, Washington, DC, is printed in tones of orange and yellow.

[See illustration on facing page]

Peasant Mother and Child, ca. 1894

Breeskin 159; Mathews/Shapiro 17

Drypoint and aquatint, Mathews/Shapiro's tenth state of ten, printed in colors, from three plates, initialed *M. C*, a fine, experimental trial proof, in light hues of green, yellow-green, russet-orange, and with grey-black to accent some of the features, and with the addition of yellow color freely brushed onto the pattern of the mother's blouse before printing, on laid paper with watermark PLANCHER BAS, the full sheet, in good condition apart from crinkling at corners from plate pressure, soft diagonal crease across upper right corner, slight oil stains in the upper margin, and minor soiling in the lower part of the large lower margin, also slight mottled discoloration on *verso*, annotated *F* in the lower left corner and *HP* at lower right

Plate: 29.7 × 24.1 cm 11⅝ × 9½ in.
Sheet: 44.6 × 28 cm 17½ × 11 in.

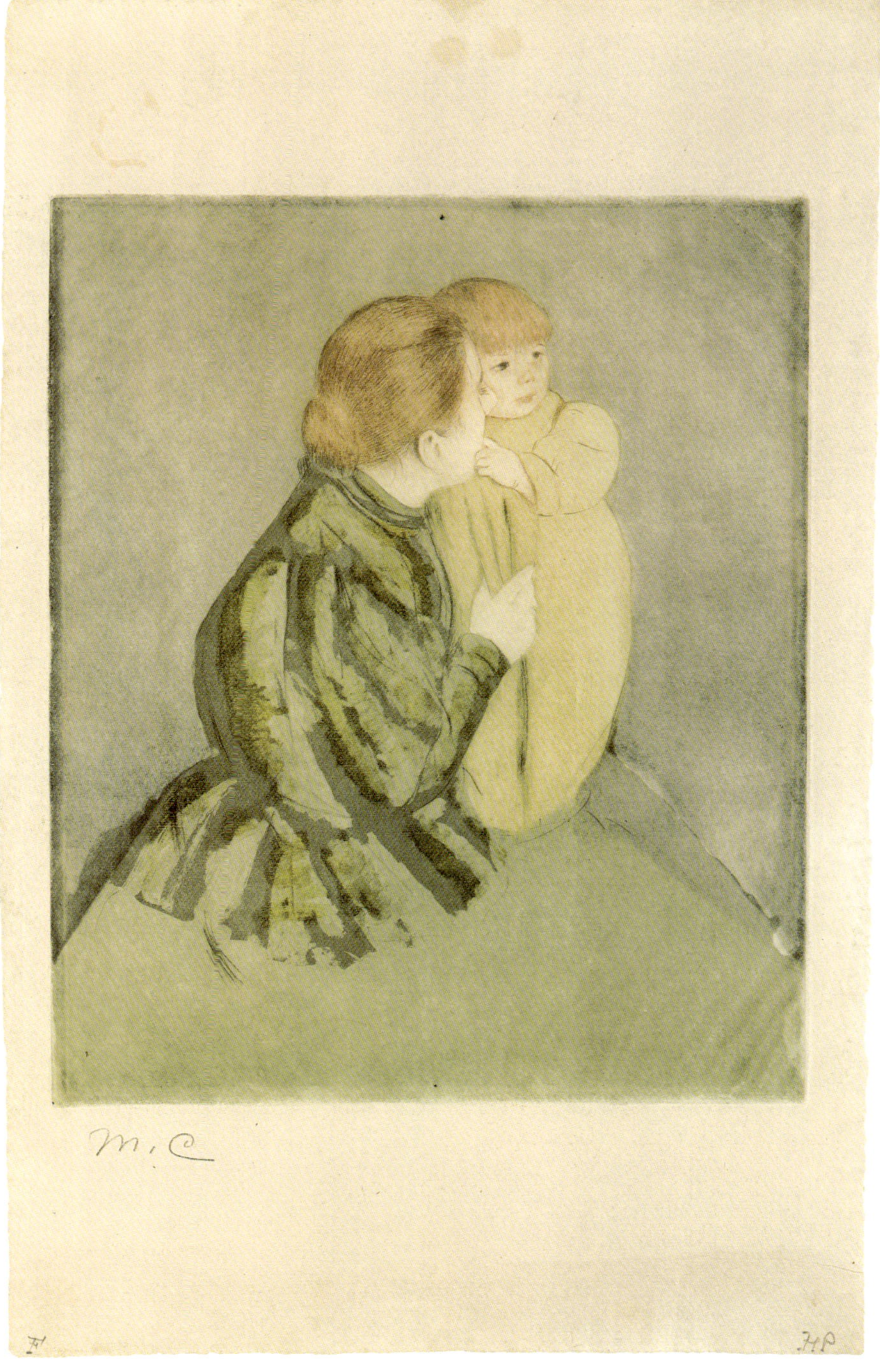

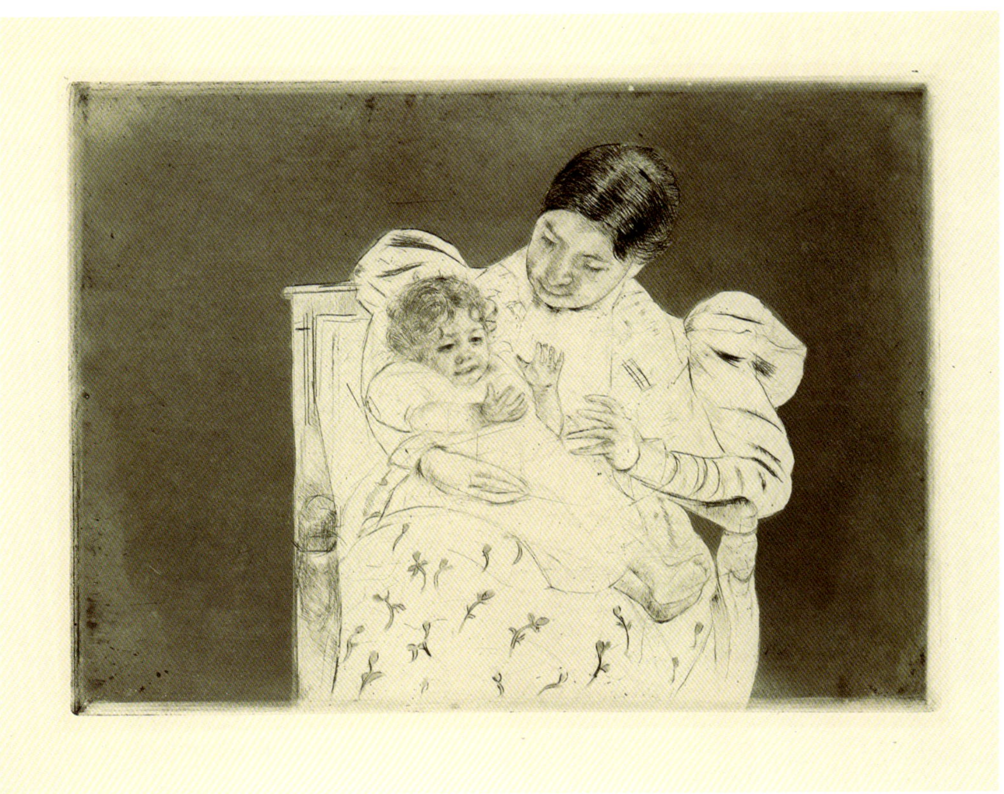

The Barefooted Child, 1896–1897

Breeskin 160; Mathews/Shapiro 22

Drypoint and aquatint, Mathews/Shapiro's fifth state of five, printed in black, from plate I alone, on wove paper with watermark Van Gelder, the full sheet, in good condition apart from a few unobtrusive, semi-vertical creases (two through image), discoloration on *verso*, and very slight light-stain (accidental plate scratches throughout)

Plate: 24.1 × 32.1 cm 9½ × 12⅝ in.
Sheet: 32.5 × 50.7 cm 12¾ × 20 in.

The Barefooted Child, 1896–1897

Breeskin 160; Mathews/Shapiro 22

Drypoint and aquatint, Mathews/Shapiro's fifth state of five, printed in colors, from three plates, signed in full, from the intended edition of 50, a fine impression, printed in unusually delicate and nuanced hues of yellow, green, turquoise, and rose, with black for accents of the design, as well as for the woman's hair and the eyes, on sturdy, laid paper with watermark ARCHES, the full sheet, in good condition apart from a small tear in the left margin, and some foxing, noticeable mainly in the margins, annotated *B.* in lower left corner

Plate: 24.6 × 32.1 cm 9⅝ × 12⅝ in.
Sheet: 30.9 × 44 cm 12⅛ × 17⅜ in.

[See illustration on facing page, top]

The Barefooted Child, 1896–1897

Breeskin 160; Mathews/Shapiro 22

Drypoint and aquatint, Mathews/Shapiro's fifth state of five, printed in colors, from three plates, from the intended edition of 50, more strongly inked on plate I and in the flesh tones and the sleeves of the woman's blouse, on laid paper with watermarks Vanderley and Pro Patria, the full sheet, in good condition (a vertical printer's crease in the sleeve at right, the lower plate mark reinforced, and with a few bits of stray purple ink in the lower margin), annotated *R* in the lower left corner

Plate: 24.2 × 31.8 cm 9½ × 12½ in.
Sheet: 32 × 39.8 cm 12⅝ × 15⅝ in.

[See illustration on facing page, bottom]

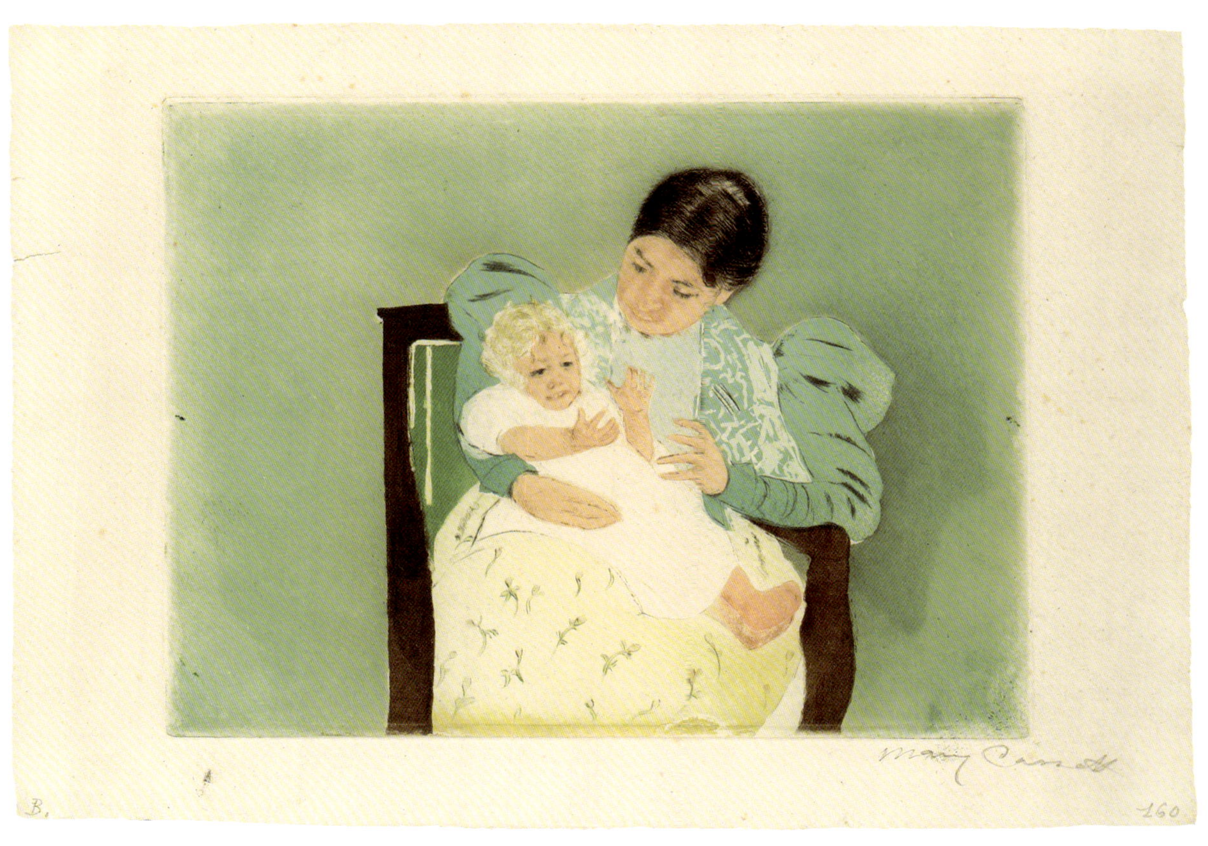

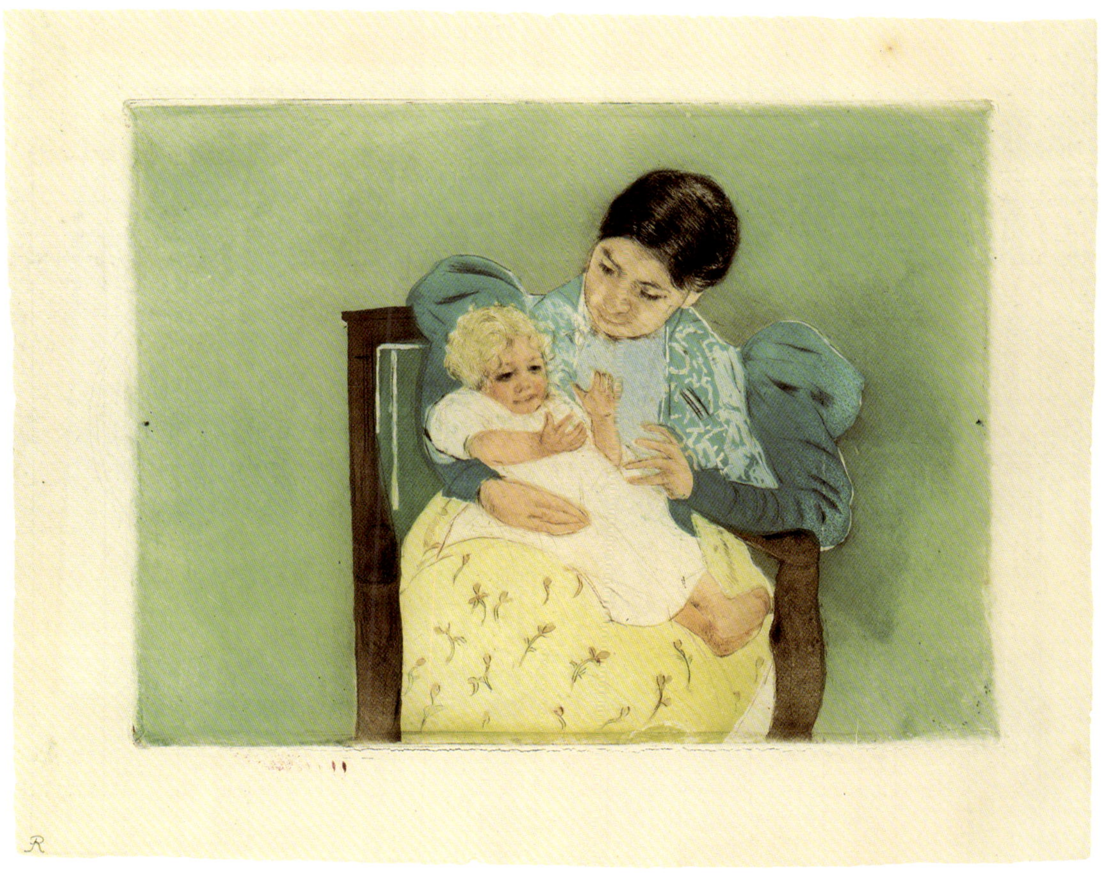

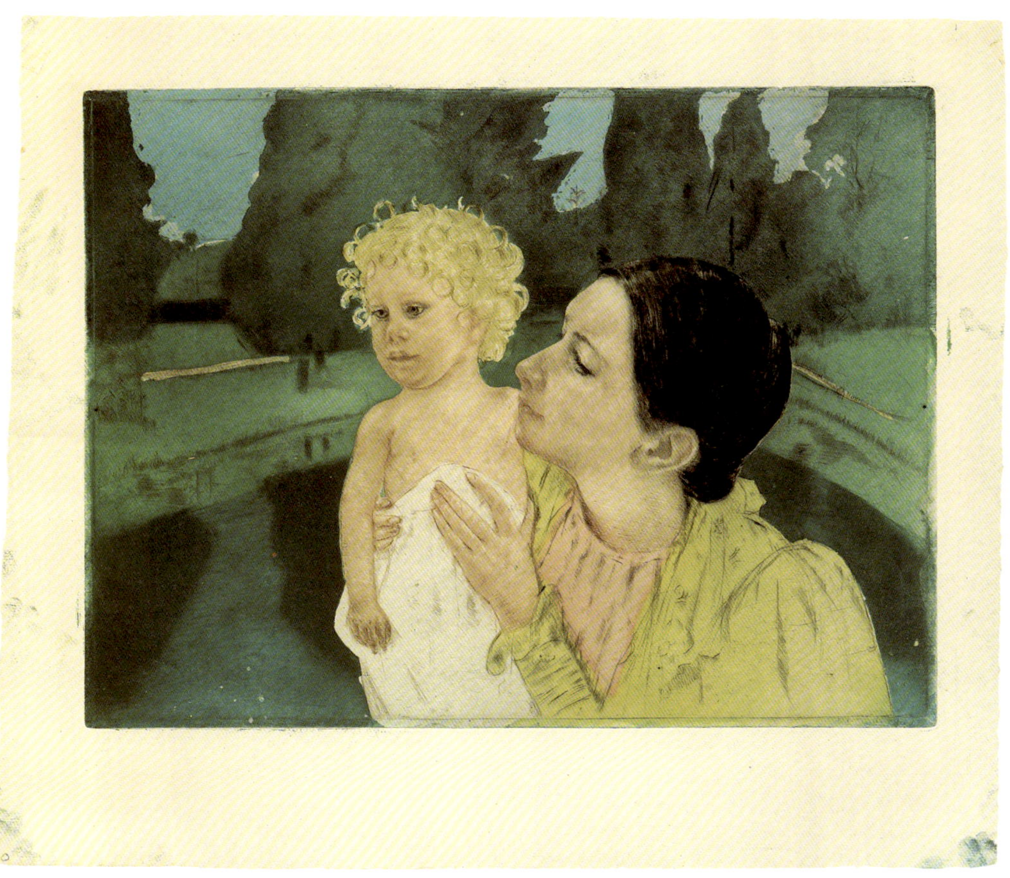

By the Pond, ca. 1896

Breeskin 161; Mathews/Shapiro 21

Drypoint and aquatint, Mathews/Shapiro's fourth state of four, printed in colors, from three plates, with the mother's black hair very richly inked, and the figures set against the deepening twilight background, on laid paper with watermarks Adriaan Rogge and fleur-de-lys in crowned shield, the full sheet, in good condition (bits of white paper hinging at top margin corners), annotated *O* at lower left

Plate: 33.1 × 42.8 cm 13 × 16⅞ in.
Sheet: 44.3 × 50.5 cm 17½ × 19⅞ in.

By the Pond, ca. 1896

Breeskin 161; Mathews/Shapiro 21

Drypoint and aquatint, Mathews/Shapiro's fourth state of four, printed in colors, from three plates, signed in full, a fine impression, printed with unusually airy tones in the background of park and sky and deeper tones in the pond to set off the figures of the mother and child, on laid paper with watermarks VanderLey and post horn in crowned shield, the full sheet, in good condition apart from stray ink in the margins (touching signature area at right), annotated *C* and *HMP* at lower left

Plate: 33.2 × 43 cm 13 × 17 in.
Sheet: 39.7 × 48.9 cm 15⅝ × 19¼ in.

By the Pond, ca. 1896

Breeskin 161; Mathews/Shapiro 21

Drypoint and aquatint, Mathews/Shapiro's fourth state of four, printed in colors, from three plates, a fine impression, printed with different and lighter tones on the face of the mother and on the child, but with later, twilight effects in the darker background, on laid paper with watermarks Adriaan Rogge and fleur-de-lys in crowned shield, the full sheet, in good condition (slight printing ink smudges in margins), annotated *M* at lower left

Plate: 33.1 × 42.7 cm 13 × 16⅞ in.
Sheet: 44.5 × 51.8 cm 17½ × 20⅜ in.

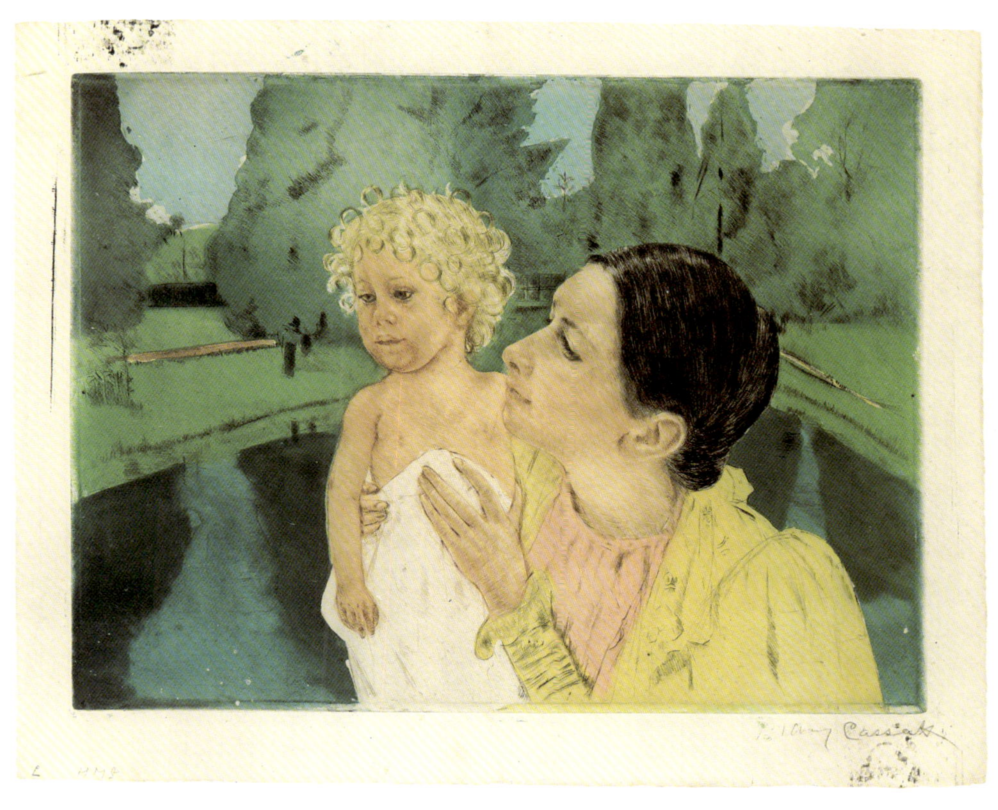

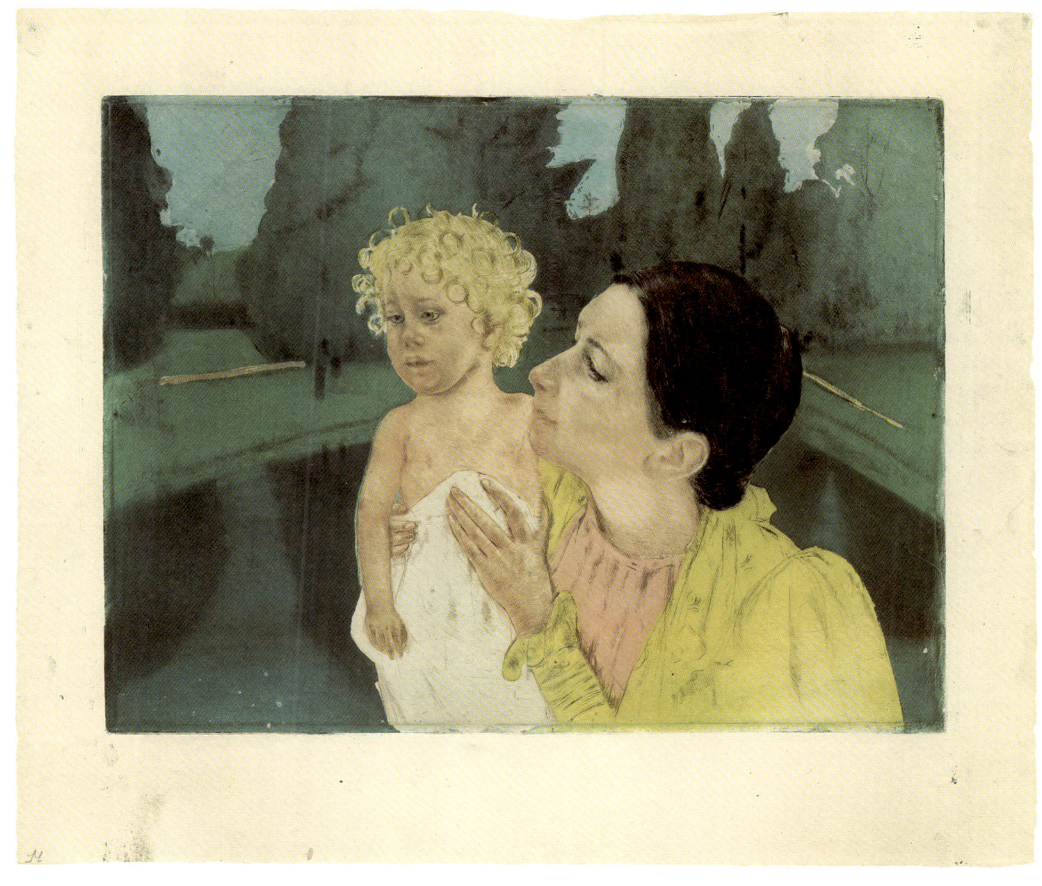

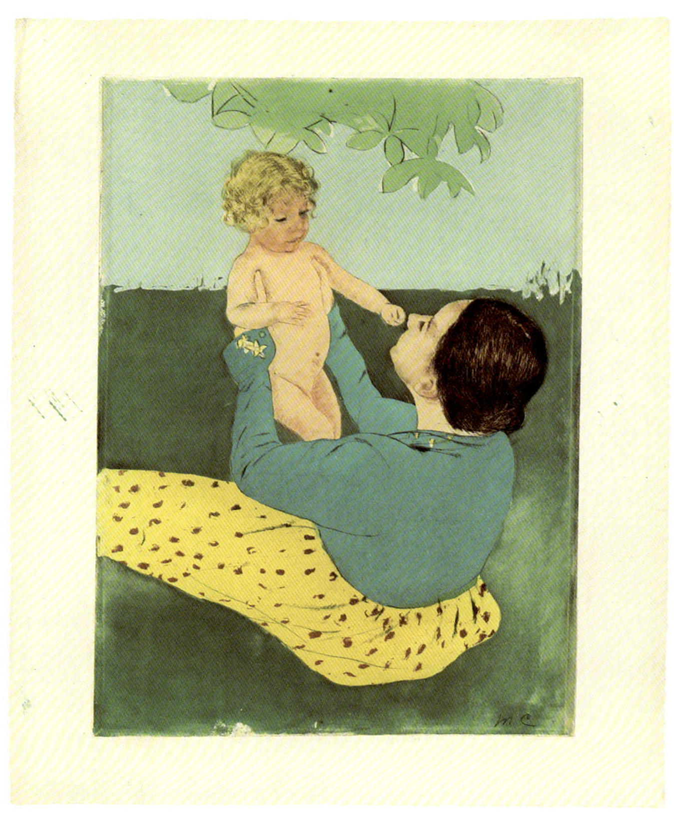

Under the Horse-Chestnut Tree,
1896–1897

Breeskin 162; Mathews/Shapiro 20

Drypoint and aquatint, Mathews/Shapiro's third state of three, printed in colors, from three plates, with the hair of the woman and child colored *à la poupée*, a fine trial proof, aside from the edition of 45, printed with a lighter and clearer green and yellow, as well as with light flesh tones, with the drypoint work defining folds of the blouse standing out more strongly against the blue, and with the hair of the woman printed in brown-black ink, on laid paper with VanderLey and Fortuna watermarks, the full sheet, in good condition except for spots of stray printing ink at top left plate corner

Plate: 40.5 × 28.8 cm 15⅞ × 11⅜ in.
Sheet: 50.2 × 39 cm 19¾ × 15⅜ in.

Under the Horse-Chestnut Tree,
1896–1897

Breeskin 162; Mathews/Shapiro 20

Drypoint and aquatint, Mathews/Shapiro's third state of three, printed in colors, from three plates, with the hair of the woman and child colored *à la poupée*, a fine, distinctively inked, trial proof, aside from the edition of 45, with rosy flesh tones, russet-brown for the woman's hair, lighter than usual blues for the blouse and sky, more subdued green for the ground and light green for the leaves above, and unusually bright brick red for the polka dots set on an almost orange-yellow skirt, initialed *M. C*, on laid paper with VanderLey and post horn in crowned shield watermarks, the full sheet, except right margin lost and made up

Plate: 40.5 × 28.8 cm 15⅞ × 11⅜ in.
Sheet: 50.2 × 39 cm 19¾ × 15⅜ in.

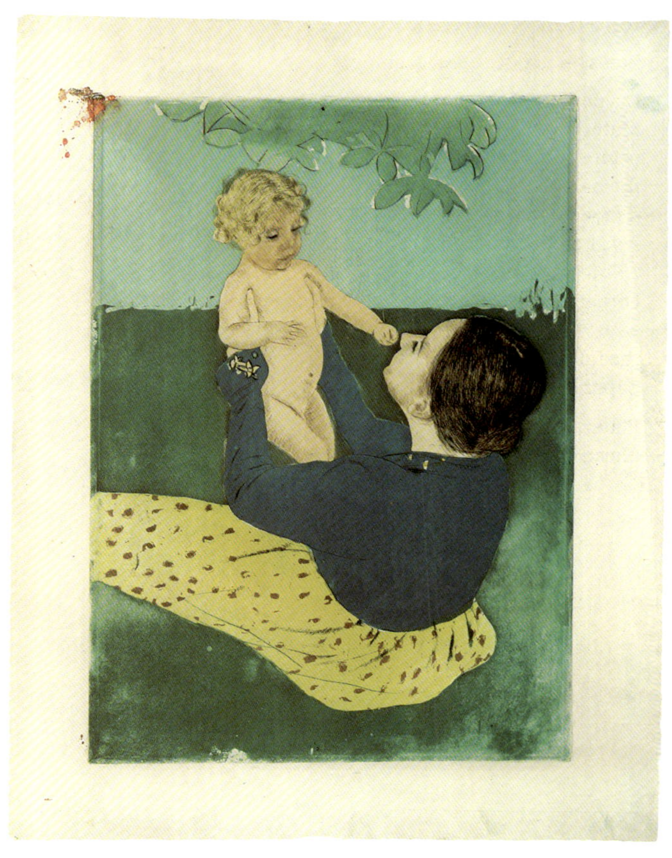

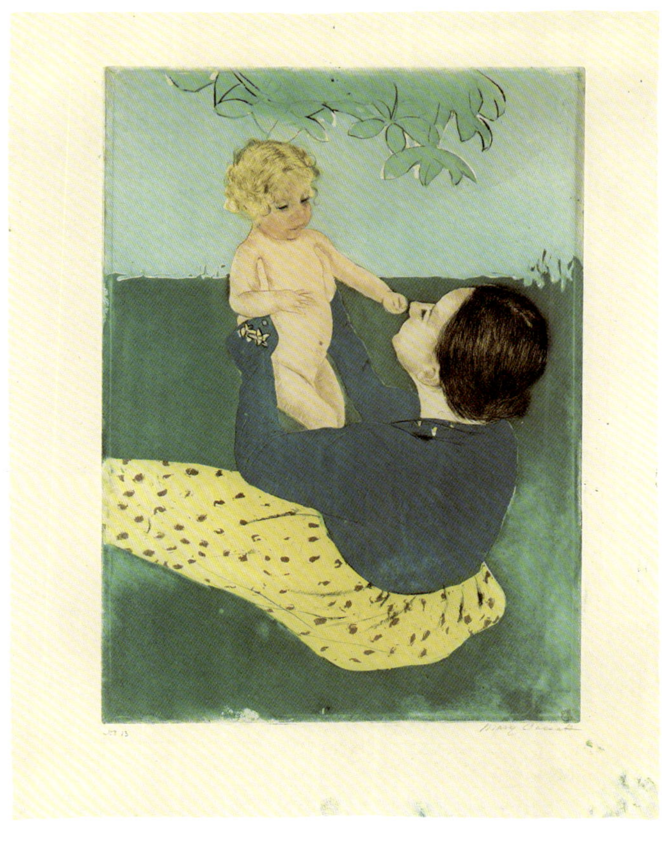

Under the Horse-Chestnut Tree,
1896–1897

Breeskin 162; Mathews/Shapiro 20

Drypoint and aquatint, a fine impression of Mathews/Shapiro's third state of three, printed in colors, from three plates, with the hair of the woman and child colored *à la poupée*, signed in full and inscribed *No 13*, from the edition of 45, published by *L'Estampe nouvelle* (stamp lower right corner of image, L. 886), 1897, on laid paper with VanderLey and Fortuna watermarks, the full sheet, in good condition (bits of paper hinging across upper corners)

Plate: 40.5 × 28.8 cm 15⅞ × 11⅜ in.
Sheet: 50 × 39 cm 19⅝ × 15⅜ in.

Under the Horse-Chestnut Tree,
1896–1897

Breeskin 162; Mathews/Shapiro 20

Drypoint and aquatint, Mathews/Shapiro's third state of three, printed in colors, from three plates, with the hair of the woman and child colored *à la poupée*, the blouse, skirt and background printed darker, and the flesh tones lighter, signed in full and inscribed *No 6*, from the edition of 45, published by *L'Estampe nouvelle* (stamp lower right corner of image, L. 886), 1897, on laid paper with VanderLey and post horn in crowned shield watermarks, with narrow margins, in good condition

Plate: 40.7 × 28.9 cm 16 × 11⅜ in.
Sheet: 42.5 × 30.3 cm 16¾ × 11⅞ in.

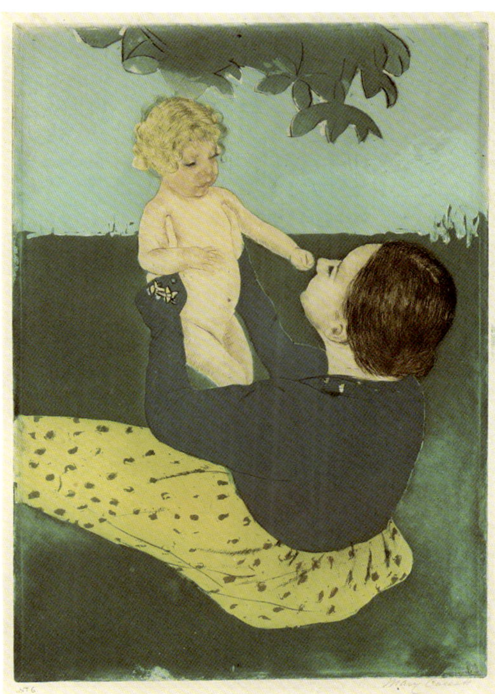

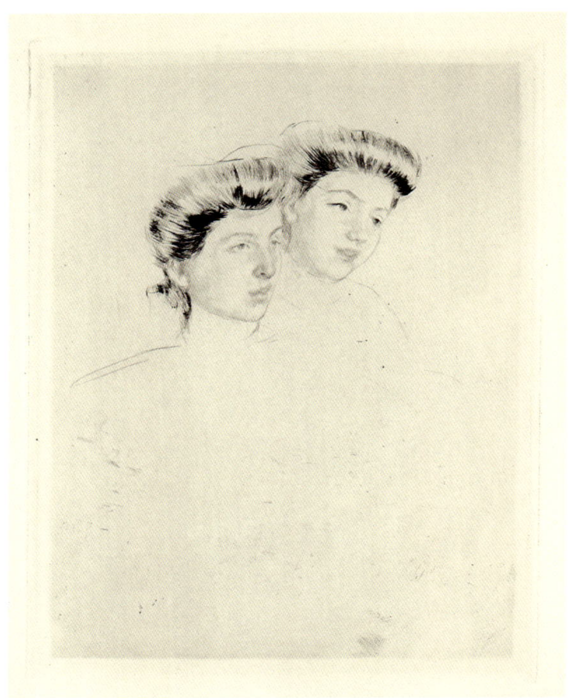

Heads of Two Young Women Looking to Right, ca. 1898

Breeskin 163+

Drypoint, according to Breeskin, one of only two known impressions, printed in black ink, with light plate tone, clean-wiped at the edges, on wove paper with Van Gelder Zonen watermark, the full sheet, in good condition except for traces of a few, soft diagonal folds

Plate: 31 × 24 cm 12¼ × 9½ in.
Sheet: 50.6 × 32.3 cm 19⅞ × 12¾ in.

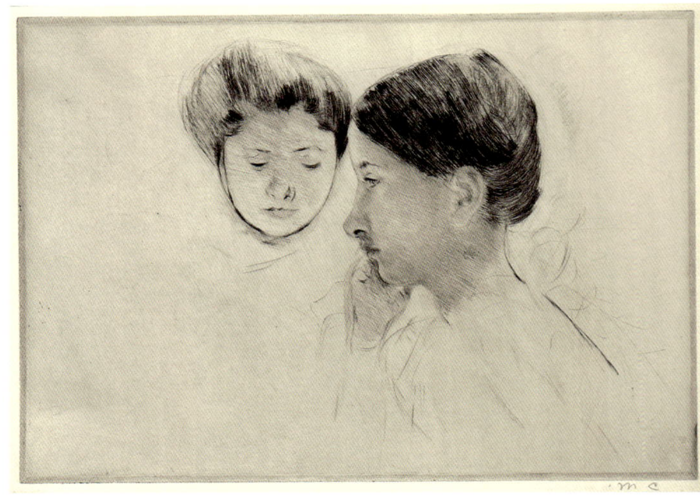

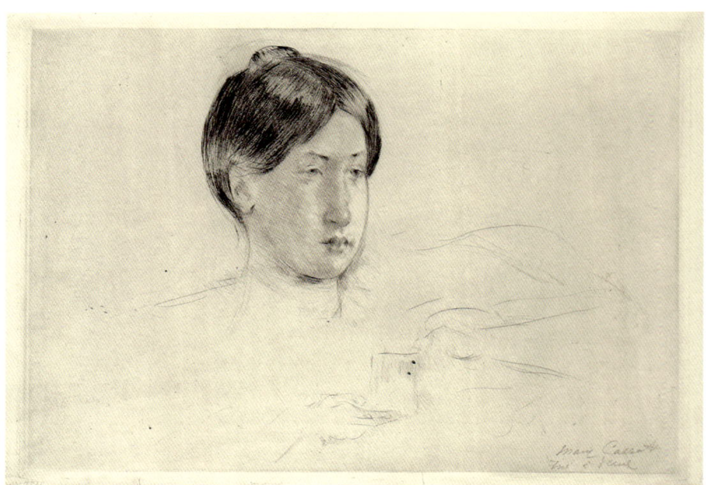

Celeste and Marjorie, ca. 1898

Breeskin 166

Drypoint, initialed *M C*, second state of two, a fine impression, printed with burr and strong plate tone, on laid paper with ARCHES watermark, the full sheet, in good condition

Plate: 29 × 41 cm 11⅜ × 16⅛ in.
Sheet: 30.7 × 44.6 cm 12⅛ × 17½ in.

Head of Celeste, ca. 1895

Breeskin 165

Drypoint, signed in full, inscribed at lower right within the platemark, *Tiré à deux*, printed in black, with burr and plate tone, wiped clean at edges, on laid paper with ARCHES watermark, the full sheet, two short tears in the lower margin, one just into the platemark, slight soiling, otherwise in good condition

Plate: 18.8 × 40.6 cm 7⅜ × 16 in.
Sheet: 30.4 × 44 cm 12 × 17⅜ in.

This impression is illustrated in Breeskin (misidentified as in the Bibliothèque Nationale). According to Cassatt's inscription, it is one of only two impressions printed.

The shading in this work and in Breeskin 166 is done in the neo-Renaissance, silverpoint manner, which the artist appears to have favored at this time.

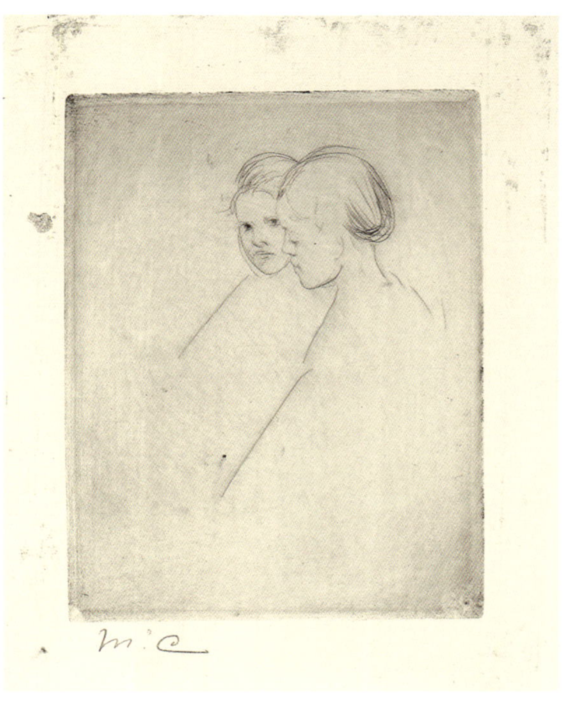

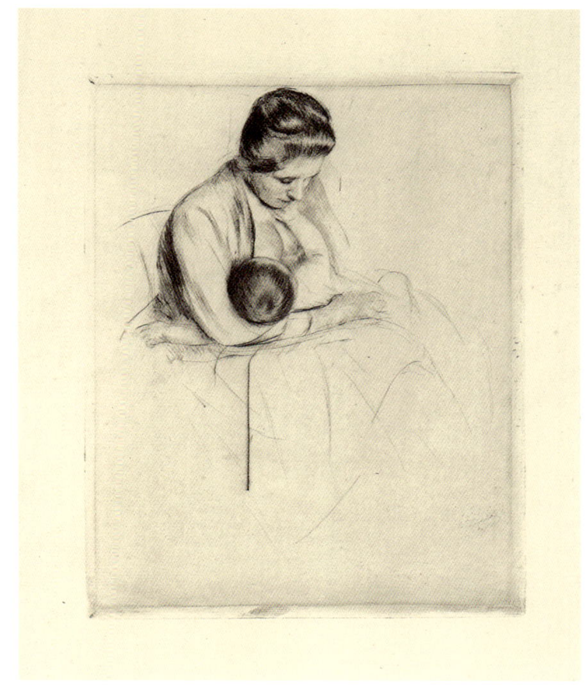

Heads of Two Little Girls, ca. 1898

Breeskin 167+

Drypoint, initialed *M. C*, printed in brown, with plate tone, on laid paper with Pro Patria watermark, the full sheet, in good condition (crinkled in upper corners from printing pressure, a tiny hole associated with the watermark, and stray offset of printing ink in the margins)

Plate: 19 × 14.7 cm 7½ × 5¾ in.
Sheet: 35 × 21 cm 13¾ × 8¼ in.

The only known impression of this work, illustrated in Breeskin.

Mother Rose Nursing Her Child, 1899

Breeskin 171

Drypoint, printed in warm, brown ink with burr and a delicate veil of plate tone, on laid paper with a watermark of crowned crossed scepters and numbers 6 8, the full sheet, in good condition apart from minor soiling and color smudges in upper and lower edges, annotated *Miss Cassatt* (script) in lower edge

Plate: 19 × 14.9 cm 7½ × 5⅞ in.
Sheet: 37.1 × 23.9 cm 14⅝ × 9⅜ in.

Mother Louise Nursing Her Child, 1899

Breeskin 172

Drypoint, second state of two, printed in black ink, with strong burr in the hair, on laid paper with a watermark of Fortuna on a base with letters VDL (Vanderley), the full sheet, in good condition, annotated *E* and *no. 24* at lower left corner

Plate: 33.5 × 22.5 cm 13⅛ × 8⅞ in.
Sheet: 39 × 25.1 cm 15⅜ × 9⅞ in.

A Woman Crocheting, ca. 1902

Breeskin 173+

Drypoint, on sturdy white wove paper with watermark BFK, the full sheet, in good condition

Plate: 14.1 × 19.9 cm 5½ × 7⅞ in.
Sheet: 25.3 × 32.2 cm 10 × 12¾ in.

Breeskin illustrated the impression in the Museum of Fine Arts, Boston, as unique. However, a few impressions of this evidently abandoned plate appear to have been printed at a later date.

[Not illustrated]

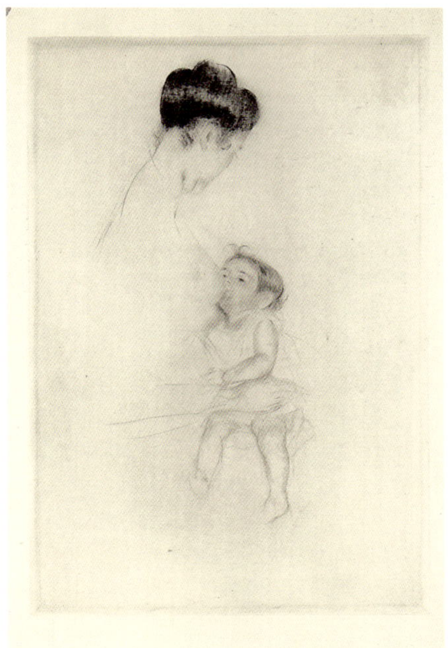

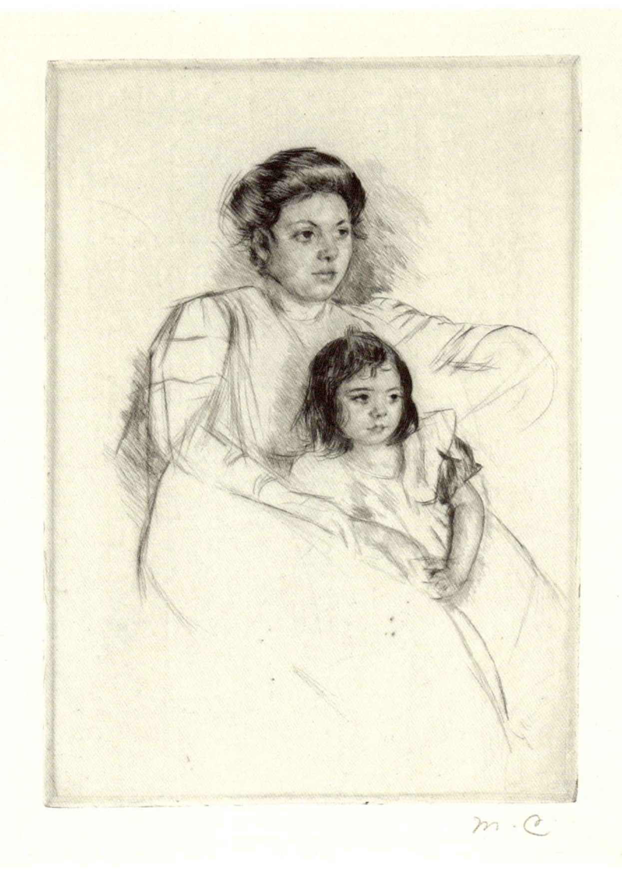

Margot Leaning against Her Mother, ca. 1902

Breeskin 175

Drypoint, a fine impression of the first state of two, initialed *M. C*, printed in black ink, with even plate tone, on laid paper with Vanderley watermark, the full sheet, in good condition (a little crinkling from plate pressure, two short tears in edge of left margin)

Plate: 25 × 17.5 cm 10⅞ × 6⅞ in.
Sheet: 35.2 × 21.4 cm 13⅞ × 8⅜ in.

PROVENANCE
Pierre Demany [b. 1887] (purple stamp, *verso*, Lugt 780b), whose collection was distinguished by its range and quality.

The Picture Book (No. 1), ca. 1901

Breeskin 176

Drypoint, first state of two, signed in full, printed in black ink, with even plate tone, on laid paper, with a watermark of script letters and countermark PM, the full sheet (as printed), in good condition apart from pale mat stain

Plate: 21.7 × 14.9 cm 8½ × 5⅞ in.
Sheet: 24.4 × 18.8 cm 9⅝ × 7⅜ in.

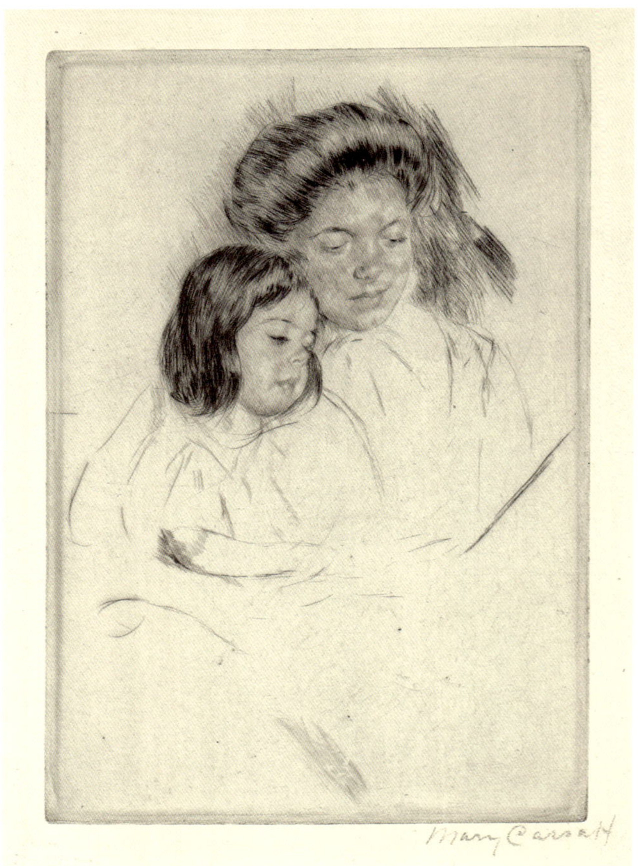

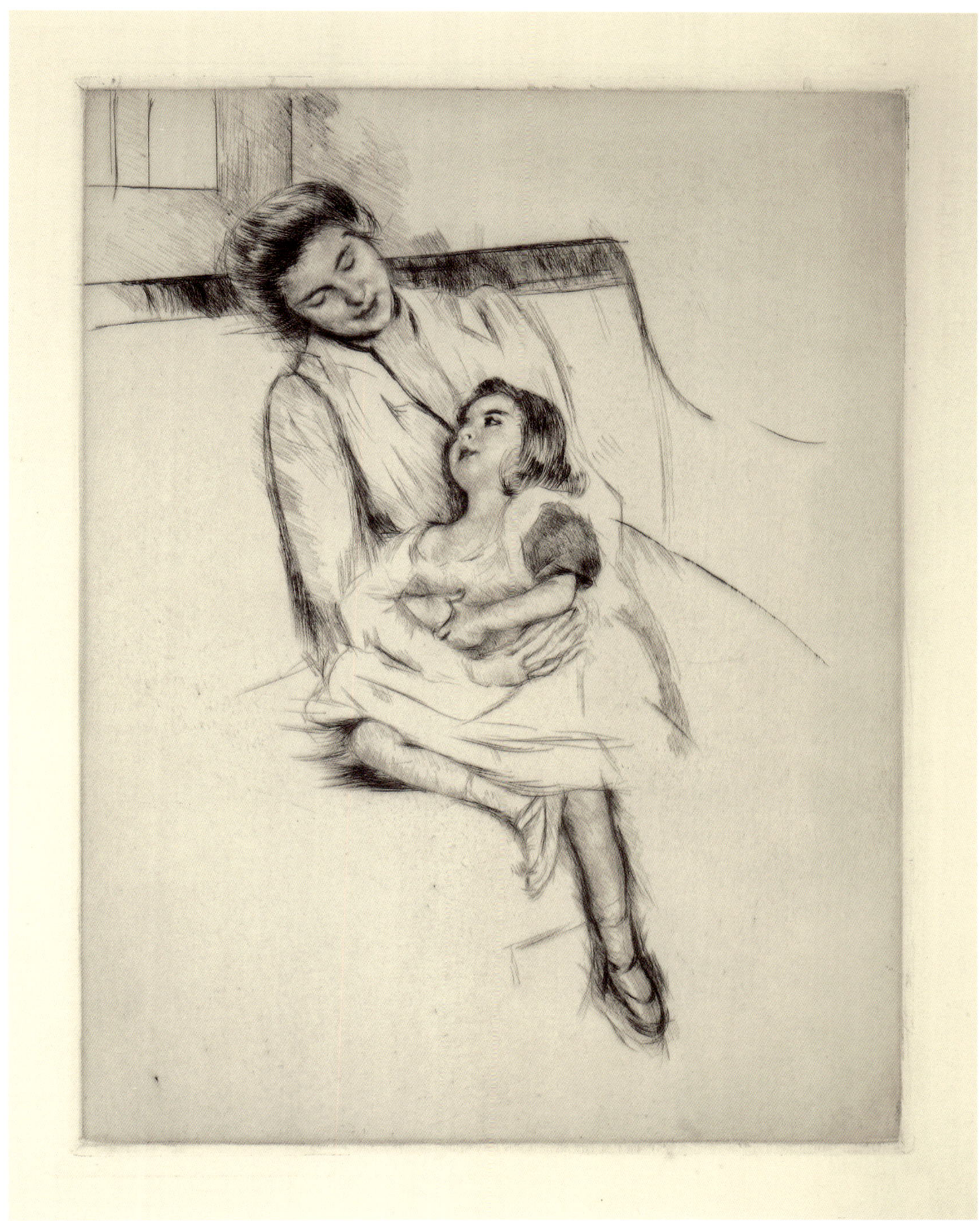

Reine and Margot Seated on a Sofa (No. 2), ca. 1902

Breeskin 177

Drypoint, Breeskin's only state, an extraordinarily fine, rich proof impression, with burr, and plate tone wiped at the bevel, before the edition of 25, on laid paper with watermark A. PORCABEUF, the full sheet, in good condition apart from some foxing, noticeable only in margins, and mottled discoloration on *verso*

Plate: 43.2 × 33 cm 17 × 13 in.
Sheet: 61.6 × 44.1 cm 24¼ × 17¼ in.

PROVENANCE

Roger Marx [1859–1913] (black stamp lower right corner, *recto*, Lugt 2229)

An earlier state exists, with only the upper part of the figures and slight indication of the sofa.

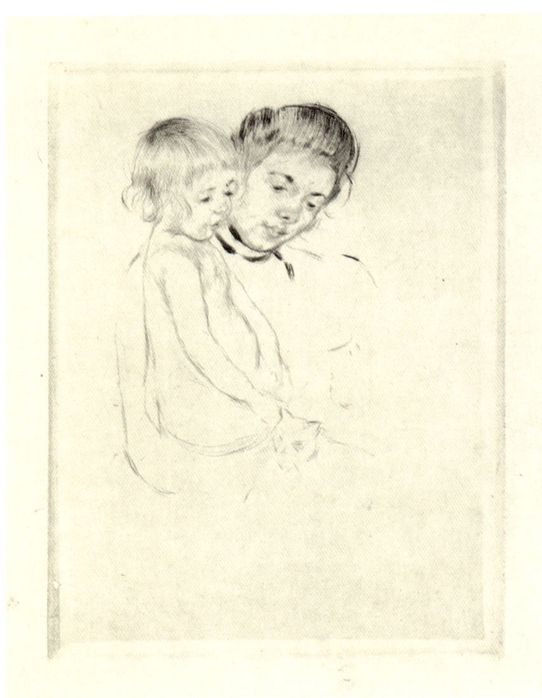

The Crocheting Lesson, ca. 1902

Breeskin 178

Drypoint, first state of two, before signature in the plate, with the stamp of *L'Estampe nouvelle* (L. 886) in the lower right plate corner, on laid paper with watermarks VanderLey and Fortuna over letters VDL, the full sheet, in good condition (trace of a horizontal center crease present from time of printing, slight soiling in margins)

Plate: 44.9 × 26.9 cm 17⅝ × 10⅝ in.
Sheet: 61.6 × 44.1 cm 24¼ × 17¼ in.

Published in the second state in a numbered edition of 50 for *L'Estampe nouvelle.* Annotated *1er Etat–Avant la Signature…* (the end of this annotation, *une épreuve,* is evidently incorrect) (see following).

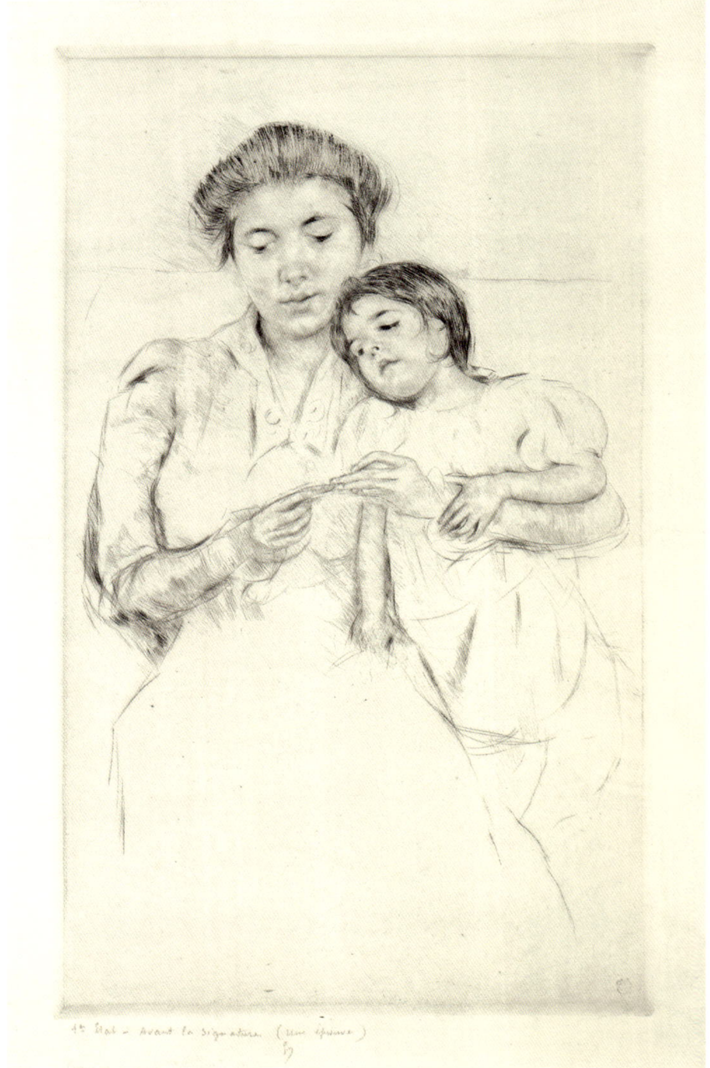

Reine and Blond Baby with a Cat, ca. 1902

Breeskin 177+

Drypoint, a fine and apparently unique impression, printed in black ink, with delicate plate tone, on laid Japan paper, with large margins, in good condition apart from slight soiling and some foxing

Plate: 23.1 × 17.1 cm 9¼ × 6¾ in.
Sheet: 33.6 × 24.2 cm 13⅛ × 9½ in.

This is the only known impression, illustrated in Breeskin.

The Crocheting Lesson, ca. 1902

Breeskin 178

Drypoint, first state of two, before the signature in the plate, a fine proof with burr and plate tone, on laid paper with watermark A. PORCABEUF, the full sheet, in good condition apart from slight soiling and handling creases

Plate: 44.9 × 26.9 cm 17⅝ × 10⅝ in.
Sheet: 61.6 × 44.1 cm 24¼ × 17¼ in.

Published in the second state in a numbered edition of 50 for *L'Estampe nouvelle*.

PROVENANCE
Roger Marx [1859–1913] (black stamp lower right corner, *recto*, Lugt 2229)

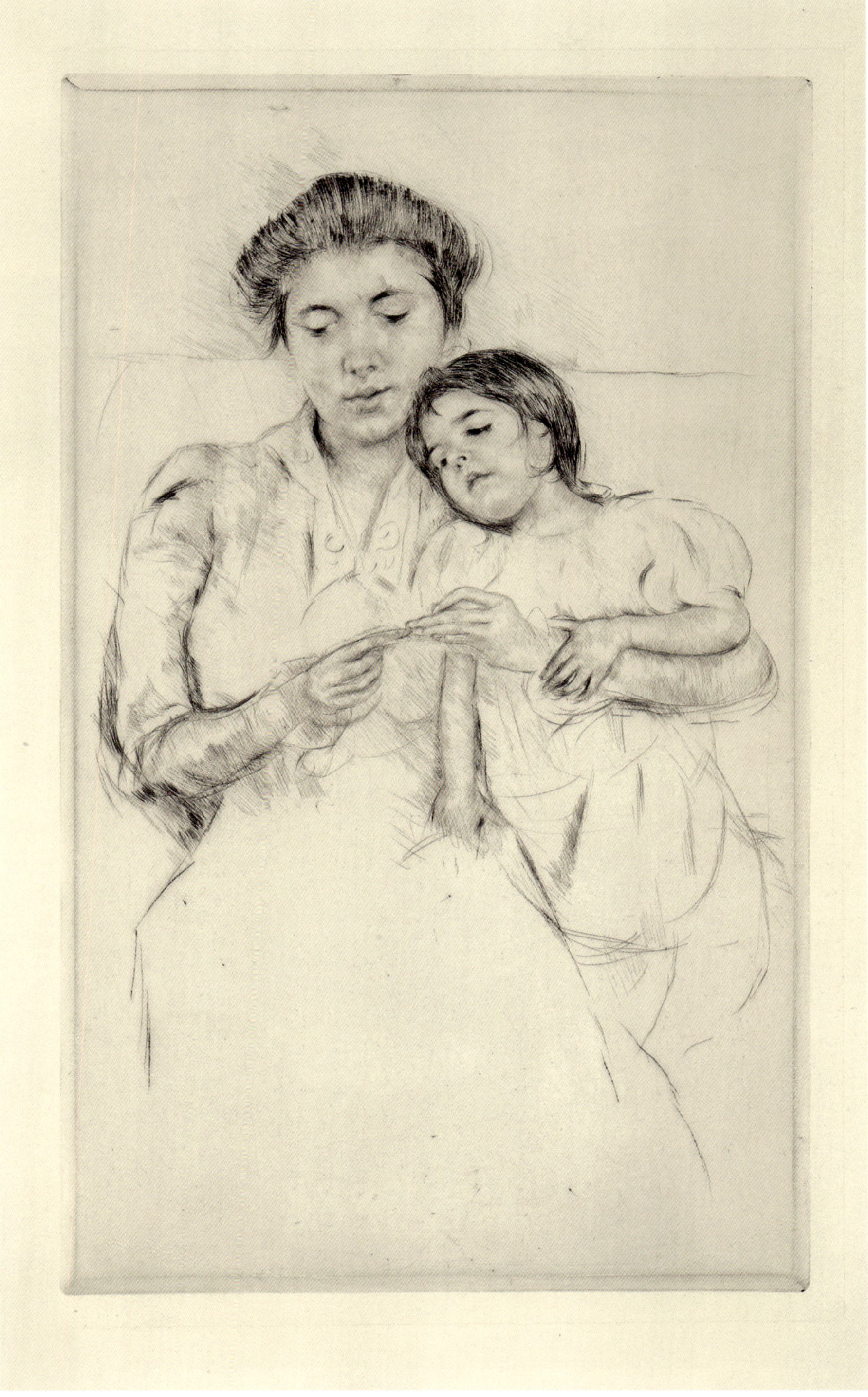

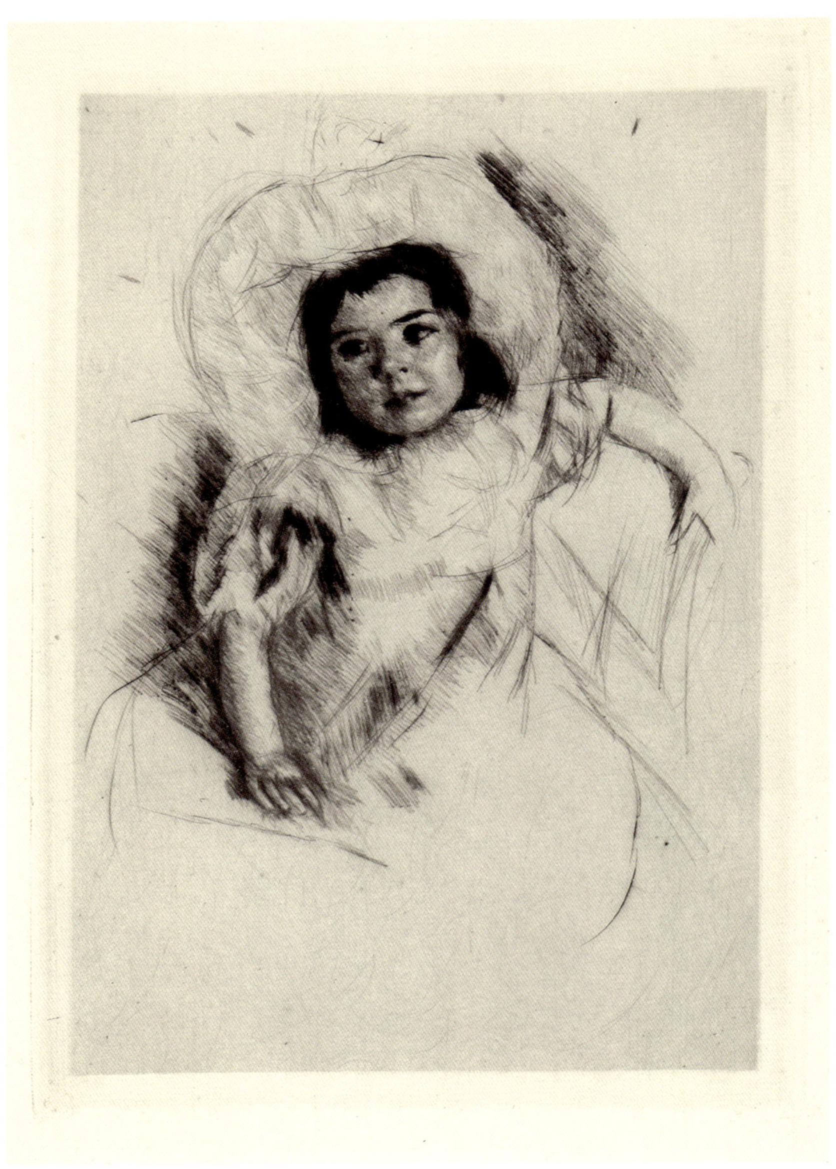

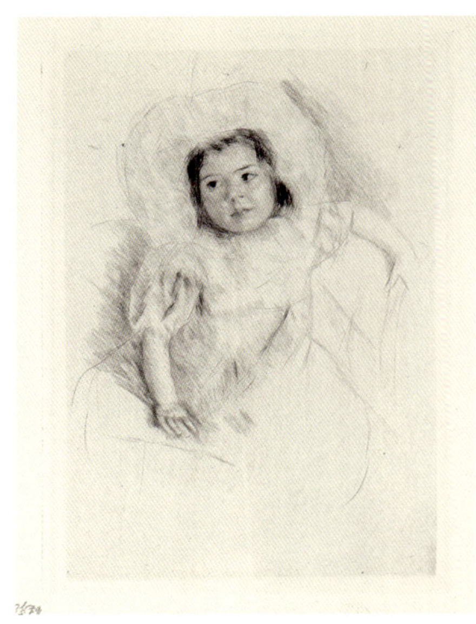

Margot Wearing a Bonnet (No. 1), 1903

Breeskin 179

Drypoint, a superb, early impression of Breeskin's only state, printed in black ink, with rich, velvety burr, and with even plate tone wiped clean at the plate edges, on laid paper, with watermark L & P, the full sheet, in good condition (inconspicuous foxing)

Plate: 23.4 × 16.4 cm   9¼ × 6½ in.
Sheet: 31.6 × 20.4 cm   12⅜ × 8 in.

Breeskin was evidently unable to locate a true early impression of this work, since the illustration in her catalogue appears to correspond with the quality of a reprint edition. (See the following.)

PROVENANCE

Roger Marx [1859–1913] (black stamp lower right corner, *recto*, Lugt 2229)

Emile Laffon [1868–1931] (blue stamp, *verso*, Lugt 877a)

Margot Wearing a Bonnet (No. 1), 1903

Breeskin 179

Drypoint, reprint, on laid paper showing top of letters, DC Blauw, watermark, with small margins, in good condition

Plate: 23.3 × 16.3 cm   9¼ × 6⅜ in.
Sheet: 24.8 × 19.9 cm   9¾ × 7⅞ in.

From a reprint edition of the preceding. This restrike usually appears in paler impressions, which are hand-colored. (See Mathews/Shapiro, Appendix, pp. 196–198.)

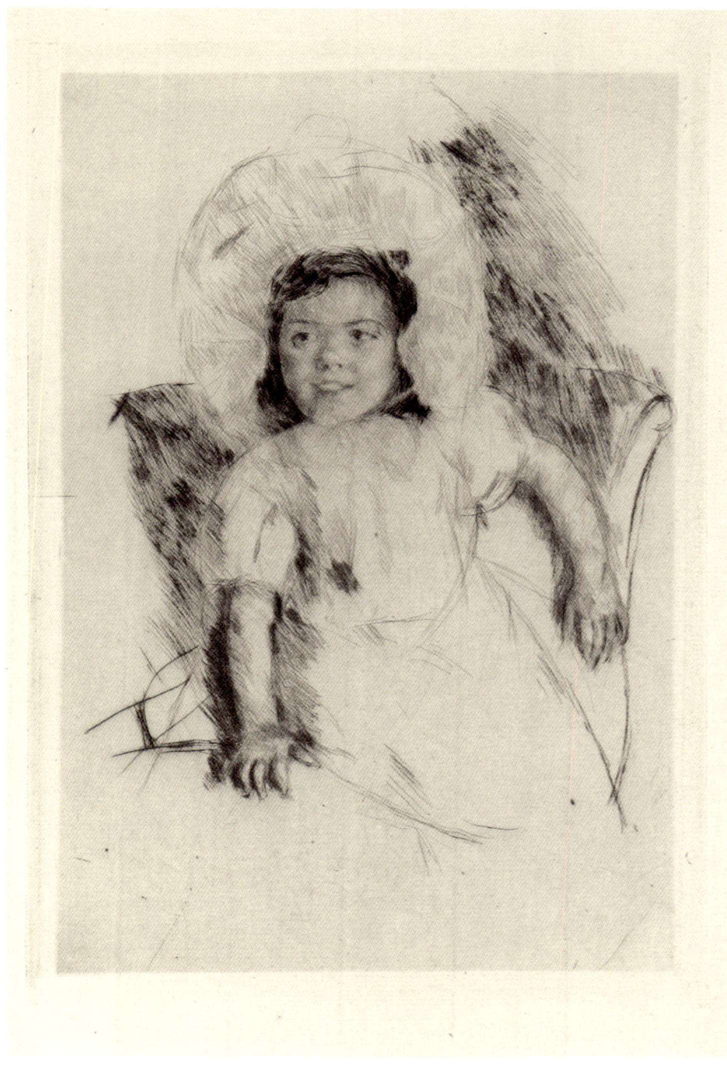

Margot Wearing a Bonnet (No. 3),
ca. 1902

Breeskin 181

Drypoint, a fine impression, printed with burr and even plate tone, wiped clean at the edges, on laid paper with Pro Patria watermark, the full sheet, in good condition (short tear in edge of right margin, and slight foxing noticeable almost exclusively in the margins)

Plate: 23.1 × 15.8 cm 9⅛ × 6¼ in.
Sheet: 35.1 × 20.9 cm 13¾ × 8¼ in.

This impression appears to show fresher burr than the example illustrated in Breeskin.

PROVENANCE
Roger Marx [1859–1913] (black stamp lower right corner, *recto*, Lugt 2229)

Margot Wearing a Bonnet (No. 5),
ca. 1902

Breeskin 183

Drypoint, signed in full, on laid paper with VanderLey watermark, the full sheet, in good condition

Plate: 17.9 × 14.3 cm 7 × 5⅝ in.
Sheet: 35.8 × 25.5 cm 14⅛ × 10 in.

Probably Breeskin's first state of two, though evidently signed at a later date. (The quality of the present impression corresponds with Breeskin's illustration of the first state.)

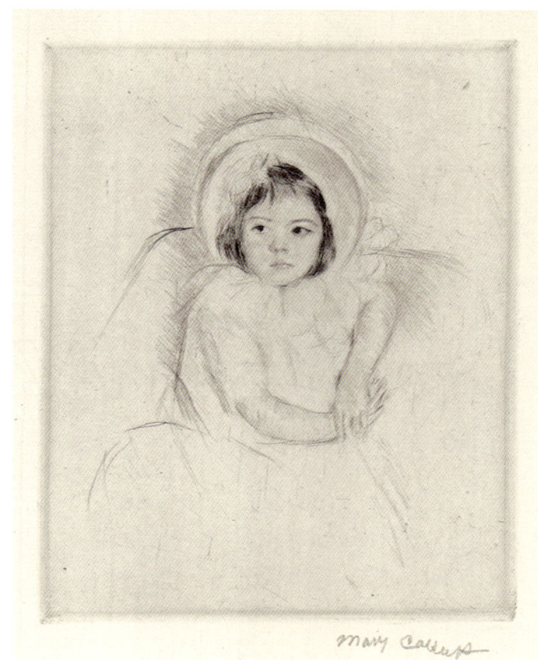

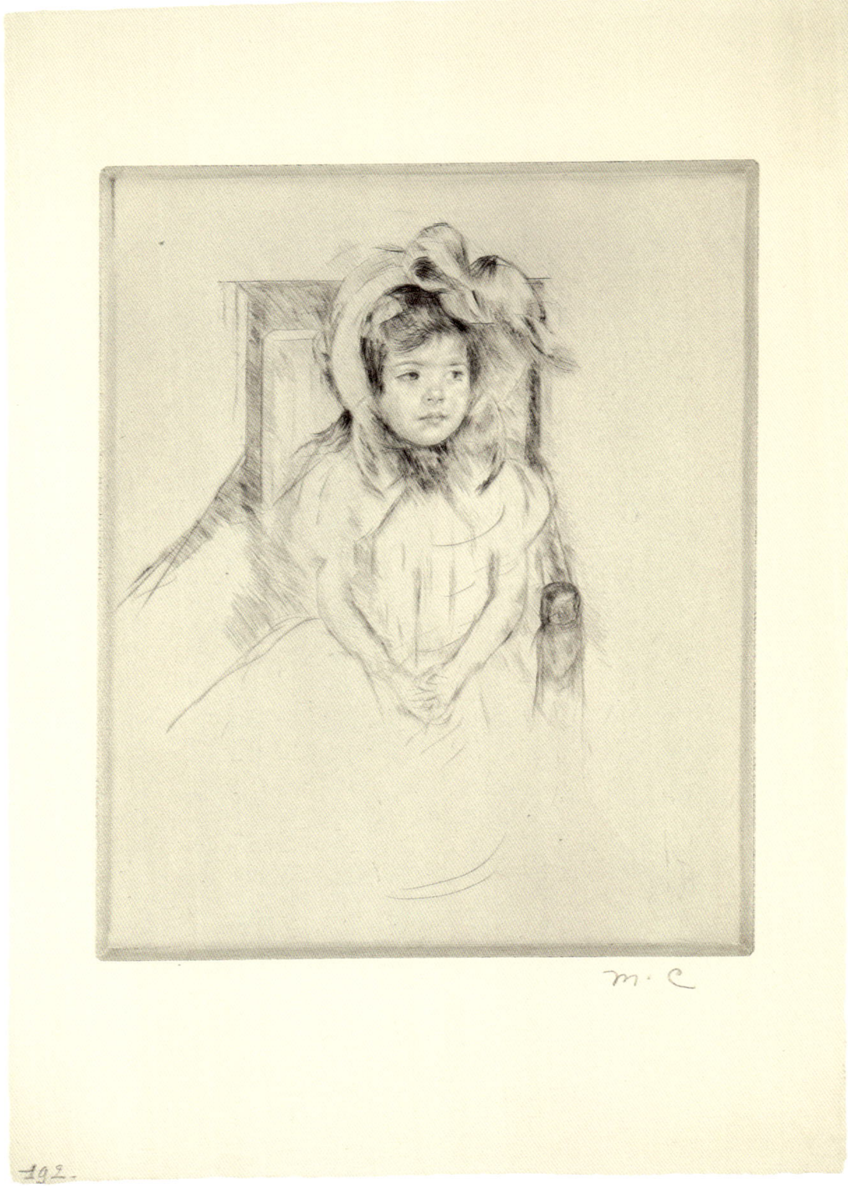

Margot in a Poke Bonnet, ca. 1902

Breeskin 184+

Drypoint, only state, on heavy, laid paper, the full sheet, in good condition apart from minor soiling

Plate: 34.2 × 22.9 cm 13⅝ × 9 in.
Sheet: 49.9 × 32.4 cm 19⅝ × 12¾ in.

This drypoint sketch on a worn plate is perhaps unique.

[Described and illustrated in Breeskin]

Margot Wearing a Large Bonnet Seated in an Armchair, ca. 1904

Breeskin 192

Drypoint, a fine impression, printed with burr and plate tone, a proof aside from the intended edition of 50, initialed *M. C*, on laid paper with watermark A. PORCABEUF, the full sheet, in good condition

Plate: 29.8 × 23.9 cm 11¾ × 9⅜ in.
Sheet: 44.1 × 31 cm 17⅜ × 12⅛ in.

The Velvet Sleeve, ca. 1904

Breeskin 194

Drypoint, only state, an exceptionally fine impression, with strong burr and plate tone, initialed *M. C*, on laid paper with Vanderley watermark, the full sheet, in good condition (slight crinkling at corners from plate pressure), annotated *A* and *HP* in the lower edge

Plate: 24.3 × 16.8 cm 9⅝ × 6⅝ in.
Sheet: 35.2 × 21 cm 13⅞ × 8¼ in.

[See illustration on facing page, top left]

The Velvet Sleeve, ca. 1904

Breeskin 194

Drypoint, only state, a fine impression, printed with burr and plate tone, initialed *M C*, on laid paper with Vanderley watermark, the full sheet, in good condition (slight crinkling at corners from plate pressure), annotated *B* at lower left (*no. 34* at lower right)

Plate: 24.4 × 16.8 cm 9⅝ × 6⅝ in.
Sheet: 34.8 × 20.5 cm 13¾ × 8⅛ in.

[See illustration on facing page, top right]

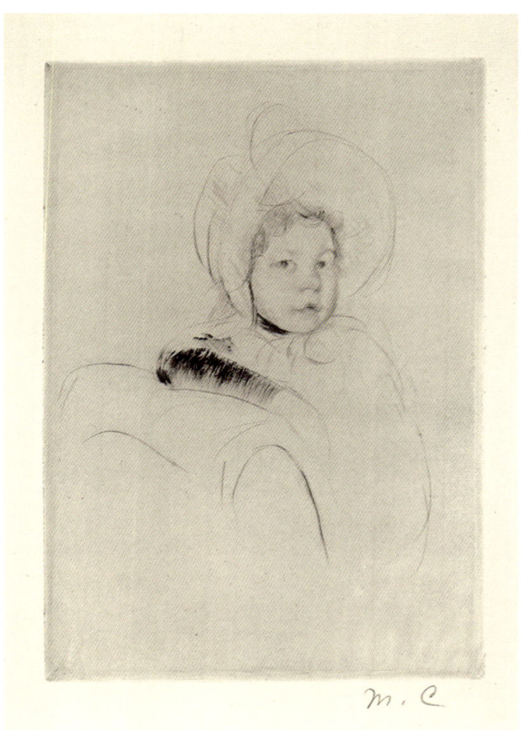

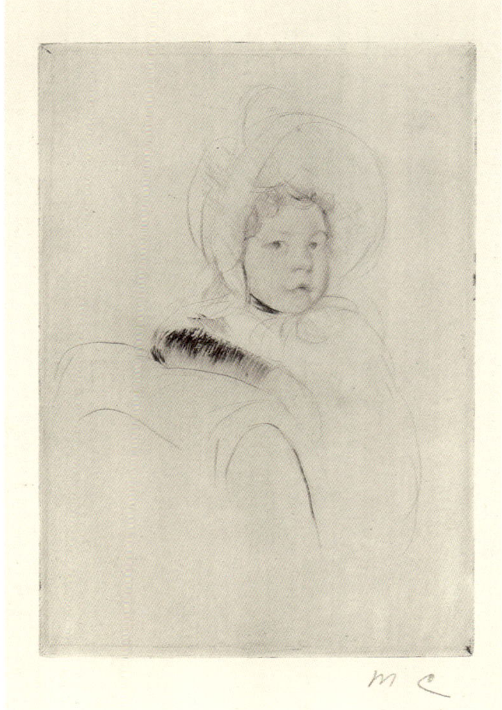

Sara Wearing Her Bonnet and Coat, ca. 1904

Breeskin 198

Transfer lithograph, a fine impression of this subject, with unusually good tonal range, on laid paper with watermarks MBM *(FRANCE) INGRES D'ARCHES*, the full sheet, in good condition apart from slight darkening of paper tone on verso, and a few iron flecks in the manufacture of the sheet

Sheet: 62.8 × 48 cm 24¾ × 18⅞ in.

[See illustration at right]

Sara Wearing Her Bonnet and Coat, ca. 1904

Breeskin 198

Transfer lithograph, on laid paper with watermarks MBM *(FRANCE) INGRES D'ARCHES*, the full sheet, in good condition apart from slight darkening of paper tone on verso, and a few iron flecks in the manufacture of the sheet

Sheet: 62.8 × 48 cm 24¾ × 18⅞ in.

[Not illustrated]

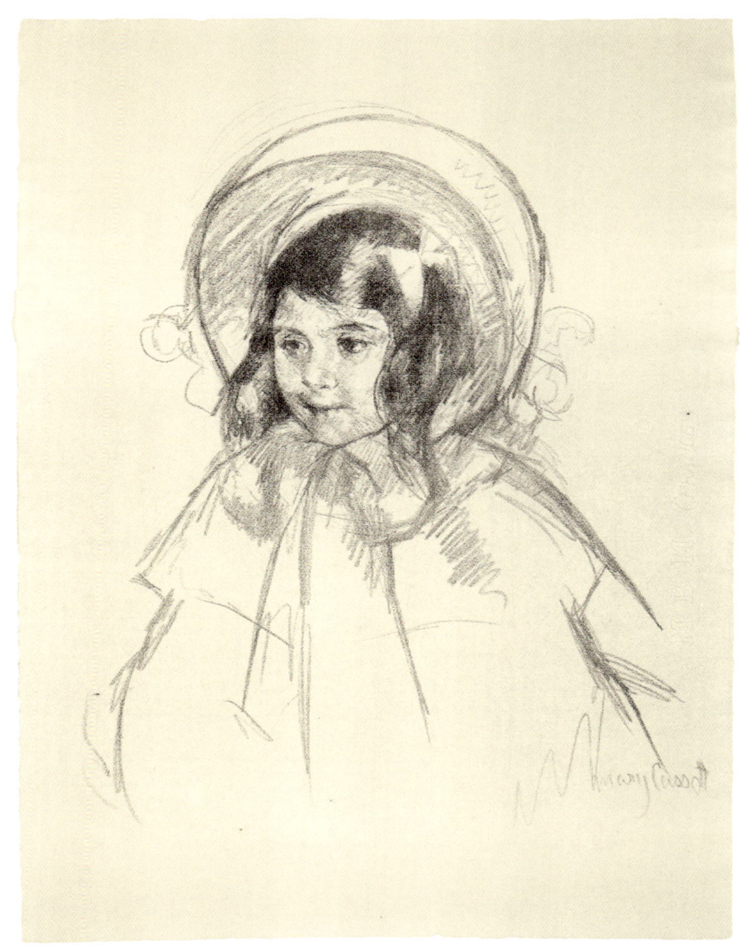

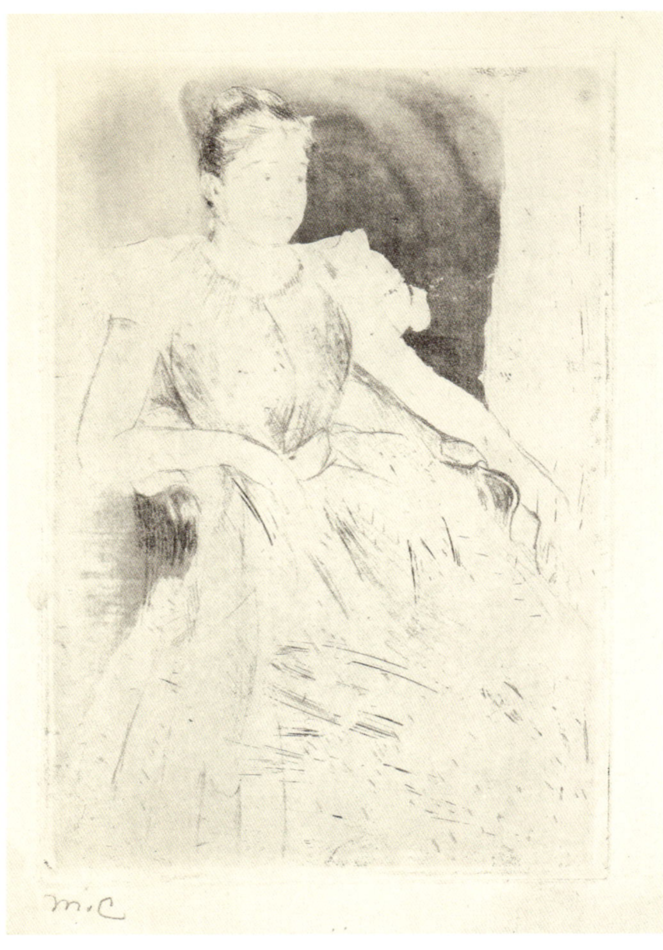

Denise Holding Her Child, ca. 1905

Breeskin 204

Drypoint, printed in colors *à la poupée,* with the tone for the lips and rosy cheek subtly distinguished from the flesh tones, and the eyes carefully accented in black ink, on laid paper, with margins, in good condition apart from some pale foxing in margins, a crease across lower right corner

Plate: 20.9 × 14.9 cm   8¼ × 5⅞ in.
Sheet: 25.8 × 20.1 cm   10⅛ × 7⅞ in.

This subject was not previously known as existing in impressions printed in colors, and, though finer than the reprints, it appears unlikely from the style of the color that this impression is early.

Katharine Kelso Cassatt, ca. 1905 [ca. 1888]

Breeskin 198+

Soft-ground and aquatint, initialed *M. C,* on laid paper with edge of letters watermark, the full sheet, in good condition apart from slight discoloration and soiling, mainly at the edges, and a small, pale stain at left platemark

Plate: 23.8 × 15.9 cm   9⅜ × 6¼ in.
Sheet: 27.9 × 22.7 cm   11 × 8⅞ in.

Breeskin dates this work, which she knew only in this apparently unique impression, ca. 1905, but a date of 1888–1889 appears more consistent with the style and technique of the works of this earlier period. The sitter has been re-identified as Cassatt's niece, rather than her mother, as previously assumed.

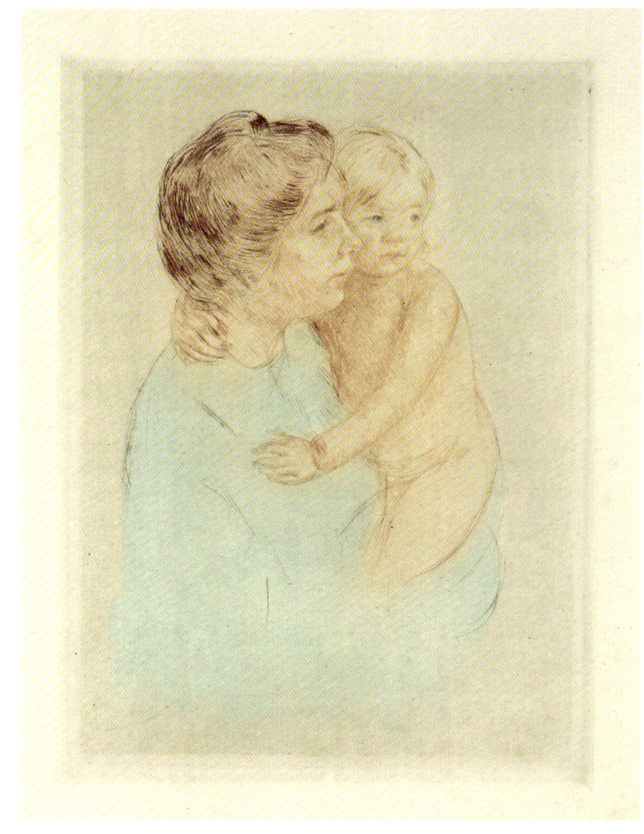

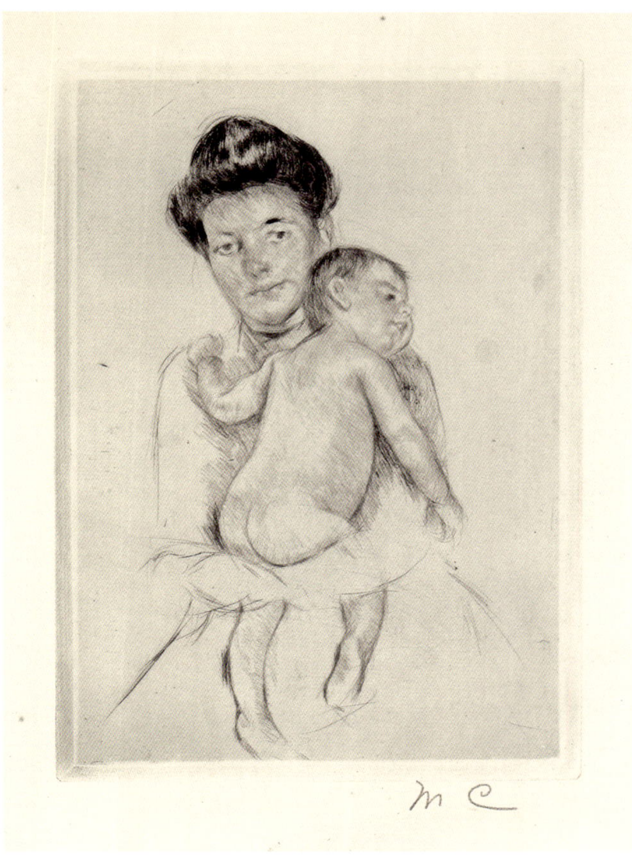

Denise in Profile to Right with a Hand Mirror, ca. 1909

Breeskin 208+

Drypoint, printed in black ink with plate tone, wiped clean at the plate edges, and showing some burr, on heavy laid paper, the full sheet, in good condition apart from some soiling in the edges

Plate: 26 × 20.7 cm 10¼ × 8⅛ in.
Sheet: 50.2 × 32.4 cm 19¾ × 12¾ in.

This is the only known impression.

[Illustrated in Breeskin]

Antoinette's Caress (No. 1), ca. 1909

Breeskin 209

Drypoint, Breeskin's first state of two (before the edition of nine in the second state printed by Delâtre in 1923), initialed *M.C*, a fine impression, showing the delicate drypoint work, and with even plate tone, on laid paper with script watermark A. Porcabeuf, the full sheet, in good condition, annotated at lower left *superbe epr.*

Plate: 20.8 × 15 cm 8¼ × 5⅞ in.
Sheet: 30.8 × 22.1 cm 12⅛ × 8¾ in.

One of perhaps only one or two early impressions.

Mother Holding Her Nude Baby, ca. 1900

Breeskin 206

Drypoint, first state of two, a fine impression, printed with burr, and with the fine drypoint work showing clearly throughout, with plate tone, partly wiped clean along the platemark, initialed *M C*, on laid paper with a coat of arms watermark, in good condition apart from a small tear in the top left corner, a soft diagonal crease running a little into the plate area from the left margin, and an irregular, inherent, nearly vertical crease in the right margin, a few small and unobtrusive stains in blank background at right

Plate: 20.9 × 14.9 cm 8¼ × 5⅞ in.
Sheet: 31.6 × 20.5 cm 12½ × 8⅛ in.

Breeskin noted the existence of an impression of this state, but illustrated only her second state, which was from the edition of nine printed in 1923 by Delâtre.

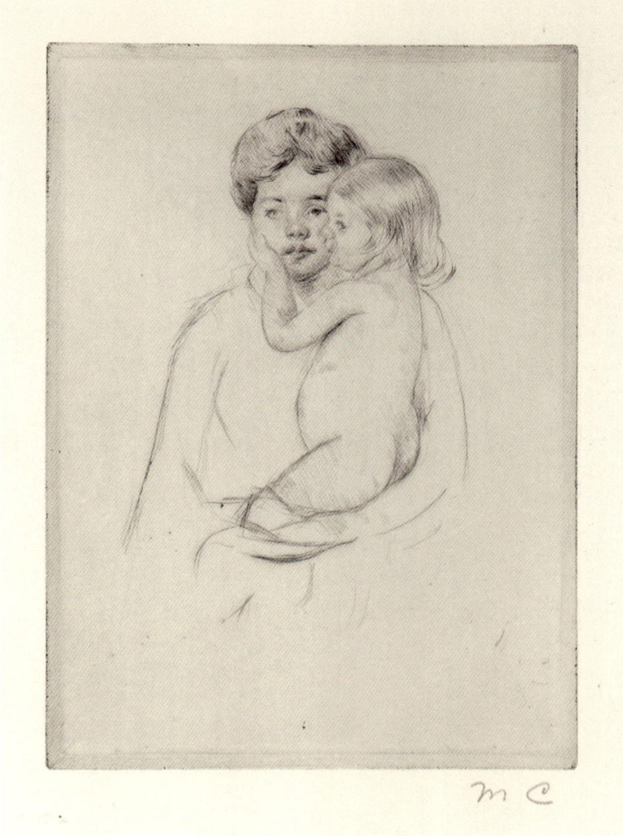

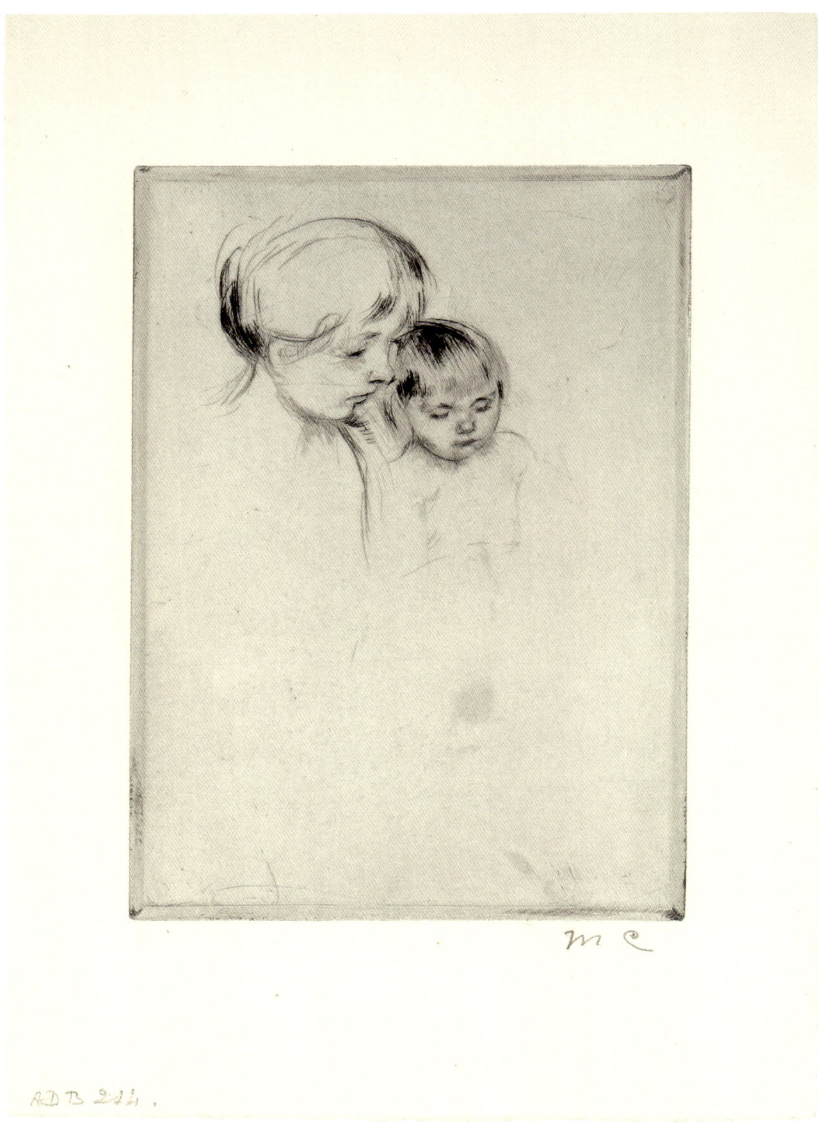

The Picture Book (No. 2), ca. 1910

Breeskin 214

Drypoint, Breeskin's first state of two (before the edition of nine in the second state printed by Delâtre in 1923), initialed *M C*, a fine impression, with burr, and showing the delicate drypoint work, with even plate tone, on laid paper with script watermark A. Porcabeuf, the full sheet, in good condition apart from a few stains in the plate area

Plate: 20.8 × 15 cm 8¼ × 5⅞ in.
Sheet: 30.8 × 22.1 cm 12⅛ × 8¾ in.

One of perhaps only one or two early impressions.

Woman Trying on a Necklace before a Mirror, ca. 1910

Breeskin 216+

Drypoint, printed with plate tone, wiped clean at the edges, on laid paper with ARCHES watermark, the full sheet, in good condition apart from slight crinkling from printing pressure, and a few handling creases

Plate: 30.8 × 23.9 cm 12⅛ × 9⅜ in.
Sheet: 43.8 × 30.6 cm 17¼ × 12 in.

The only known impression of this work.

[Illustrated in Breeskin, but with incorrect number, 218+]

Woman Posed with Hand at Back of Head, ca. 1910

Breeskin 217

Drypoint, a rare, early impression, printed with plate tone, wiped clean at the edges, on laid paper with ARCHES watermark, the full sheet, in good condition apart from slight crinkling from printing pressure, and a few handling creases

Plate: 30.8 × 23.9 cm 12⅛ × 9⅜ in.
Sheet: 43.8 × 30.6 cm 17¼ × 12 in.

[See illustration on facing page, lower left]

Woman Posed with Hand at Back of Head, ca. 1910

Breeskin 217

Drypoint, reprint, on heavy, white wove paper with RIVES watermark, the full sheet, in good condition

Plate: 30.8 × 24 cm 12⅛ × 9⅜ in.
Sheet: 49.7 × 32.3 cm 19⅝ × 12¾ in.

The existence of this reprint is not noted by Breeskin.

[Not illustrated]

Heads of Denise and Child, ca. 1910

Breeskin 218+

Drypoint, on heavy laid paper, the full sheet, in generally good condition apart from a few handling creases, and some soiling and a few short tears in the very large margins

Plate: 30.2 × 36.8 cm 11⅞ × 14½ in.
Sheet: 49.8 × 65 cm 19⅝ × 25⅝ in.

The only known impression of this work, illustrated in Breeskin, but with incorrect number.

Slight Sketch of Mother's Head, ca. 1910

Breeskin 219

Drypoint, on laid paper, with large margins, in good condition

Plate: 33.4 × 22.5 cm 13⅛ × 8⅞ in.
Sheet: 42.6 × 29.7 cm 16¾ × 11⅝ in.

[See illustration below, right]

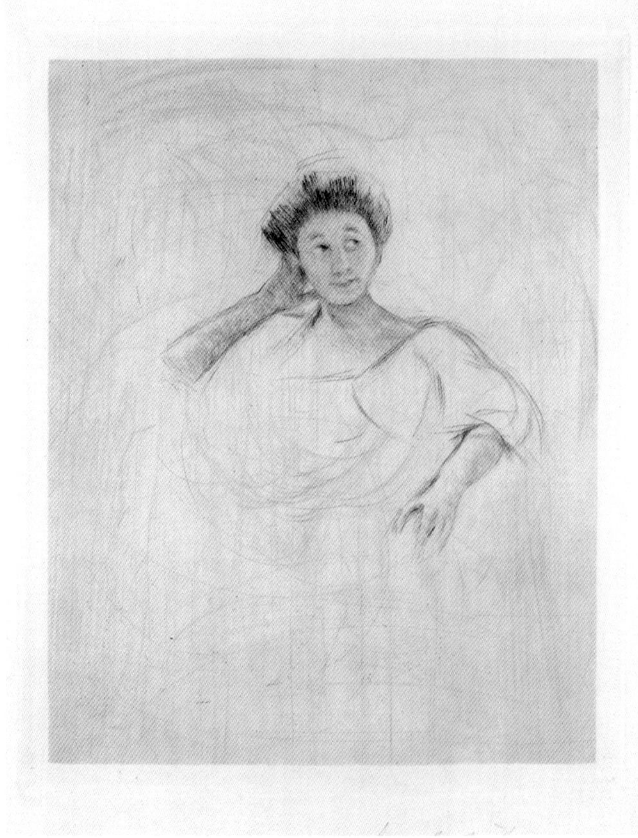

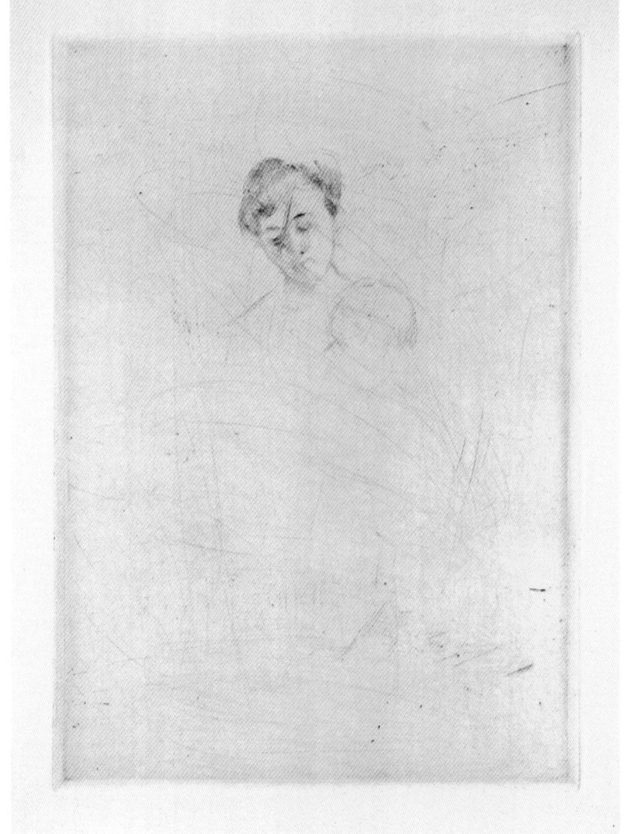

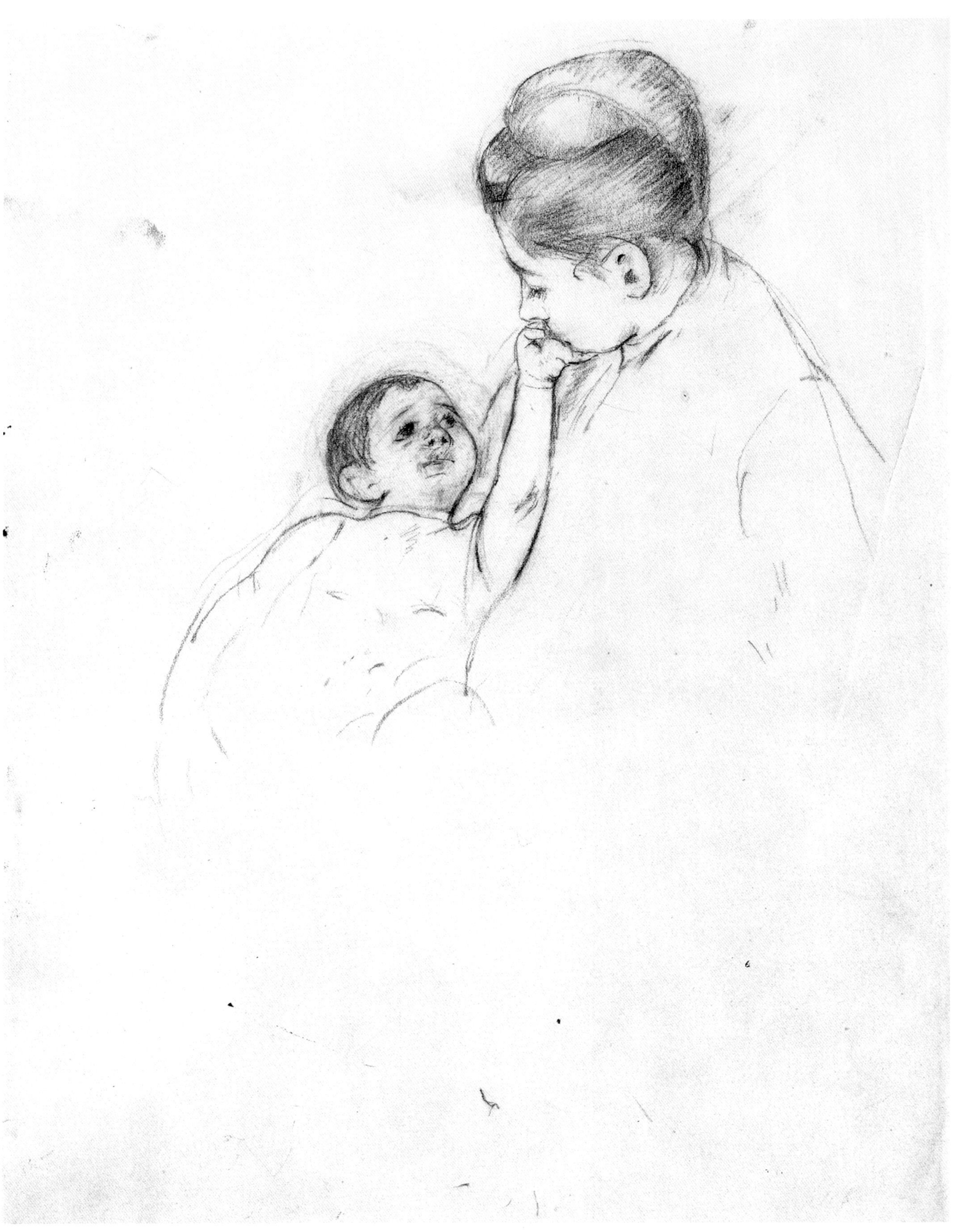

Mary Cassatt: Drawing on Drawing

Mary Cassatt: Prints and Drawings from the Artist's Studio not only provides an in-depth view of the achievement in graphic art of this important and innovative artist but also adds greatly to our understanding of Cassatt's working methods. This publication affords us the opportunity to re-examine her relationship with and distinction from her colleagues in the modern art scene of later nineteenth-century France while providing a glimpse of the originality and determination of an artist whose creative life is still very much a mystery and subject to wide interpretation. Despite the ever-increasing number of publications about the artist, the relative scarcity of documentation coupled with her own reticence and isolation from the very artistic circle in which she played a significant part has made it a necessity for critics and scholars to draw their conclusions from her work itself. And many of the assumed facts about that work, concerning title, date, provenance, and subject, are still undergoing scrutiny as the work of the Catalogue Raisonné Committee advances.

Given the changing currents of artistic and political dialogue the interpretation of Cassatt's work has been highly subjective. There is a great deal we still need to discover about what Cassatt intended and how well she accomplished her goals. Mary Cassatt has long been thought of as an Impressionist and as a painter of a rather narrow range of subjects. The complicated evolution of her working method, style, and subject matter is, in fact, still being charted. The 1989 exhibition *Mary Cassatt: The Color Prints* first seriously explored how Cassatt carried the creation of a work of art through many stages towards final completion and documented the unconventional approach she brought to her uniquely realized color prints and to other aspects of her graphic art as well. More recently, the essay "Innovation and Tradition in Mary Cassatt's Pastels: A Study of Her Methods and Materials" by Harriet Stratis published in connection with the exhibition, *Mary Cassatt: Modern Woman*, provided fresh and important insights into Cassatt's relentless exploration of the pastel medium, an area in which she proved to be an imaginative and successful practitioner. Both of these investigations reveal much about Cassatt's unique artistic personality as well as serving to tie her even more

The First Caress, 1890–1891

Not in BrCR

Black chalk, on thin, buff, wove paper

Sheet: 32.1 × 24.8 cm   12⅝ × 9¾ in.

This work and another drawing, *The First Caress* (BrCR 800; Avery Collection, New York Public Library), may be preparatory studies for the pastel, *Baby's First Caress* (BrCR 189; New Britain Museum of American Art, New Britain, CT).

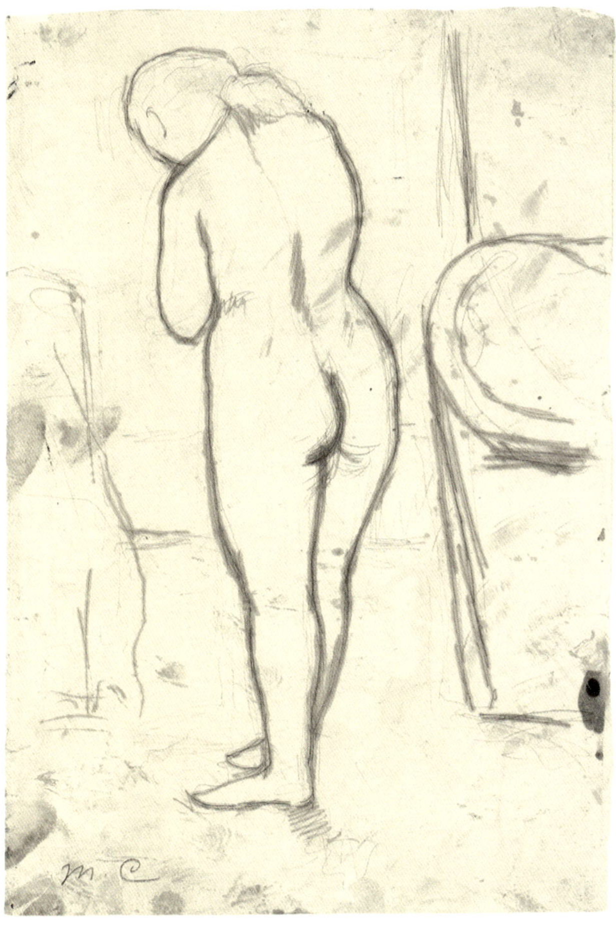

BrCR 706

Drawing for "Standing Nude," ca. 1879

BrCR 706

Pencil, on thin, buff, wove paper, traced over for soft-ground etching (with offset of soft-ground on *verso*, showing through)

Initialed in pencil, *M. C*, and annotated in blue pencil on verso, *PH 93*

Sheet: 28.2 × 18.3 cm   11⅛ × 7¼ in.

The preparatory drawing for the soft-ground etching, *Standing Nude (Dark)* (Breeskin 8).

The etching is known only in a state with the figure alone (covered with a dark grain), and with the background details removed.

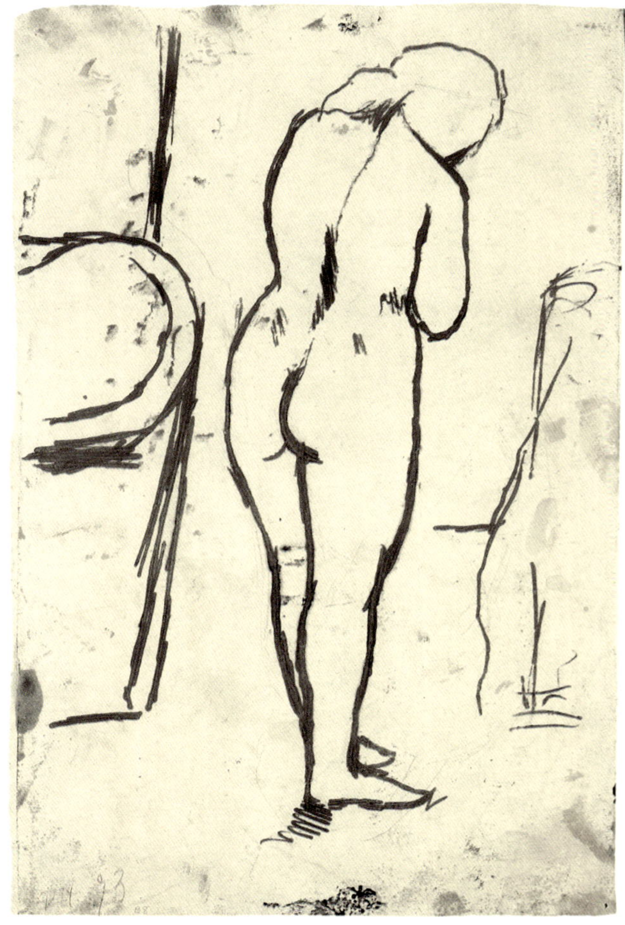

BrCR 706 *verso*

closely to her era, no matter how individual or idiosyncratic her subject matter might appear.

The "studio collection" both underscores and amplifies the appreciation of the imaginative meanderings of Cassatt's artistic personality and also suggests another important area of study: the changing role of drawing in her work. Only a small clutch of drawings by Mary Cassatt exists to provide insight into this topic. These remaining sketches present a tantalizing mystery: are they merely a few surviving pieces from what was a larger body of drawn works, or do they attest to the limited role of drawing for an artist who, as an "Impressionist," worked directly in front of her subject, shortening the distance between perception and picture making? Given this small number of extant drawings, the presence of more than 30 in the present collection affords the opportunity for us to examine afresh Cassatt's subtle dexterity and her immediate response to subject, and to pose the question about where drawing fits in her artistic process. Cassatt had, very early in her career, rejected the preeminence of drawing, especially the dry conventions of rendering promulgated by the Academy as the cornerstone of artistic achievement. Traditional art education saw drawing as the fundamental tool for the depiction of forms, the definition of space, and the overall harmony and order of a composition.

Despite Cassatt's fondness for and continuing study of historical art, her own work followed a different path. She utilized the knowledge garnered from her art studies but depended on her own visual experiences as well as the lessons learned firsthand in the studio in directing her creative course. From the beginning of her studies, Cassatt was impatient to work with oil paint to translate her visual experience into an expressive and personal statement. As her work evolved in response to an increasingly modern sensibility, drawing became, at best, a modest tool in the creation of her art. Paradoxically, it would be her growing enthusiasm for printmaking in the decade of the 1880s that ultimately established drawing as a significant pursuit.

While Mary Cassatt apparently did not follow the traditional path of developing a painting from preliminary drawings and designs, she did employ drawings and sketches as an adjunct to her search for suitable subjects for her art. As she fell under the sway of the circle of advanced artists in Paris in the 1870s and turned to depictions of modern life, she produced a handful of small pencil sketches that document the world around her. These sketches were sometimes bounded by lines, suggesting that they were also compositional notations and provided a stimulus for the choice of subject for some of her canvases of the 1870s and 1880s. Taken at the theater or opera as well as recording friends and family engaged in quiet domestic and polite social activities, they also served as a visual diary. They are often quickly rendered, concerned more with mass, figural relationships, and the aspect of light in a particular environment than with a close rendering of the subject and setting.

Drawings played a more pivotal role in the creation of prints, in which Cassatt became increasingly involved in the 1880s. Many of her prints were directly related to drawings that were created either as original compositions or as graphic translations of previously executed pastels and oil paintings. Nearly all of her most complex drawings relate directly to major print compositions. Her prints, in turn, increasingly depended for their success on her skills as a draftsman as well as on her experimental attitude and technical expertise.

Sometimes drawings were utilized even more directly, as when they were used to transfer the composition to the plate. A drawing was laid on the prepared plate and the major lines traced over. In the process, the ground was removed from the plate and picked up by the paper. The reverse of sheets such as *Drawing for "Standing Nude"* (p. 128), employed in this way, still show the soft ground that was transferred during this procedure.

Cassatt was energetic and productive as a printmaker and undoubtedly she produced more drawings than are currently known, lending credence to her claim in a letter of about 1906 that she had destroyed a quantity of her own work. That fate makes the handful of surviving works all the more precious.

The subjects of her prints and the drawings related to them are diverse and apparently random, suggesting that Cassatt was testing both the process itself and the range of images that would be appropriate and effective as prints. Her Impressionist colleagues had frequently repeated specific scenes and subjects, developing them into what could be described as "series works." By contrast, and in spite of her intense and focused activity in printmaking, Cassatt's work appears more exploratory and searching. This tendency would change somewhat after the turn of the century when her art shifted in ambition and focus.

Most of the drawings in the "studio collection" date from around 1903–1904. (These are all undated but can be assigned an approximate date based on their relationship to paintings and pastels.) Along with other drawings known from this period, they form a uniquely comprehensive body of drawings that stands in virtual isolation in the whole of Cassatt's oeuvre. The creation of these drawings at a time when she was transforming her art suggests that she saw drawing as a useful tool in this process. While they may have survived by accident and may be only a small portion of a much larger group of now lost drawings, the fact that these drawings come from a period of creative transition might equally imply that this was a momentary exercise.

It is clear that during this period Cassatt was struggling to renew her art in relation to her own past history as well as in response to newer artistic ideas with which she was out of sympathy. As a hard-working and dedicated professional, she strove to keep her work fresh, vigorous, and up-to-date while remaining true to her own artistic principles. Around 1900, in response to increasingly radical artistic innovations, she can be seen to turn inward. She was less concerned with "modern" issues and themes and ignored the external stimuli of the current artistic landscape, thus allowing her art to evolve out of its own imperatives. As her friends and colleagues in the Impressionist circle grew apart or died, Cassatt worked increasingly in isolation, immune to the latest innovations and becoming, in certain ways, more academic, even while embracing some avant-garde compositional and color strategies. Some of these ideas she had garnered from her printmaking experience and especially from the innovations of her color print work. The drawings and prints therefore can be seen as providing a significant index of Cassatt's artistic concerns as well as the vehicle for successive transitions in her work.

Having begun somewhat timidly as a printmaker and in great measure under the influence of Degas, she brought the same dedication to first mastering and then pushing the boundaries of the process that she showed elsewhere in her art. Her series of printmaking campaigns became, at times, all consuming. She focused on technical and aesthetic goals in a still novel field of endeavor, working side by side with the printer in proofing various stages and frequently reworking plates until she was satisfied with the image. Each episode of her printmaking found resonance in the rest of her work, whether it be her early, "Impressionist" work in soft-ground etching, her adoption of a linear format in her drypoints (often mixed and overlaid with earlier tonal modes), underscoring the importance of drawing in contrast to the loose brushwork of Impressionism, or her ultimate foray into color etching, which increased her understanding of the abstract patterned aspect of the picture plane. But it was probably this last phase of color printmaking that most profoundly influenced her later artistic path. The deepened understanding of abstract values in line, color, and composition propelled her towards the creation of the pictorially complex but successfully integrated compositions that characterize her twentieth-century work.

While it is likely that she approached her paintings and pastels as an immediate process involving the close translation of experience into the fabric of art, the creation of prints is indirect and product oriented, with multiple interim stages leading to the final result. The work is achieved over time but the artist's evolutionary engagement disappears in the ultimate coalescence of the final work. Her painting and pastels after the turn of the century seem to also reflect the influence of that multi-layered approach that is integral to the printmaking process. She began to see painting as a process of picture making, in which a motif would be explored from various points of view and themes repeated until their possibilities had been exhausted. In adopting this approach, she also recalled her early academic training as well as her own personal study of old masters. Her art, while maintaining its modern edge, thus also revealed its traditional underpinnings and was increasingly the combined product of observation and fabrication melded into a final synthesis. Drawing took on an importance in the way states of a print carried the image forward to its final resolution. In addition to these "preliminary" drawings, Cassatt also produced summary oil sketches and partially realized pastels that she would carry only as far as necessary to capture the effect or character she sought. These were not false starts but rather cumulative byways on the road towards the realization of an image felt but not yet articulated. While this process was logical in the preparation of complex or elaborate compositions, it is somewhat surprising to see her proceeding in the same way for less ambitious works.

The current group of drawings should be viewed in light of this process and, indeed, helps us to understand it. A few of these drawings are multi-figure compositions, relating to finished works, and these might well have served the more traditional role as compositional studies, but most of the drawings in this group are renderings of individual figures—often a child who might eventually appear in either a single-subject work or in a multi-figure composition. While not intended as portrait likenesses, these drawings detail the specifics of expression and costume with an accuracy that suggests Cassatt's continuing interest in observation while working to translate her subject into a motif. In many of these drawings it is the face alone that is the artist's focus, while the rest of the body, if present at all, is barely sketched in. Numerous pastels and oils of this period follow a similar format, demonstrating a remarkable degree of finish in the face in relation to the rest of the picture.

In her drawings, Cassatt was concerned with both light and volume. In spite of the limitations of her medium, she achieved a fleshy appearance, giving vitality and character to her subjects. Her line is both searching and assured. She struggled at times to fix boundaries and to render volume convincingly while in other drawings she succeeded with the barest notational lines. What impresses finally about these drawings is that, despite their often modest scale, they demonstrate a confidence and a finesse that belies the likely hurried pace of their rendering. Many of these drawings are of children and this rapidity may reflect the limited time of a sitting with a juvenile subject. It is, in fact, possible that Cassatt depended heavily on these drawings to work up more complex paintings and pastels, abstracting these numerous pencil notations into a more definitive statement in the studio. This could also help to explain how Cassatt avoided easy sentimentality while conveying the tender fragility of her young models. It is the character of childhood or the complexity of interrelationships between women and children as much as the children themselves that the artist succeeds in both memorializing and monumentalizing. In her smallest drawing and her grandest canvas, she translates minor incident and domestic intimacy into an engaging pictorial exercise and a distinctly modern expression.

Jay E. Cantor
Director
Mary Cassatt Catalogue Raisonné Committee

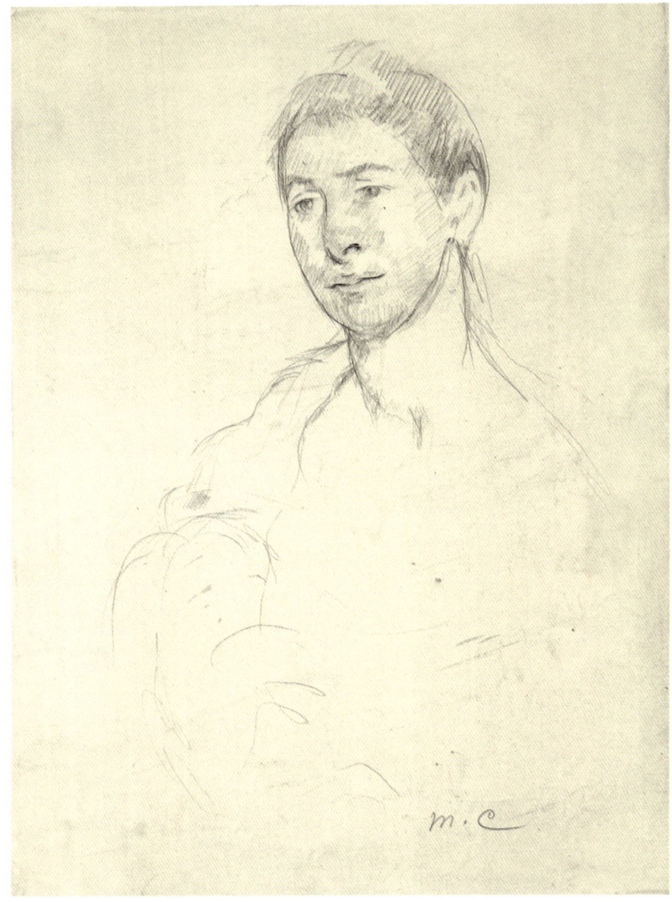

BrCR 819

Sketch for "Two Little Girls," ca. 1903–04

BrCR 833

Pencil, on thin, white, wove paper
Initialed *M. C,* annotated in blue chalk in the right edge, *133*

Fold line: 19.7 × 18.3 cm 7¾ × 7⅛ in.
Sheet: 25 × 32.3 cm 9⅞ × 12¾ in.

A sketch related to the drawing, *Two Little Girls* (BrCR 834; last known when sold at Sotheby Parke Bernet, Inc., Los Angeles, 1973). Both drawings may be studies for the pastel, *Two Little Girls* (BrCR 280; Indianapolis Museum of Art).

Study of a Woman's Head, ca. 1892

BrCR 819

Pencil, on wove paper with watermark J. W. ZANDERS 1886
Initialed *M. C,* annotated in blue chalk in the right edge, *PH 90*

Fold line: 42 × 30 cm 16½ × 11¾ in.
Sheet: 48 × 39.3 cm 18⅞ × 15½ in.

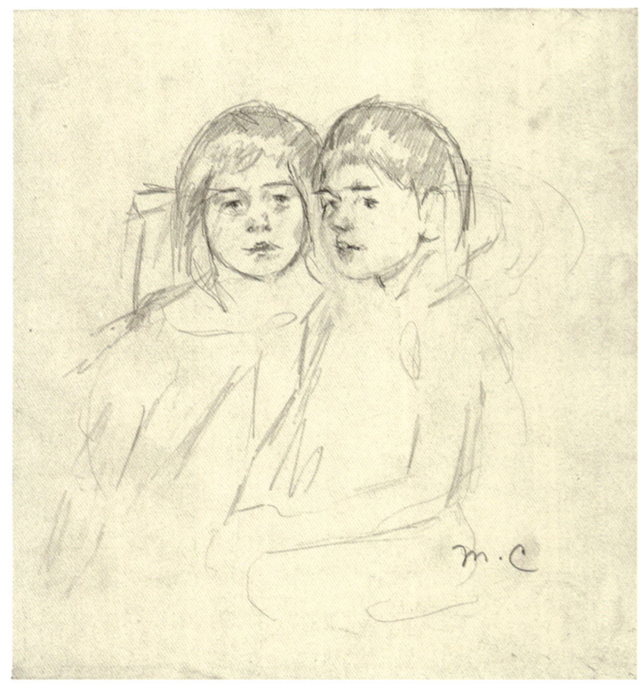

BrCR 833

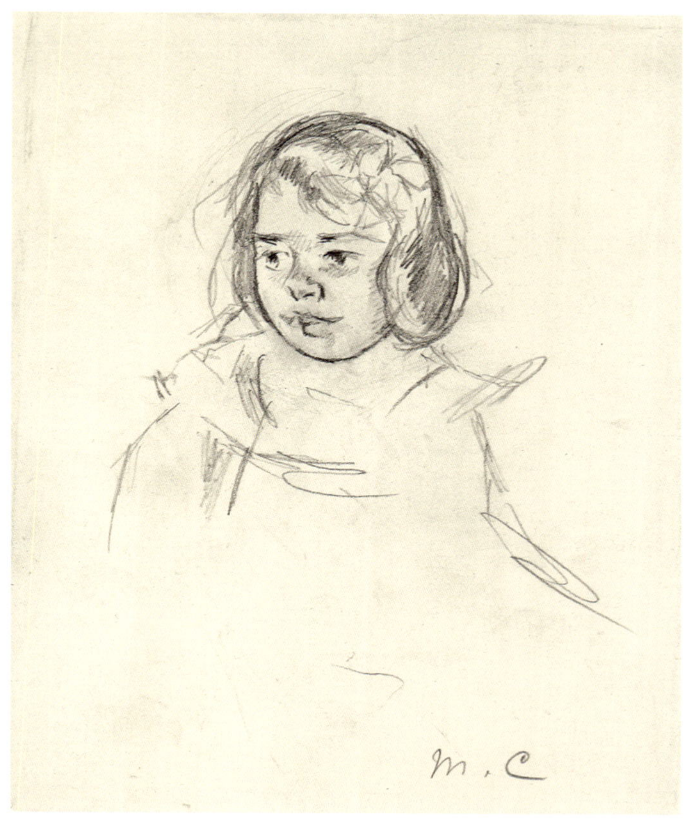

BrCR 850

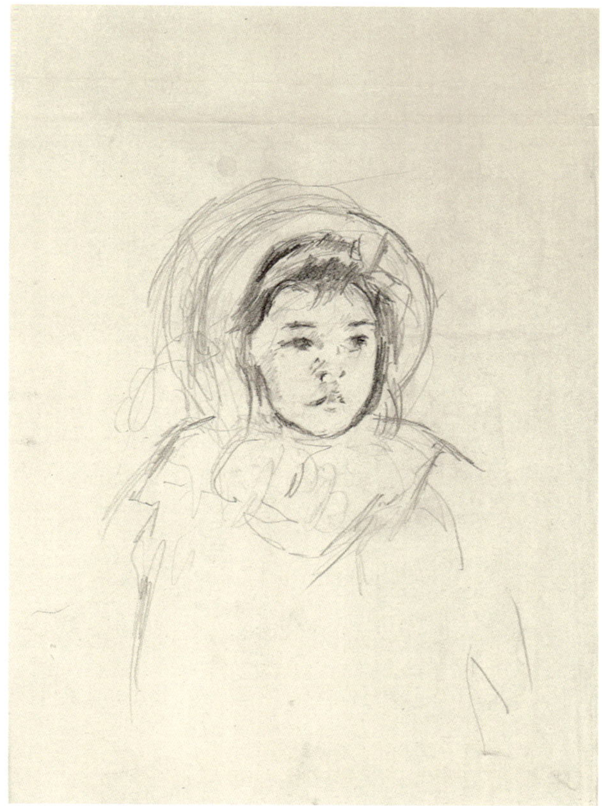

BrCR 850 *verso*

Sketch for "Sara Smiling" (No. 1), ca. 1903–04

Verso: another sketch of the same child

BrCR 850

Pencil, on thin, white, wove paper
Initialed *M. C*, annotated in blue chalk in the upper edge, *verso*, *123*
Fold line: 18.5 × 15 cm   7¼ × 5⅞ in.
Sheet: 31.5 × 20.2 cm   12⅜ × 8 in.

Sketch for "Sara Smiling" (No. 2), ca. 1903–04

BrCR 851

Pencil, on thin, white, wove paper
Initialed *M. C*, annotated in blue chalk in the upper edge, *111*

Fold line: 22.5 × 15.5 cm   8⅞ × 6⅛ in.
Sheet: 30.2 × 23.8 cm   11⅞ × 9⅜ in.

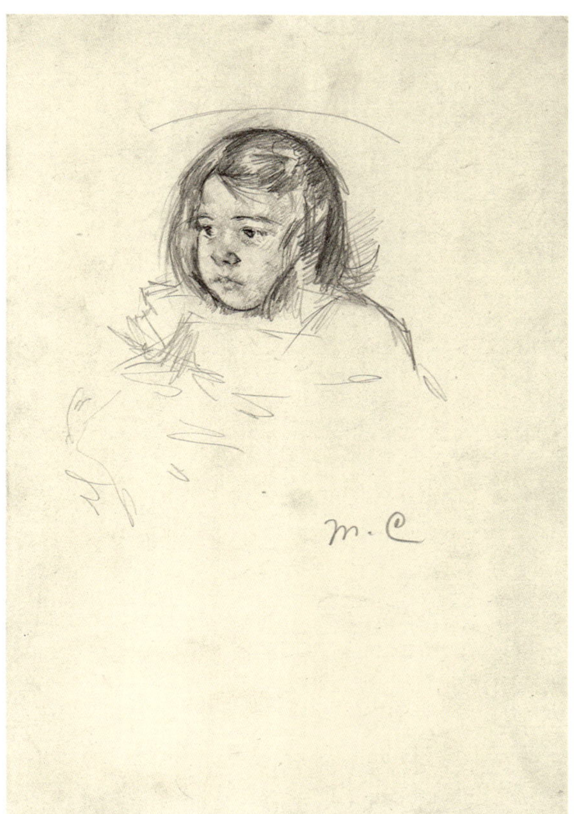

BrCR 851

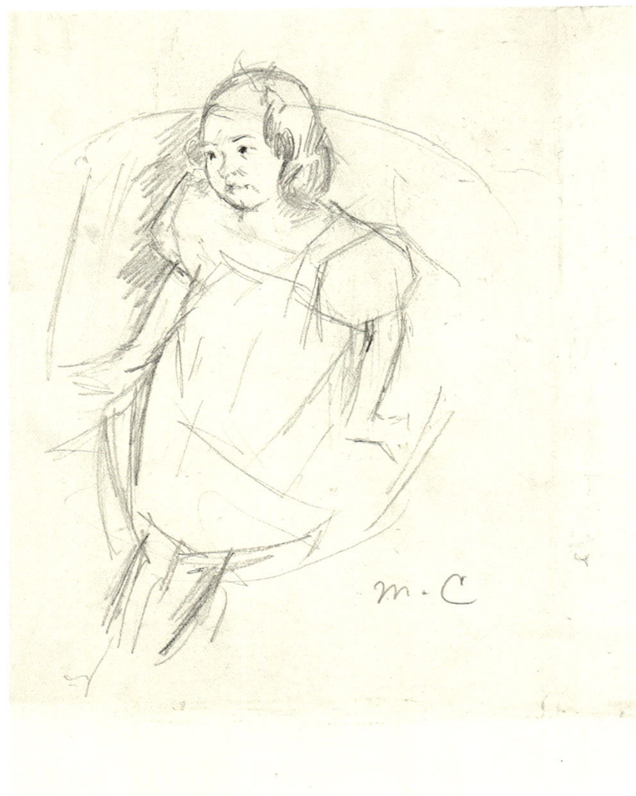

BrCR 853

Little Girl in a Party Dress,
ca. 1903–04

BrCr 853

Pencil, on thin, white, wove paper
Initialed *M. C,* annotated in blue chalk in the upper edge, *verso, 109*

Fold line: 20.3 × 15.5 cm   8 × 6⅛ in.
Sheet: 36 × 21.7 cm   14⅛ × 8½ in.

Study for "Portrait of Margot in a Large Red Bonnet," ca. 1903–04

BrCR 866

Pencil, on thin, white, wove paper
Initialed *M. C,* annotated in blue chalk in the lower right edge, *134*

Fold line: 18.2 × 13.3 cm   7⅛ × 5¼ in.
Sheet: 25 × 31.3 cm   9⅞ × 12¼ in.

Sketch related to the pastel (BrCR 425) in the Sterling and Francine Clark Art Institute, Willamstown, MA.

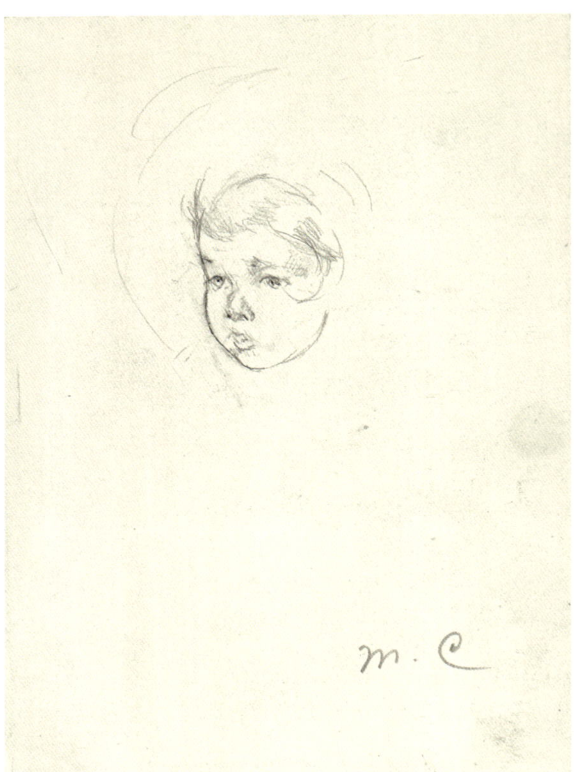

BrCR 866

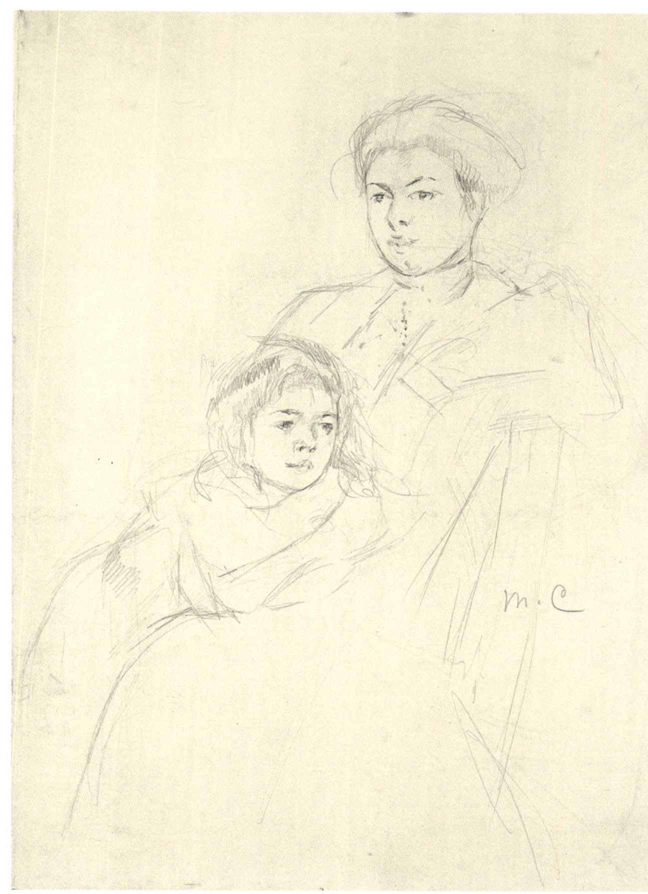

BrCR 862

Margot Leaning against Reine's Knee (No. 1), ca. 1903–04

BrCr 862

Verso: the figures lightly traced in blue, and an upside-down sketch of a head

Pencil, on wove paper
Initialed *M. C*, annotated in blue chalk in upper edge, *PH 88*

Fold line: 37.5 × 26.5 cm 14¾ × 10⅜ in.
Sheet: 50.2 × 32.5 cm 19¾ × 12¾ in.

Two diagonal blue lines on the mother's blouse, either accidental or related to the stripe on the sleeve in the related drypoint, *Margot Leaning against her Mother* (Breeskin 175).

Margot Leaning against Reine's Knee (No. 2), ca. 1903–04

BrCR 863

Pencil, on wove paper
Initialed *M. C*, annotated in blue chalk in upper edge, *PH 86*

Fold line: 37.5 × 27 cm 14¾ × 10⅝ in.
Sheet: 50.2 × 32.5 cm 19¾ × 12¾ in.

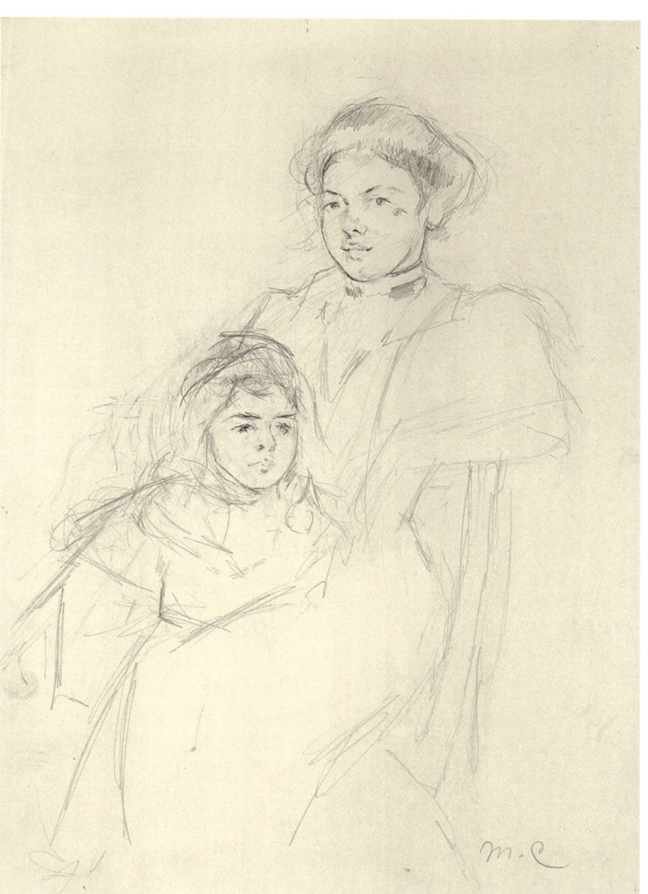

BrCR 863

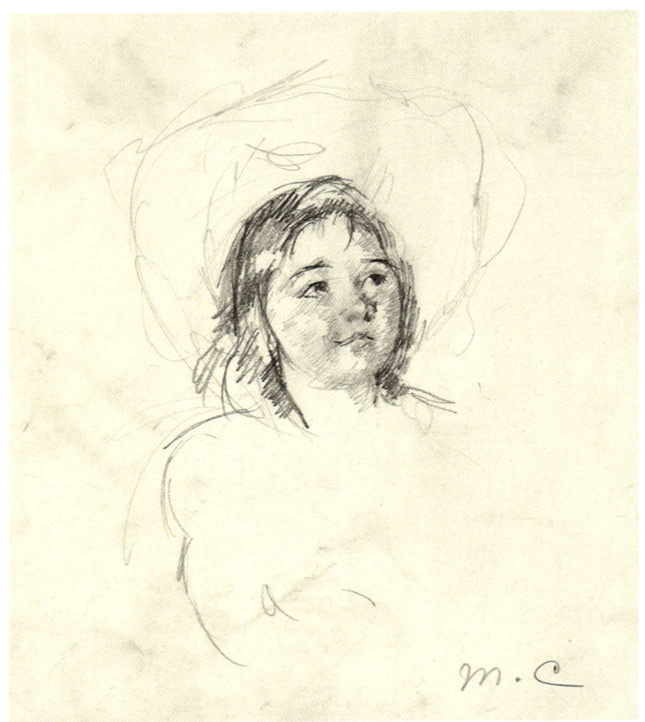

BrCR 874

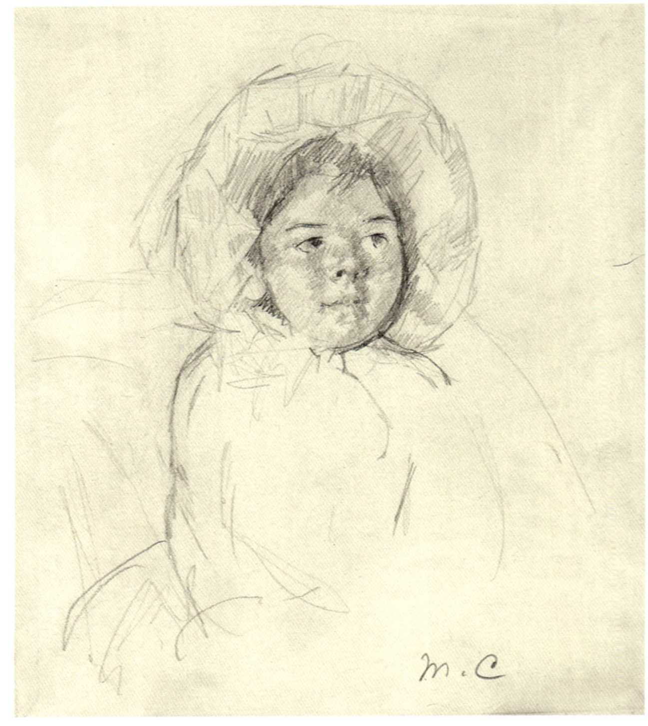

BrCR 875

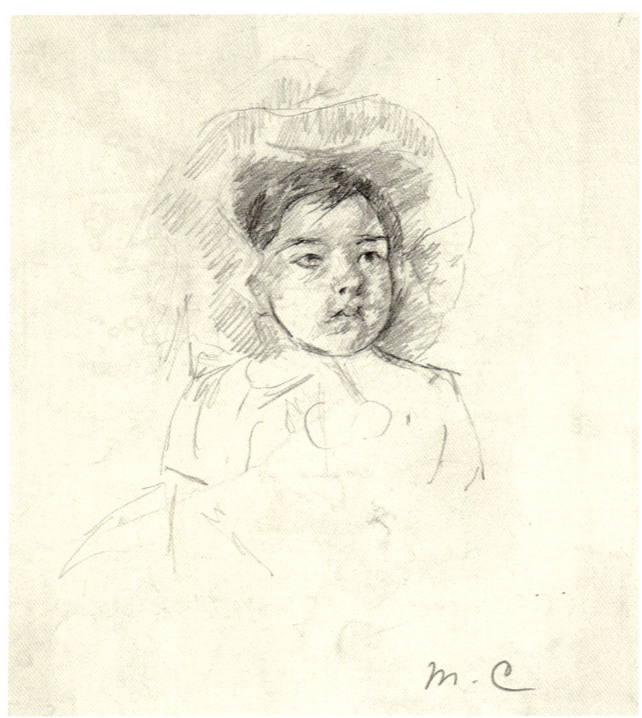

BrCR 876

Margot in a Ruffled Bonnet (No. 1),
ca. 1903–04

BrCR 874

Pencil, on thin, white, wove paper
Initialed *M. C,* annotated in blue chalk in the lower edge, *verso, 128*

Fold line: 18.5 × 16 cm 7¼ × 6¼ in.
Sheet: 31.3 × 20.1 cm 12¼ × 7⅞ in.

Margot in a Ruffled Bonnet (No. 2),
ca. 1903–04

BrCR 875

Pencil, on thin, white, wove paper
Initialed *M. C,* annotated in blue chalk in the lower edge, *verso, 129*

Fold line: 18.5 × 16 cm 7¼ × 6¼ in.
Sheet: 31.3 × 20.1 cm 12¼ × 7⅞ in.

Margot in a Ruffled Bonnet (No. 3),
ca. 1903–04

BrCR 876

Pencil, on thin, white, wove paper
Initialed *M. C,* annotated in blue chalk in the lower edge, *verso, 125*

Fold line: 18.5 × 16 cm 7¼ × 6¼ in.
Sheet: 31.1 × 20.2 cm 12¼ × 8 in.

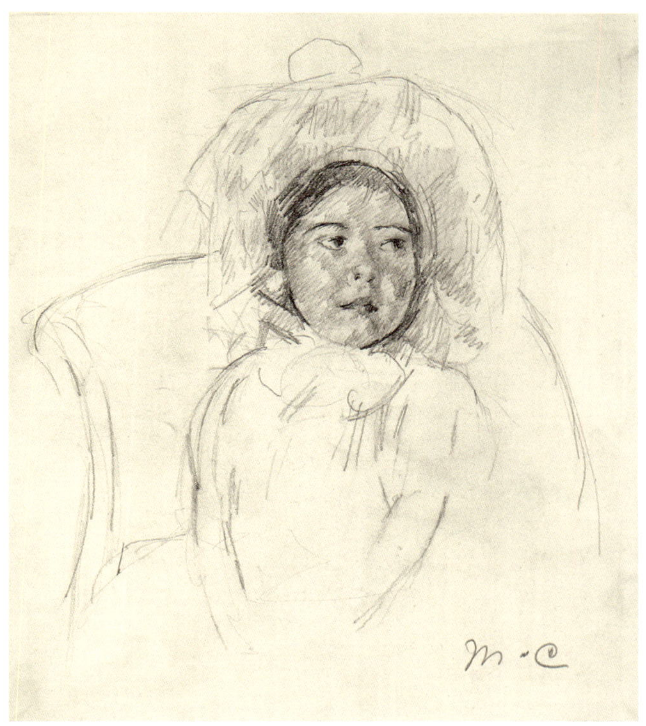
BrCR 877

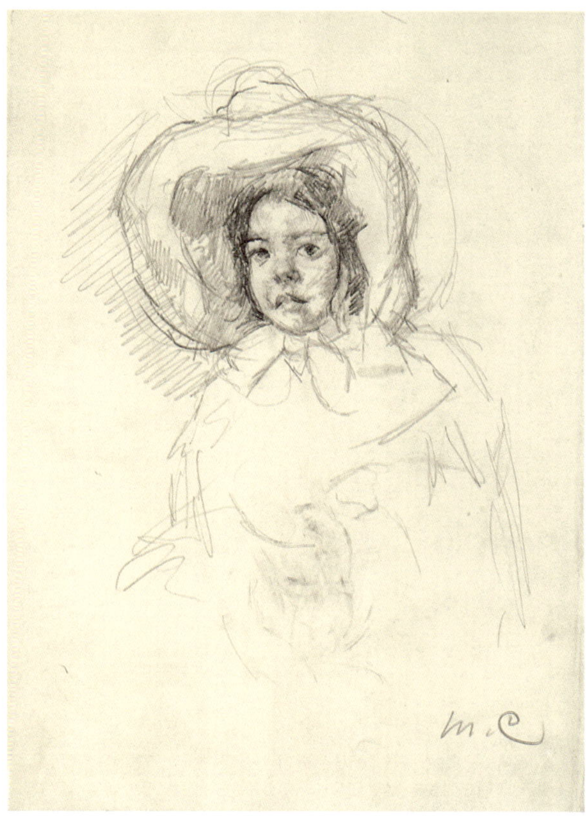
BrCR 881

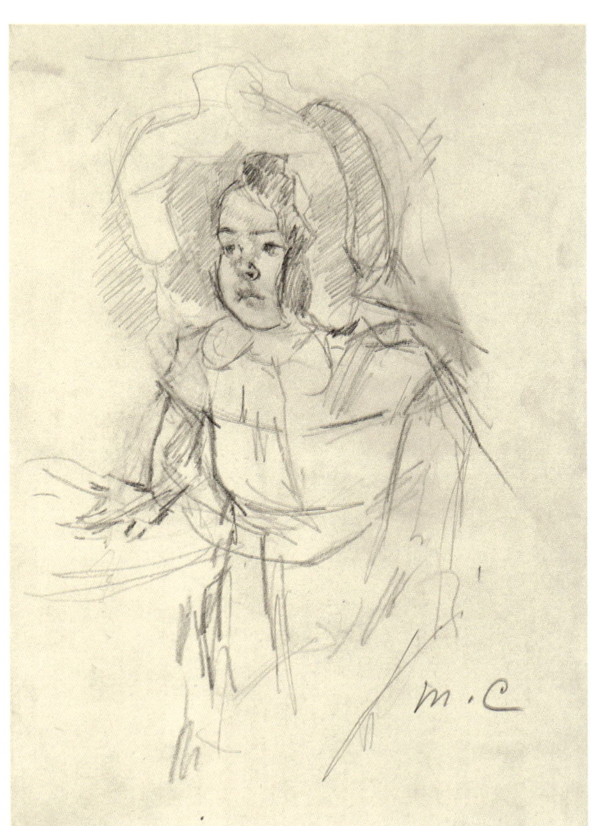
BrCR 882

Margot in a Ruffled Bonnet (No. 4),
ca. 1903–04

BrCR 877

Pencil, on thin, white, wove paper
Initialed *M. C*, annotated in blue chalk in the upper edge, *verso, 127*

Fold line: 18.3 × 16 cm 7¼ × 6¼ in.
Sheet: 31.2 × 20.2 cm 12¼ × 8 in.

Margot in a Floppy Bonnet (No. 1),
ca. 1903–04

BrCR 881

Pencil, on thin, white, wove paper
Initialed *M. C*, annotated in blue chalk in the lower edge, *126*

Fold line: 22.3 × 15.5 cm 8¾ × 6⅛ in.
Sheet: 31.3 × 20.3 cm 12⅜ × 8 in.

Margot in a Floppy Bonnet (No. 2),
ca. 1903–04

BrCR 882

Pencil, on thin, white, wove paper
Initialed *M. C*, annotated in blue chalk in the lower edge, *verso, 116*

Fold line: 22.2 × 15.5 cm 8¾ × 6⅛ in.
Sheet: 31.4 × 20.1 cm 12⅜ × 7⅞ in.

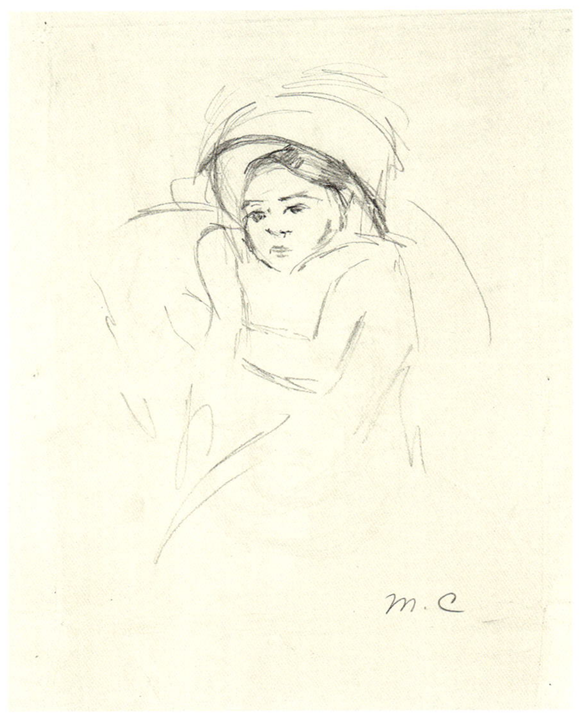

BrCR 884

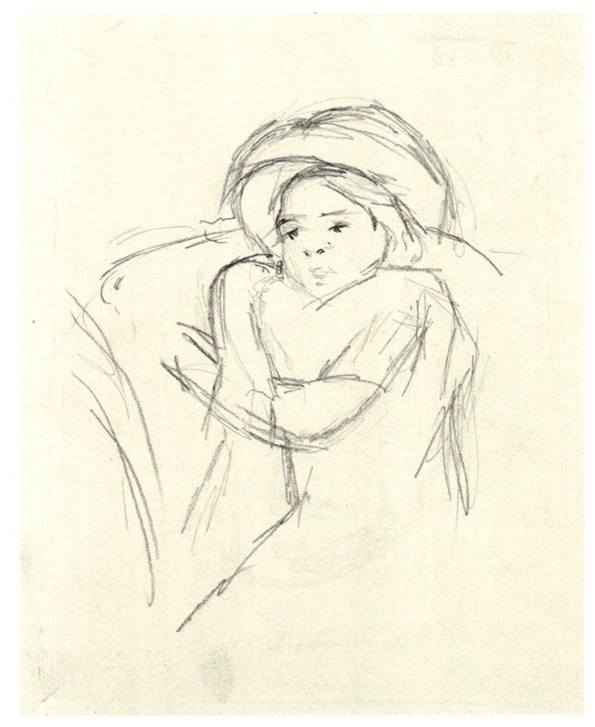
BrCR 884 *verso*

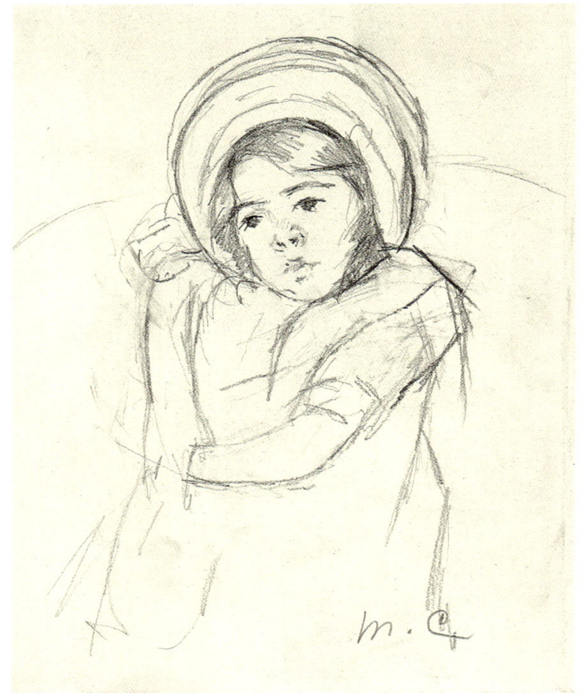

BrCR 886

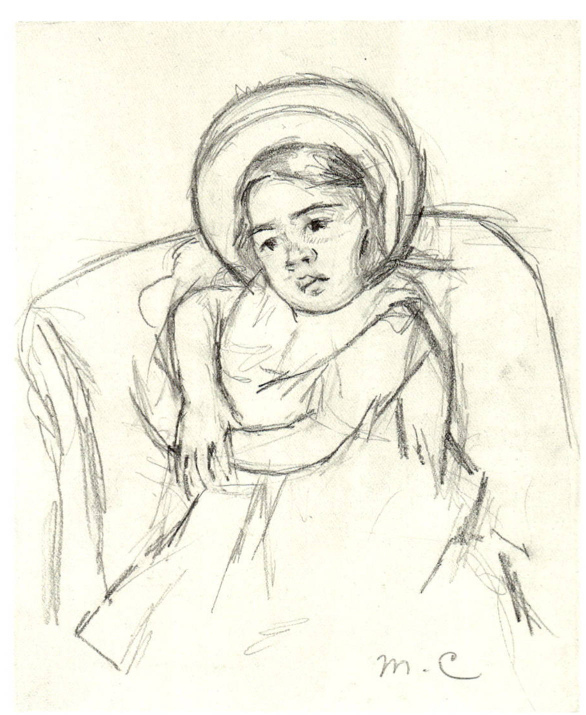

BrCR 888

Margot in a Floppy Bonnet (No. 3), ca. 1903–04

BrCR 883

Pencil, on thin, white, wove paper
Initialed *M. C*, annotated in blue chalk in the upper edge, *verso, 124*

Fold line: 22.2 × 15.5 cm 8¾ × 6⅛ in.
Sheet: 29 × 20.1 cm 11⅜ × 7⅞ in.

Sketch of Margot Wearing a Bonnet (No. 1), ca. 1903–04

Verso: composition sketch of same subject

BrCR 884

Pencil, on thin, white, wove paper
Initialed *M. C*, annotated in blue chalk in the upper edge, *115*

Fold line: 19.6 × 15.5 cm 7¾ × 6⅛ in.
Sheet: 31.4 × 20.2 cm 12⅜ × 8 in.

Sketch of Margot Wearing a Bonnet (No. 3), ca. 1903–04

BrCR 886

Pencil, on thin, white, wove paper
Initialed *M. C*, annotated in blue chalk in the lower edge, *verso, 112*

Fold line: 19.3 × 15.5 cm 7⅝ × 6⅛ in.
Sheet: 36.2 × 23 cm 14¼ × 9 in.

Sketch of Margot Wearing a Bonnet (No. 5), ca. 1902

BrCR 888

Pencil, on thin, white, wove paper
Initialed *M. C*, annotated in blue chalk in the lower edge, *113*

Fold line: 19.6 × 15.5 cm 7¾ × 6⅛ in.
Sheet: 23 × 18 cm 9 × 7⅛ in.

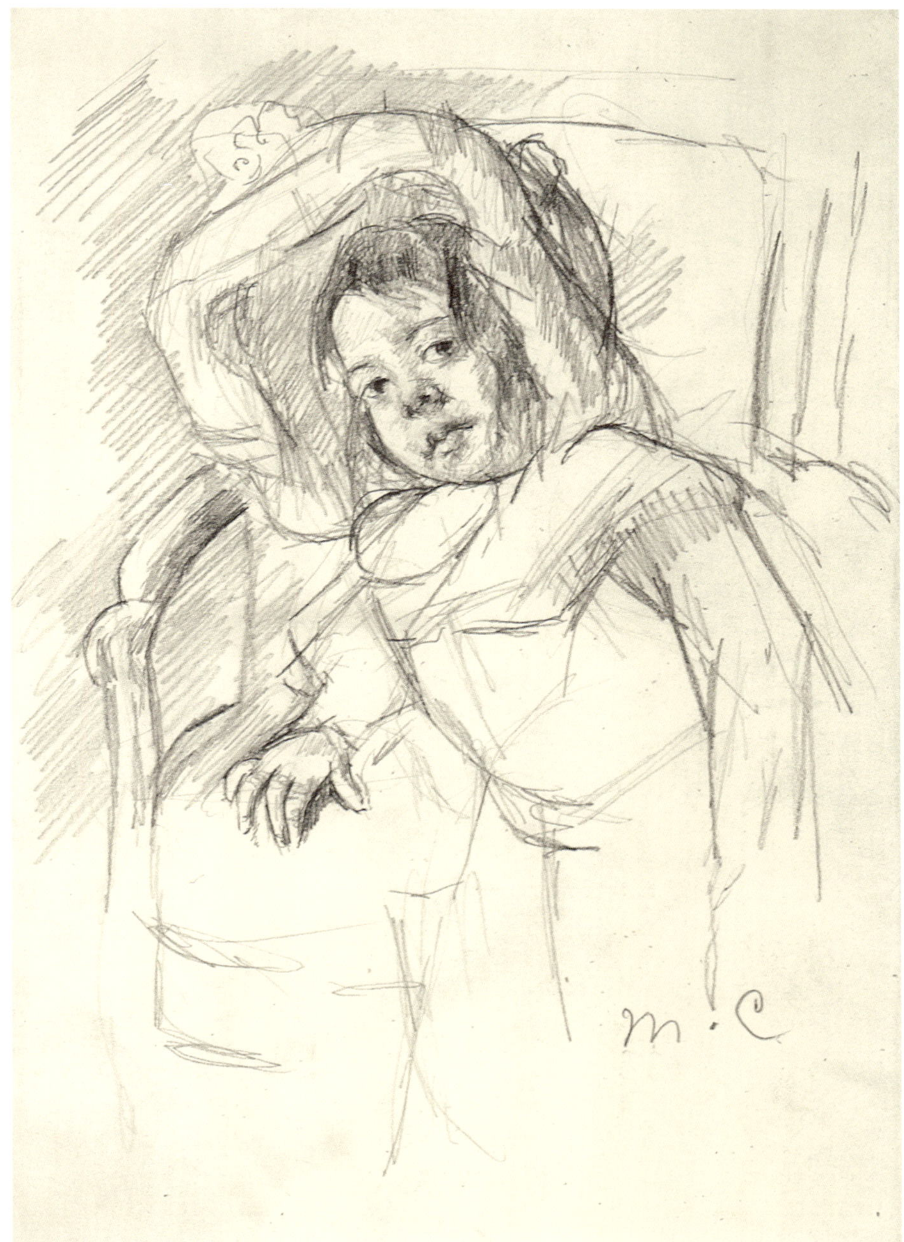

BrCR 883

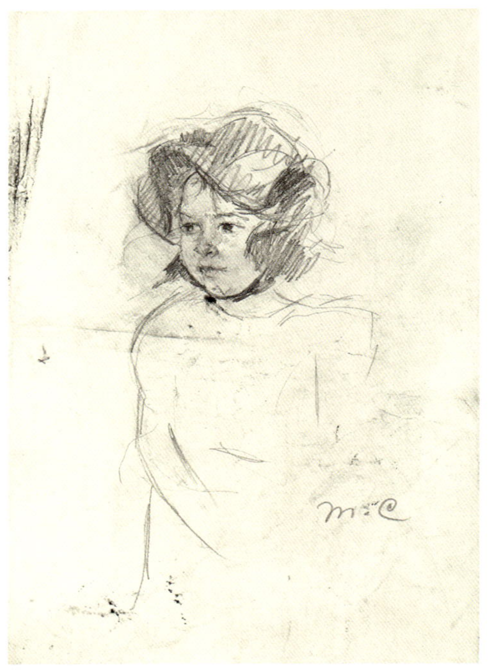

BrCR 889

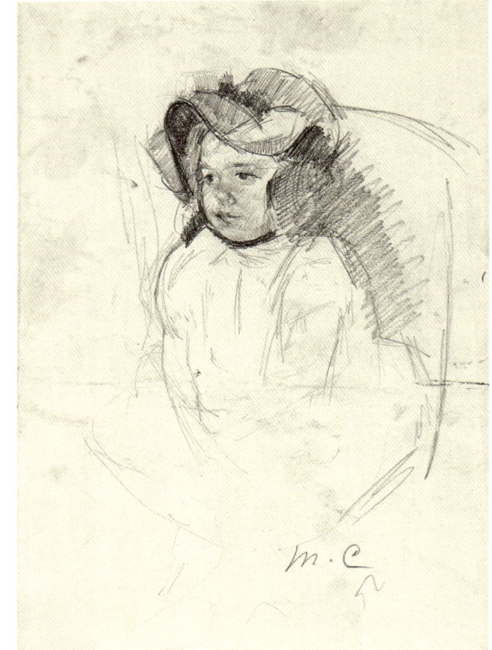

BrCR 890

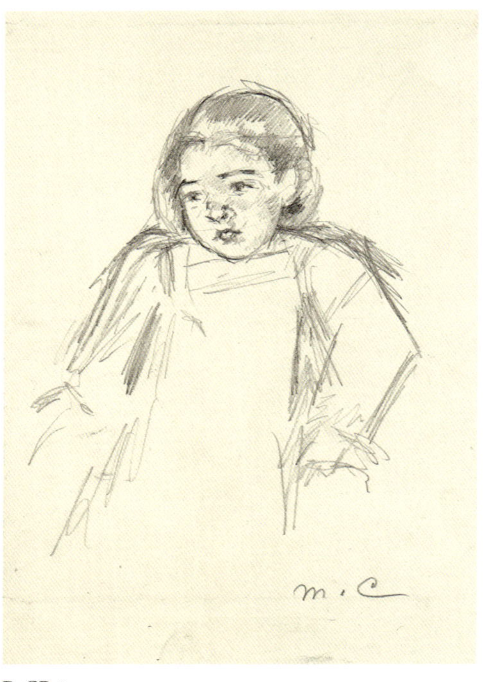

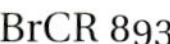

BrCR 893

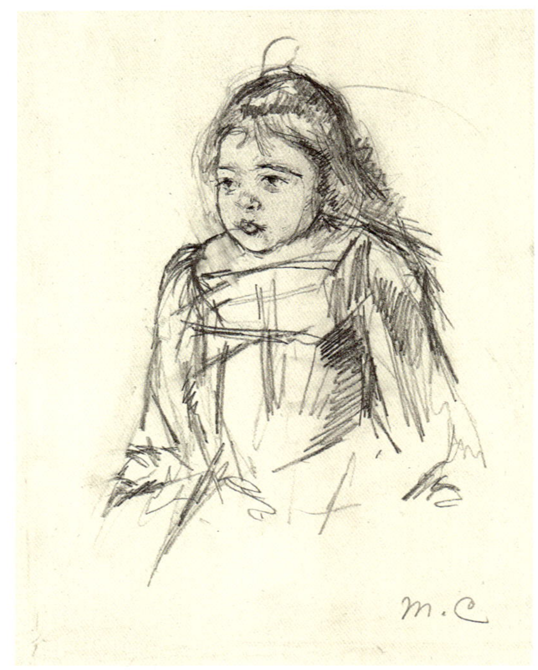

BrCR 894

Margot in a Bonnet with a Wavy Brim (No. 1), ca. 1903–04

BrCR 889

Pencil, on thin, white, wove paper
Initialed *M. C,* annotated in blue chalk in the upper edge, *verso, 122*

Fold line: 22.2 × 15.2 cm 8¾ × 6 in.
Sheet: 31.2 × 20.2 cm 12¼ × 8 in.

Margot in a Bonnet with a Wavy Brim (No. 2), ca. 1903–04

BrCR 890

Pencil, on thin, white, wove paper
Initialed *M. C,* annotated in blue chalk in the lower edge, *verso, 121*

Fold line: 22 × 15.2 cm 8⅝ × 6 in.
Sheet: 31.2 × 20.2 cm 12¼ × 8 in.

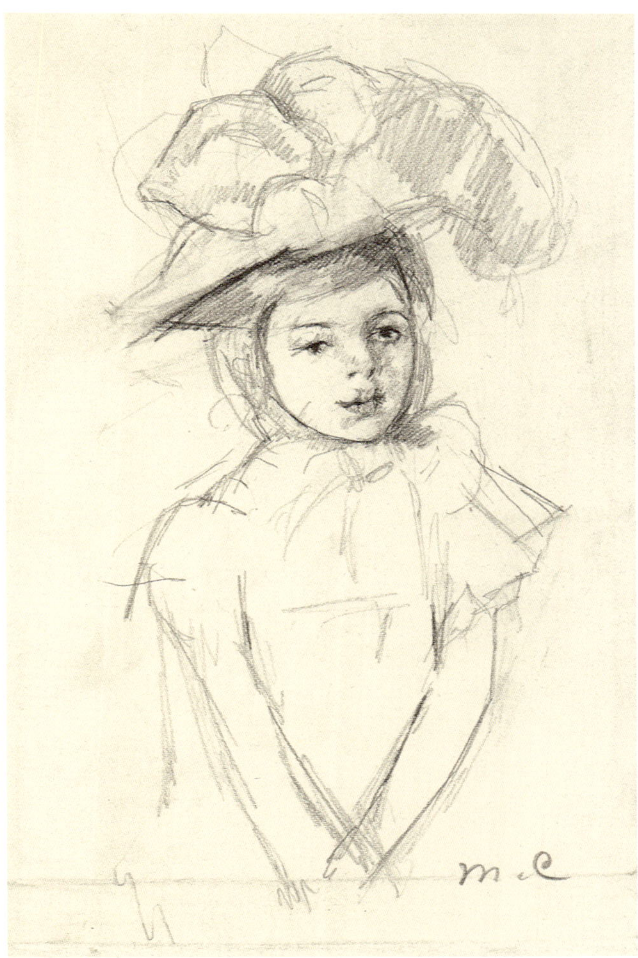

BrCR 897

Half-length of a Little Girl in a Pinafore, ca. 1903–04

BrCR 893

Pencil, on thin, white, wove paper
Initialed *M. C,* annotated in blue chalk in the upper edge, *verso, 106*

Fold line: 19.5 × 15.5 cm   7⅝ × 6⅛ in.
Sheet: 31.5 × 20 cm   12⅜ × 7⅞ in.

Sketch of a Little Girl Looking Left, ca. 1903–04

BrCR 894

Pencil, on thin, white, wove paper
Initialed *M. C,* annotated in blue chalk in the upper edge, *verso, 110*

Fold line: 19.5 × 15.5 cm   7⅝ × 6⅛ in.
Sheet: 31 × 20 cm   12¼ × 7⅞ in.

Sketch of Simone in a Festive Hat (No. 3), ca. 1903–04

BrCR 897

Pencil, on thin, white, wove paper
Initialed *M. C,* annotated in blue chalk in the upper edge, *verso, 118*

Fold line: 16.9-18 × 12.2 cm   6⅝-7 × 4¾ in.
Sheet: 31.5 × 25.1 cm   12⅜ × 9⅞ in.

Sketch of Simone in a Festive Hat (No. 4), ca. 1903–04

BrCR 898

Pencil, on thin, white, wove paper
Initialed *M. C,* annotated in blue chalk in the left edge, *117*

Fold line: 18 × 12.2 cm   7 × 4¾ in.
Sheet: 32.5 × 25 cm   12¾ × 9⅞ in.

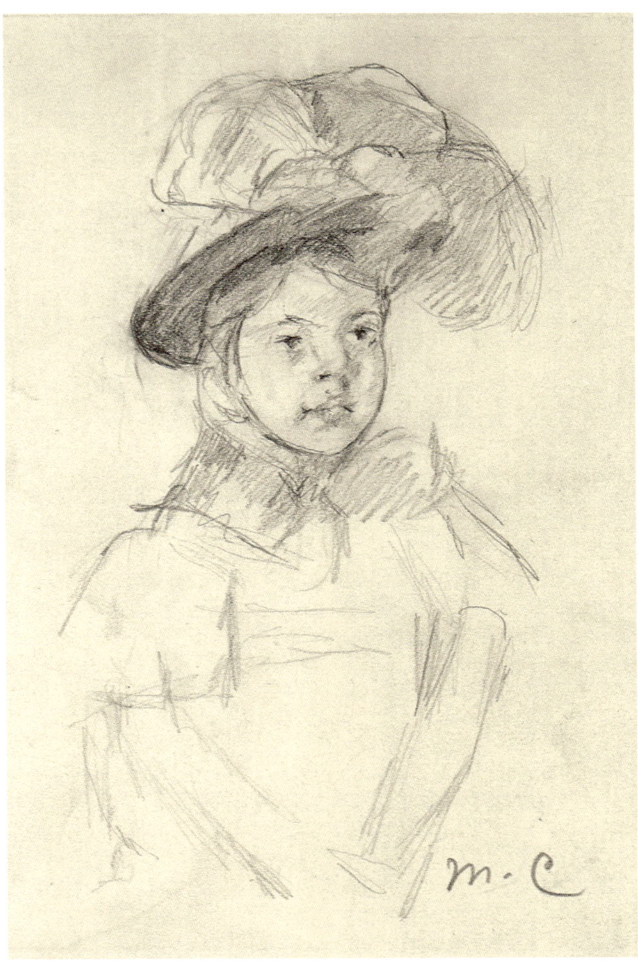

BrCR 898

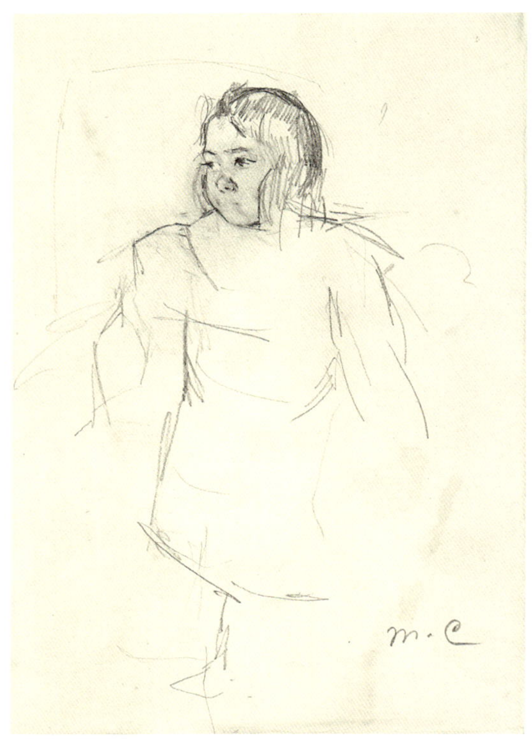

BrCR 899

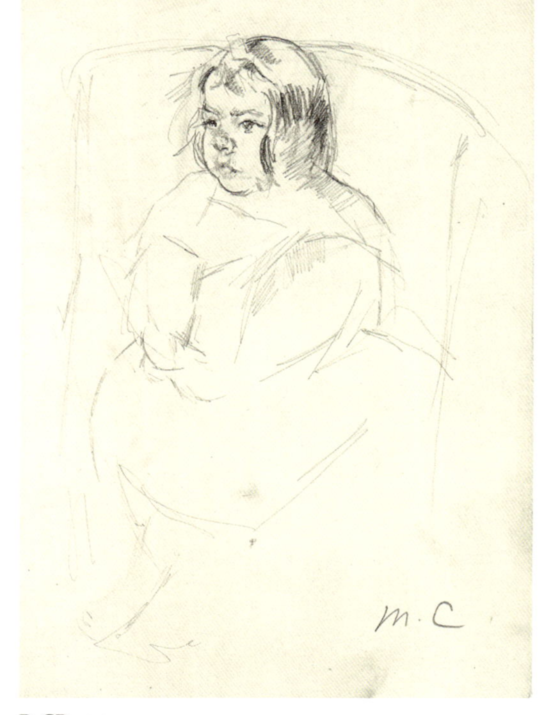

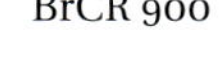

BrCR 900

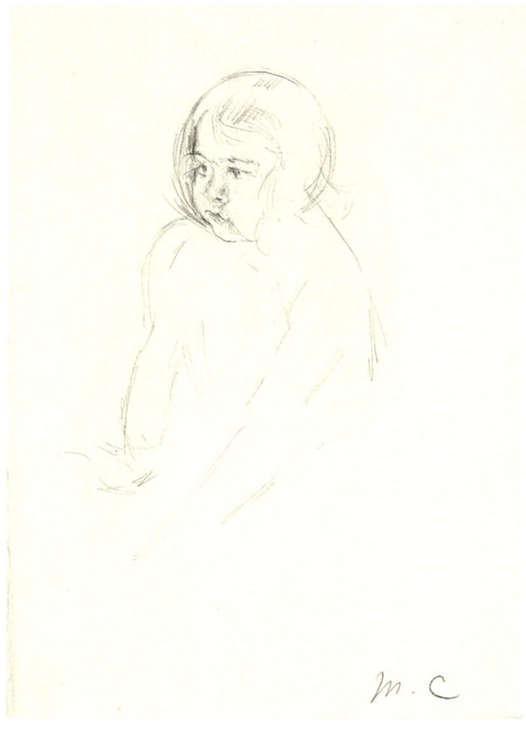

BrCR 902

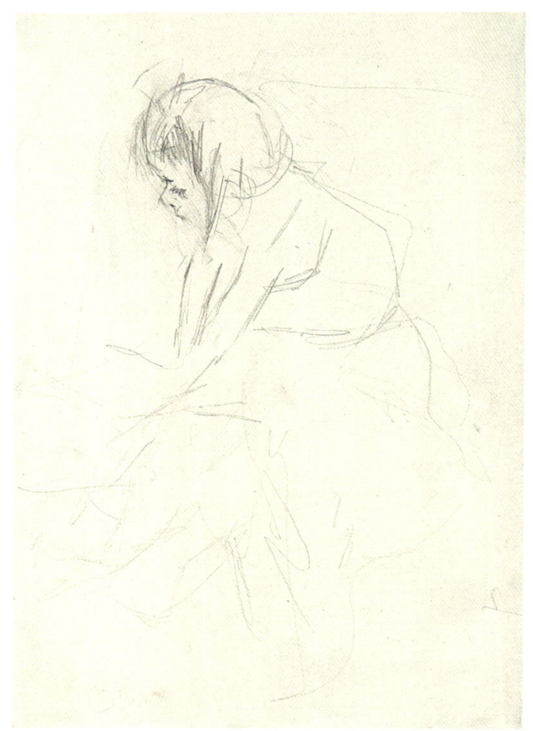

BrCR 902 *verso*

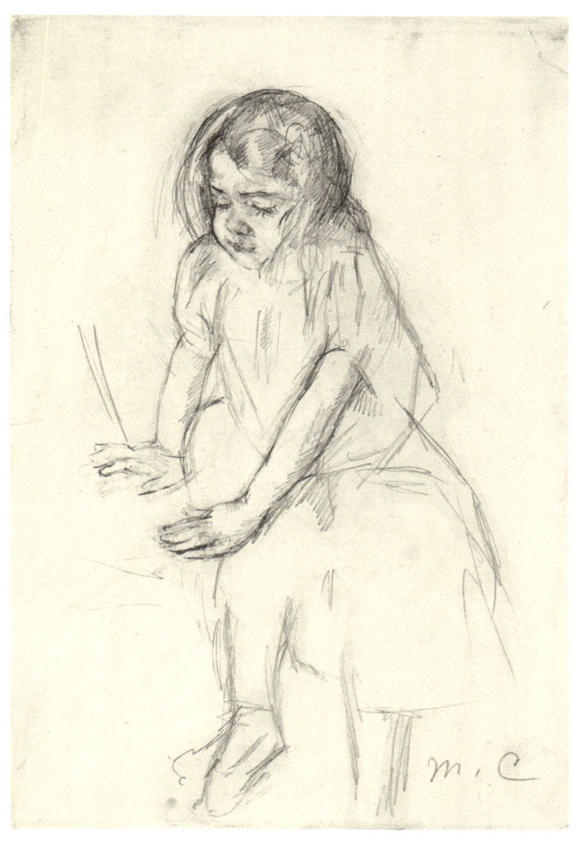

BrCR 903

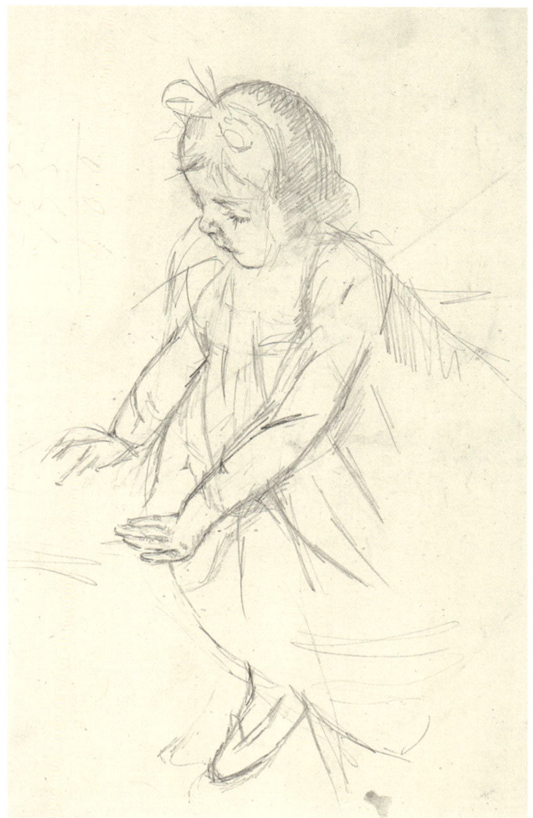

BrCR 903 *verso*

Sketch for "Simone Seated with Hands and Feet Crossed" (No. 1), ca. 1903–04

BrCR 899

Pencil, on thin, white, wove paper
Initialed *M. C,* annotated in blue chalk in the lower edge, *verso, 105*

Fold line: 22.3 × 15.5 cm 8¾ × 6⅛ in.
Sheet: 31.2 × 20.2 cm 12¼ × 8 in.

Sketch for "Simone Seated with Hands and Feet Crossed" (No. 2), ca. 1903–04

BrCR 900

Pencil, on thin, white, wove paper
Initialed *M. C,* annotated in blue chalk in the upper edge, *verso, 108*

Fold line: 22.3 × 15.5 cm 8¾ × 6⅛ in.
Sheet: 31.4 × 19.1 cm 12⅜ × 7½ in.

Head of Little Girl Leaning on Her Hands, ca. 1903–04

Verso: loose sketch of similar subject

BrCR 902

Pencil, on thin, wove paper
Initialed *M. C,* annotated in blue chalk in the left edge, *103*

Fold line: 22.3 × 15.5 cm 8¾ × 6⅛ in.
Sheet: 32.5 × 25 cm 12¾ × 9⅞ in.

Full-Length Sketch of a Little Girl Leaning Forward on Her Hands, ca. 1903–04

Verso: a related drawing

BrCR 903

Pencil, on thin, wove paper
Initialed *M. C,* annotated in blue chalk in the upper edge, *verso, 104*

Fold line: 22.3 × 15.5 cm 8¾ × 6⅛ in.
Sheet: 31.7 × 20.5 cm 12½ × 8 in.

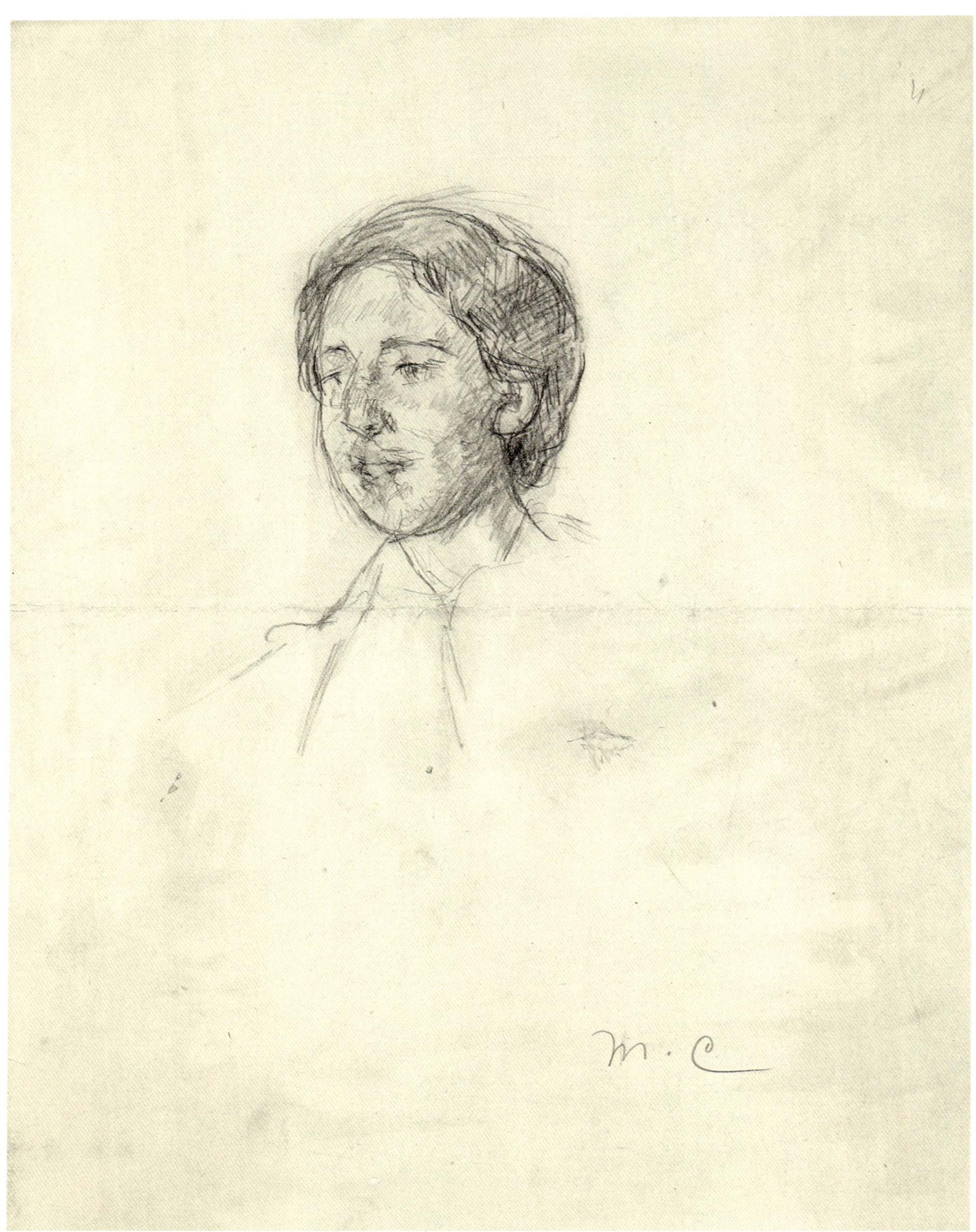

BrCR 928

Head of a Woman with Scratches of Shading over Her Face, ca. 1903–04

BrCR 928

Black conté crayon, on thin, white, wove paper
Initialed *M. C,* annotated in blue chalk in the top edge, *101*

Fold line: 31.5 × 24.5 cm 12⅜ × 9⅝ in.
Sheet: 40.4 × 30.8 cm 15⅞ × 12⅛ in.

SELECTED BIBLIOGRAPHY

The interested reader will find a wealth of important and insightful information about Mary Cassatt as a printmaker in Adelyn Breeskin's excellent essay and introduction to the revised edition of the catalogue raisonné of the graphic work, and in the publications noted in our bibliography, in particular, Mathews and Shapiro's catalogue for the exhibition, *Mary Cassatt: The Color Prints*, 1989, and in the essays by the many distinguished contributors to the exhibition catalogue, *Mary Cassatt: Modern Woman*, 1998.

Barter. Judith A., et al. *Mary Cassatt: Modern Woman.* Chicago and New York: The Art Institute of Chicago in association with Harry N. Abrams, Inc., 1998. Exhibition catalogue.

Breeskin, Adelyn D. *The Graphic Art of Mary Cassatt.* Washington, D.C.: Museum of Graphic Art and Smithsonian Institution Press, 1967. Exhibition catalogue.

———. *The Graphic Work of Mary Cassatt, A Catalogue Raisonné.* New York: H. Bittner and Co., 1948. 2d ed., Washington, D.C.: Smithsonian Institution Press, 1979.

———. *Mary Cassatt, A Catalogue Raisonné of the Oils, Pastels, Watercolors, and Drawings.* Washington, D.C.: Smithsonian Institution Press, 1970.

Collection des estampes modernes composant la collection Roger Marx. Sale catalogue. Paris: Hotel Drouot, April 27–May 2, 1914.

Dumas, Ann, et al. *The Private Collection of Edgar Degas.* New York: The Metropolitan Museum of Art, 1997. Exhibition catalogue.

Frelinghuysen, Alice Cooney, et al. *Splendid Legacy: The Havemeyer Collection.* New York: The Metropolitan Museum of Art, 1993. Exhibition catalogue.

Ives, Colta Feller. *The Great Wave: the Influence of Japanese Woodcuts on French Prints.* New York: Metropolitan Museum of Art, 1974. Exhibition catalogue.

Lugt, Frits. *Les Marques de collections de dessins et d'estampes.* Amsterdam: Vereenigde drukkerijen, 1921. Facsimile ed., San Francisco, CA.: Alan Wofsy Fine Arts, 1975.

———. *Les Marques de collections de dessins et d'estampes – Supplément.* The Hague: M. Nijhoff, 1956. Facsmile ed., San Francisco, CA.: Alan Wofsy Fine Arts, 1988.

Mathews, Nancy Mowll and Shapiro, Barbara Stern. *Mary Cassatt: The Color Prints.* New York: Harry N. Abrams, Inc. in association with Williams College Museum of Art, 1989. Exhibition catalogue.

Mathews, Nancy Mowll. *Mary Cassatt.* New York: Harry N. Abrams, 1987.

———. *Mary Cassatt: A Life.* New York: Villard Books, 1994. Reissue, New Haven and London: Yale University Press, 1998.

Mathews, Nancy Mowll, ed. *Cassatt and Her Circle: Selected Letters.* New York: Abbeville Press, 1984.

———. *Mary Cassatt: A Retrospective.* New York: Hugh Lauter Levin Associates, 1996.

Reed, Sue Welsh and Shapiro, Barbara Stern. *Edgar Degas: The Painter as Printmaker.* Boston: Little, Brown and Company, 1984. Exhibition catalogue.

Shapiro, Barbara Stern. *Mary Cassatt: Impressionist at Home.* New York: Universe Publishing, 1998.

INDEX OF ILLUSTRATIONS

Prints

Drawings

Design by Marcus Ratliff
Composition by Amy Pyle
Digital photography and color separations by Martin Senn
Lithography by Meridian Printing